OUTBURSTS
IN
ACADEME

OUTBURSTS IN ACADEME

MULTICULTURALISM AND OTHER SOURCES OF CONFLICT

Edited by
Kathleen Dixon

Assisted by
William Archibald

and
Jane Varley

BOYNTON/COOK PUBLISHERS
HEINEMANN
Portsmouth, NH

*To all those who have put their talents into the service
of the public good. Two who have inspired the editing
of this book are the late Jacqueline Anderson, beloved
friend and colleague, and the recently retired Jay
Robinson, respected mentor and scholar. May their
years of quiet activism continue in the works of a new
generation.*

Boynton/Cook Publishers, Inc.
A subsidiary of Reed Elsevier Inc.
361 Hanover Street
Portsmouth, NH 03801–3912
http://www.heinemann.com

Offices and agents throughout the world

© 1998 by Boynton/Cook Publishers, Inc.

Library of Congress Cataloging-in-Publication Data
Outbursts in academe : multiculturalism and other sources of conflict / edited by Kathleen Dixon.
    p. cm.
  Includes bibliographical references.
  ISBN 0-86709-477-X
  1. Multicultural education—United States.   2. Critical pedagogy—United States.
3. Feminism and education—United States.   4. Education, Higher—Political aspects—
United States.   5. Minorities—Education (Higher)—United States.   I. Dixon, Kathleen,
1955– .
LC1099.3.088   1998   98-29882
370.117—dc21   CIP

Editor: Lisa Luedeke
Production: Abigail M. Heim
Cover design: Jenny Jensen Greenleaf
Manufacturing: Louise Richardson

Printed in the United States of America on acid-free paper
02   01   00   99   98   DA   1   2   3   4   5

Contents

Acknowledgments

This book followed hard on the heels of my first book, *Making Relationships: Gender in the Forming of Academic Community* (Peter Lang Publishing, 1997) and so I am grateful that the dean of arts and sciences at the University of North Dakota, John Ettling, granted me funds to offset the subvention fees for *Making Relationships:* His generosity allowed me to turn my attention to *Outbursts in Academe.* The UND Faculty Research Committee (as it was known at the time) awarded me a grant that I used to hire graduate students Bill Archibald (whose steadfastness bears special mention) and Jane Varley as editorial assistants: Thanks to that committee and to my assistants. Colleagues within the UND Department of English have been encouraging in various ways, some by reading parts of the manuscript, some by offering book publishing advice. Thanks go to Michael Anderegg, Michael Beard, Steve Dilks, Elizabeth Hampsten, Bob Lewis, and Sherry O'Donnell. UND students frequently have been inspirational; I would like to mention Kara Luger, an appreciative reader of "Revisiting White Feminist Authority," and former students Scott Lyons and Doreen Stärke-Meyerring, who were there at the beginning of *Outbursts in Academe.* I remember it well and fondly. Sandy Barclay, mistress of the UND Composition Domain, provided consistent good help and good cheer as we neared the end of the process of putting the book together. Ursula Hovet—without whom nothing gets done in the UND Department of English—and undergraduate Alicia Rodewald also helped us conclude the work.

I am grateful to all those who agreed to contribute to *Outbursts in Academe.* Among those are John Schilb and Elizabeth Flynn, who by now have read partial manuscripts of both my books; I have greatly profited from their expertise. Series editor Chuck Schuster gave excellent advice: Thanks much for that, and for taking a chance on a rather unconventional book. Abby Heim at Heinemann has been most helpful at the copyediting stage.

Carol Winkelmann, friend, colleague, and contributor, has sparred with me for years (intellectually, of course): This book would not exist without her. Pat Escarraz has endured the consequences of many of my obsessions; *Outbursts in Academe* is the only one fit to print.

Introduction

Outbursts: The Theory and a Guide to Reading

Kathleen Dixon and William Archibald

This book is intended primarily for an audience of progressive teachers, especially those who teach in U.S. colleges and universities. We aim to reach those who are skeptical of the thing called Theory, but who remain committed to classroom teaching and ideals of social change. We wish as well to persuade those who find themselves attracted to Theory that it can be spelled with a small *t,* and that practice and theory really can be mutually informative. Most of the theory used by the authors in *Outbursts in Academe* has been digested and applied without fanfare. However, the applications do constitute original research; the very concept of *outbursts* as isolatable, researchable moments in the lives of teachers and students constitutes an original contribution to critical theory. Thus, this volume will be of interest to many feminist- and cultural-studies researchers seeking new ways to theorize contemporary culture.

Most of the contributors to *Outbursts* are specialists in language study and pedagogy. They may research and teach rhetoric and composition, American or British literature, African-American studies, Indian studies, women's studies, sociology, or education. Many consider themselves practitioners of cultural studies. Cultural-studies adherents notice that people arrange themselves or are arranged into many smaller and larger, complex, and overlapping social groups. Differences within and among groups are often accompanied by differences of power. All "texts" (whether written or oral or belonging to "high" or "pop" culture) are expressions of these cultures and are analyzed in relation to their cultural and historical contexts.

This volume is occasioned at least partly by its particular historical moment. To academics committed to cultural studies or multicultural or feminist projects, it may seem that the political stagnancy or outright regression of the 1980s has metamorphosed into an almost incomprehensibly complex and dynamic period.

College student bodies are, in some parts of the country, less diverse than in the past (because of the decrease in federal financial aid) and, in others, more so (because of the changing demographics of regions like the West Coast and the Southwest). Whatever their color or background, undergraduates may evince opinions that might be labeled *feminist* or *progressive,* yet oppose *politically correct* attitudes, as does mainstream pop culture, which itself broadcasts newly accepted leftist values and simultaneously undermines them.

Meanwhile, many progressive faculty are themselves divided. At a recent conference on her campus, Jane Gallop's theorizing of the "personal" could be seen against the backdrop of students' protests: they charged conferees with tacit support of sexual harassment (i.e., two sexual harassment complaints had been brought against Gallop—from two women graduate students). At about the same time, Butler's *Gender Trouble: Feminism and the Subversion of Identity* (1990) was aiding the breakdown of the category of "woman," upon which much of the basis for feminist conceptualizing rested. Women of color had been forming their own support groups, caucuses, and publishing companies (partly in response to neglect in white feminist organizations). As well, some women of color engaged in a kind of theorizing that did not grow out of European philosophy, but rather issued from the history and present-day experiences of their cultural or tribal groups (e.g., Leslie Marmon Silko's understanding of oral tradition, 1986). And still many women of color chose to perform their political work with men of color rather than (and sometimes in addition to) white women—whether or not the men identified themselves as feminists. In addition, the growth of cultural studies and the turn toward autobiographical writing in the humanities and social sciences have begun to make apparent differences in class background among academics.

The result of all this work: *black, white, woman, latina, Native American, working class, middle class*—none of these is a unitary concept and not even "progressive" academics agree on which terms to use when. One could certainly consider these disagreements salutary or indicative of a growth in democracy. There may be less political cohesion, but there are certainly more voices being heard. By the 1990s, many organizations and scholarly journals still presided over primarily by white middle-class feminists find it *de rigueur* to publish women of color and to consider race and class as categories of analysis coequal with gender or sex. *Multiculturalism,* a term of the popular media as well as the academic culture, is perhaps to the 1990s what *feminism* was to the 1970s.

But that does not mean people know yet how to talk to one another across (and sometimes even within) boundaries of color, class, and gender. Both students and professors are confused and conflicted as groups and as individuals. I am thinking of a question-and-answer session after a paper presentation by Tania Modleski at a recent conference on multiculturalism. (The presentation has been published as an essay [Modleski 1997].) Somewhere in her critical reading of Anna Deavere Smith's performance of the Los Angeles riots, Modleski compared the piercing of a Caribbean infant girl's ears to the botched silicone implant operation on a U.S. middle-class white woman's face. When asked (by a white woman) if she knew, or thought she ought to know, more about the cultural practices of the Caribbean family, what the ear-piercing might mean to the growing girl, and what the particularities of the situation were, Modleski replied that yes, maybe she should learn more. But in a most emphatic outburst she also cried, "You can particularize yourself out of a movement!"

It is thus that the fractures become fractious. They ought not to be smoothed over or dismissed with knee-jerk moralizing, but rather noticed, pointedly, made to matter to a group of people still fond of abstractions and "impersonal" knowledge. Our understanding of ourselves is slight, but we forge on anyway, haggling among ourselves within our power blocks, defining *movements,* creating policies on sexual harassment, mandating *diversity* in an article for scholarly publication. We pause, briefly, when some outsider—perhaps a student, perhaps a colleague whom we have not heard from (or listened to) in the past— objects, observing that the emperor has no clothes. Such pauses are crucial; we might wish to create more of them.

We cannot and should not stop acting, but we must learn to become self-reflexive; that is, we must develop the capacity to observe and critique ourselves *as political actors. Outbursts in Academe* stands as a pause in our activity, an invitation to study ourselves. It brings together essays that showcase the university as an animated and confusing "site of struggle" among students and faculty.

An *outburst* is a moment when the often latent conflicts among faculty and among students, between students and faculty, or within individuals bubble to the surface, erupting in class discussions, small-group work, office-hour conversations, conference presentations, evaluations of teachers, written assignments, academic publications, or e-mail conferencing. An *outburst* is a response to a conflict that expresses a person's orientation to that conflict and to the social and political conditions that underlie it.

Frequently, the outburst is unexpected and, therefore, will take an unexpected form—yet, upon reflection, we usually can identify its culturally inscribed character. Outbursts can be verbal—both oral and written. They may be loud and short, like a shout, or long and monotonous, like a hectoring. They can be gestural or even pre-gestural (e.g., a blush, a stammer). We may believe that we see the traces of an outburst in an absence (e.g., a student who drops a course; the silence that greets one person's outburst).

Outbursts are not reducible to mere expressions of "resistance" to "oppression." An emotional display made in a classroom or at a conference might feel good at the moment, feel bad later, advance one's cause, and set it back simultaneously. Furthermore, one person's outburst may create the conditions for another person's silence. Just who is allowed to perform an outburst when, where, and in the company of whom is part of what this volume seeks to determine.

Outbursts frequently provoke other outbursts. Rarely are these essays reports of single instances, but rather of multiple outbursts and their contexts.

Outbursts in Academe is a written document, but it often draws from oral language, from the popular culture of academe (yes, we argue that academe *does* express itself in popular as well as "high" culture), from classroom discussions, question-and-answer sessions at conferences, and gossip in the hallways. In methods and methodologies, it draws widely from social-science and humanities fields. The loose center is a descriptive and interpretive methodology/method taken from qualitative social-science research and literary critical studies. Kathleen Dixon's work, for example, frequently describes classroom situations and analyzes them using theories from cultural and gender studies (which are themselves eclectic; thus, the "studies" appellation). Doreen Stärke-Meyerring's work relies on the survey method. Most are of the descriptive and interpretive variety mentioned previously, employing linguistic, psychoanalytic, deconstructive, semiotic—and other—approaches. All are centrally concerned with power relations between or among people of different genders, races, classes, nationalities, ages, and so on. Indeed, it is the conflict that results from differential power relations that usually creates the outburst in the first place. The collection as a whole probably should be considered a contribution to cultural studies, although individual authors may claim allegiance to a number of theories or discourses (including Marxist, feminist, Afro-centric), some of which may contradict the seemingly inclusive *cultural studies* epithet (e.g., some feminists question the foundations of the Birmingham School of Cultural Studies, finding it more Marxist than feminist; an Afro-centrist might wear the mantle of *essentialist* that a post-structuralist would question).

Outbursts in Academe might be seen as a multicultural *Gendered Subjects: The Dynamics of Feminist Teaching* (Culley and Portuges 1985) for the 1990s. Many of the articles treat feminist pedagogy and/or other types of progressive pedagogy or activism within the academy; but, unlike the earlier collection, *Outbursts* will not represent an upbeat unity, and gender is not the only variable under consideration for analysis. *Outbursts* shares the general cultural studies perspective and orientation toward pedagogy of such books as *Race, Identity, and Representation in Education,* edited by McCarthy and Crichlow (1993); Berlin and Vivion's *Cultural Studies in the English Classroom* (1992); and a volume edited by Fitts and France, *Left Margins: Composition and Cultural Studies* (1995). *Outbursts,* however, is primarily composed of analyses of contemporary culture as they play themselves out within academe. Not just classrooms, but also the consciousness of particular individuals becomes the object of analyses. We not only look at the way students enact culture and power in the classroom, but also how professors and teachers enact multicultural identities in the company of students and colleagues. *Outbursts* differs from other recent books on academic culture (like *Working-class Women in the Academy: Laborers in the Knowledge Factory,* edited by Tokarczyk and Fay [1993]), in that it insists on looking at the whole complex of social categories (i.e., class, race, gender, and many others). Also, *Outbursts* relies less on self-dramatized oral histories than some of these books and more on a balance of theory and story.

Are outbursts good things? With regard to the expansion of democracy, to the inculcation of self-reflexive ideologies (rather than merely self-perpetuating ones), to the creation of dialogic possibilities across groups separated by various and complicated power differences, some outbursts might be seen as progressive, some regressive; indeed, any one outburst could be both at once. What the leftists have wrought, the rightists too have taken up. Australian-born art critic Robert Hughes (1993) put his finger on something real when he referred to the United States as one giant "culture of complaint." We all know now how to agitate for our rights; what seems harder is to listen to one another. The proliferation of loudly competing ideologies is confusing, distracting, annoying— yet, potentially exciting, intellectually challenging, and downright inspirational. So many individual voices speaking! So many "interest groups" advocating! Can they be articulated within a larger perspective that is not merely nostalgic (plenty of feminists, as well as pro-family advocates, are nostalgic) or above the fray (plenty of academics, including some deconstructionists, still take this Platonic route)? Is there a collection of perspectives that can bring people and ideas together, at least provisionally?

Maybe academe and, more specifically, cultural studies have something to contribute to the agitated public rhetoric of the times. It seems that outbursts are inevitable in this place and time, regardless of what we teachers and researchers do. But we should note that a veritable hothouse of desire for outbursting is sure to result from those classrooms, conference presentations, and scholarly articles that interrogate the meanings of power relations, that foreground the categories of race, class, and gender in political analysis. We must study the conditions of the outbursts and their consequences so that we can patch together a public rhetoric for our times. We think of this book as a kind of rhetorical laboratory out of which such a text might grow.

Guide to Reading *Outbursts in Academe*

This book is based on a slim hope. To wit: that a publication produced by multiple authors writing from hotly contested perspectives can be a book at all and that that book, if purged of—well, at least, partly purged of—jargon and specialized vocabulary could be fairly agreeably consumed by most readers. Nonetheless, we expect this text will give rise to at least as much discomfort as it purports to analyze within its pages.

We persist in believing that slim hope is better than no hope at all, and that something entitled *Outbursts in Academe,* if not fulfilling most readers' notion of a good read (whatever that might be, and it certainly would be varied), will further an intellectual project of self-reflection in some way or another.

Let us offer a *Guide to Reading Outbursts in Academe. Outbursts* is unusual in that the essays within it were not solicited by topic. Instead, the essays partake in extending the theorizing of the phenomenon of *outbursts* begun in the introduction. The extensions are not always readily discernible *as* extensions: the proportions of *Outbursts'* body, so to speak, are not always lovely, not a work of God or even of God's Renaissance humanist (e.g., "how noble in stature"). Some of the essays might well stand on their own (to continue the body metaphor) and might be read intelligibly without recourse to the introduction of this book.

Most, however, are heavily reliant on the theorizing of outbursts and might surprise an academic reader accustomed to certain discursive markers (e.g., certain conventions of argumentation or, indeed, of autobiography). Some of the essays contained within this book are less arguments or polished autobiography than alternations of outbursts and moody ruminations. Some operate on several levels of thought and chronology: A conference presentation is quoted at length, the ensuing discussion reported by the author/presenter; then, a critical turn is made upon the "report." In such a piece, the discovery of the "outburst/s" may occur suddenly at the end, like a newly sprouted tail.

What *Outbursts in Academe* is attempting to do is represent something of the variety of experiences people are undergoing in an environment of "posts," "neos," "inters," and "multis"—postmodern, post-Colonial, neoliberal and neoconservative, multicultural, multipositional, interdisciplinary, and so on. The focus is on academe, although we firmly believe that these experiences will ring true for other locales. More specifically, the authors focus on places within the liberal arts (mostly English departments) or schools of education where work is being done on the articulations among student, academic, and popular cultures.

Most of the authors are self-conscious about the political nature of their profession (here, we are thinking of the way the noun grows out of the verb, *to profess*), and most profess a commitment to egalitarian movements—civil rights movements, feminist movements, and the like. But never let it be supposed that these *profess-ors* are or can be of the same mold! Or that their respondents at conferences or in the classroom meekly accept their (presumedly) more passive position. If *author-ity* once was thought to reside in the author— remember Paulo Freire's depiction (1990) of the teacher as *narrator,* who narrates while his students listen?—it scarcely can be so in this historical moment at the end of this (Judeo-Christian) millennium. Just as one begins to limn some outlines of thought, someone else, or some group of others, pounces on the inchoate thing. Those of us who have wanted to "erase" or "traverse boundaries" have gotten our wish: Who can even follow one's own "train of thought" nowadays? (And how anachronistic! Perhaps it would be better to reference the television "clicker"—a "click of thought.") In such a world, how is politically committed scholarship and teaching to proceed?

If the book cannot quite answer that question, it does offer interpretive strategies for making useful, if provisional, meaning out of vital and unruly forces. The authors invite the reader to lurk about amid a selection of contemporary academic culture. Because this invitation is an unusual one, we offer this *Guide to Reading.*

Each part of *Outbursts in Academe* includes two or more essays, usually written by untenured academics; each part ends with one or more formally invited responses to the essays, usually written by more established academics. Additionally, editor Dixon has composed responsive pieces labeled "Interviews," which sometimes mediate between essays and responses, sometimes between views that have been articulated in these pages and others that have not. Please beware that any given essay or response might wrench apart some connection previously made, popping off an appendage of the *Outburst* body. The editor's own reading of the book tends toward *re-membering,* and that is part of what happens in the *inter-views.* Perhaps it is only fair to provide the *reader* with at least some picture of her fishing around for a suitable tool, scrounging together some rough archetype of hope.

Part One

Immodest Proposals

1

Cyborg Bodies: Race, Class, Gender, and Communications Technology

Carol Winkelmann

LaShawnla is like our dream girl for this class. A young cyberpunk. She is one who thinks clearly and creatively, using quantum-electronic appliances and brain know-how, in the newest, updated, top-of-the-line model of our species. She is one who can break what people think women's role in society should be. I truly feel LaShawnla knows what it means to be a cyborg. She's a pioneer of our complex scientific world.

Nikki, a student

My name is nothing. Men should be given vacetimes [sic] for treating women badly. Sometimes I just want to give up.

Shelter Woman

I say use your femininity to overthrow world governments, or at least use it to make things better for yourselves and for women, especially minority women and men, in the future.

440896, a male student, to Sheila

If it was ever possible ideologically to characterize women's lives by the distinction of public and private domains—suggested by images of the division of working-class life into factory and home, of bourgeois life into market and home, and of gender existence into personal and political realms—it is now a totally misleading ideology, even to show how both terms of these dichotomies construct each other in practice and in theory. I prefer a network ideological image, suggesting the profusion of spaces and identities and the permeability of boundaries in the personal body and in the body politic. *Networking* is both a feminist practice and a multinational corporate strategy—weaving is for oppositional cyborgs.

Writing is preeminently the technology of cyborgs, etched surfaces of the late twentieth century. Cyborg politics is the struggle for language and the struggle against perfect communication, against the one code that translates all meaning perfectly, the central dogma of phallogocentrism.

Donna J. Haraway

Electronic Excursions:
Middle-Class Academics Surf the Net

As I begin this essay, I would like to locate myself, if momentarily, for you. It is an impulse born, I am sure, of my postmodern socialist-feminist ethnolinguistic identity. My name is Carol Winkelmann and my virtual home address is: winkelma@xavier.xu.edu. Even without the other trappings, my address reveals at least one salient feature about me—that is, I am an academic with access to information technology. More of the salient features: I am a white middle-class female and currently an associate professor of English at a nearly all-white private Jesuit university in a dialect-interface area labeled in the linguistic atlases as the Lower North/Upper South. When I teach ethnolinguistics, sixteenth- and seventeenth-century women's literacy, and electronic literacy to my predominantly white middle-class Catholic students during the day, I am in the Lower North. At night, when I drive across the Ohio River to my home in the hills of Kentucky, I am in the Upper South. More than any other place I have ever lived and worked, such distinctions are important.

Of course, few of my colleagues and neighbors are aware of the great and finally ill-fated linguistic atlas project of my academic predecessors: the great maps of dialect areas, regions marked off by twisty lines, long unbroken strings delineating one language area from another. There, they say *faucet;* here, we say *spigot.* To the locals, however, the murky Ohio River (once running red with the blood of butchered animals, as city legend would have it) marks the important distinctions: We over here are Buckeyes and those folks over there are not. On both sides of the river, identities count. These are the borderlands where Appalachians, German Catholics, African Americans, and Shawnees—not to mention heterosexuals, homosexuals, and bisexuals—mix dangerously. The annual KKK cross on the city square during the Christians' nativity season is only one more reminder of the regulation of Us/Other relations. In this area of the country—like many others—surely the borders are strictly patrolled.

This is an essay about border traversings. In it, I want to tell you my version of a story, a moment of interaction, a chance intersection, between the participants of a seminar on electronic literacy I taught at my university and an African American woman living in the shelter for battered women where I volunteer.

This is also a study of a series of outbursts: angry outbursts among privileged people in an electronic terrain, each authoring and coauthoring narratives of desire. Any rendition creates tension and invites dispute, of course. All reading is rewriting, all articulation is interested. And all the multiple layers of meaning in any articulation are open to dispute, conflict, and interruption. So it is with this story.

This is a tale, as well, about social relations enforced and mediated by technology and about how all the participants, including myself, had their preconceived notions about *Otherness* techno-digested. My students and I never expected the events of this story to happen as they did; as you will see, technology created and disintegrated whole narratives of race, class, and gender.

Finally, this text is a polemic about cyborg politics and the struggle against perfect communication. I am interested in creating an *infidel heteroglossia:* multitudinous perspectives on life, a multitude of Other-minded discursive practices that will signify the end of the sometimes seemingly uncontested rule of patriarchal, militaristic, and anti-ecological discourses so long harmful to the earth, the animals, and the marginals—that is, the children, the women, the indigenous, and the other silenced, exploited, and poverty-stricken populations on the planet.[1]

As a teacher, I am interested in sponsoring this irreverent discourse with the use of technology; hence, my seminar on electronic literacy involves border-traversing, boundary transgressions unusual or usually unarticulated in this conservative environment of the Lower North/Upper South region. The curriculum of the seminar entails the philosophical, sociological, linguistic, literary, and technical. Among other topics, we consider the history of writing technology, the nature of electronic literacies, the effects of computerization on the workplace and the academy, the current popular culture assimilations and interpretations of technology, the interaction of humans and computers in cyberpunk science fiction, the problems of access for those who are marginalized, the range of feminist responses to technology, and the (in)significance of gender in the computer culture. In addition to book-learning and face-to-face interaction, there is a continual hands-on aspect to the course. During this particular semester, the students learned how to use the Internet, including applications and protocols such as Usenet, e-mail, gopher, ftp, veronica, and ircs. They learned kermit; they wrote hypertexts.

At a conservative university, it does not take much effort to unleash an irreverent discourse. The seminar is popular, but the participants—thus far, white middle- to upper-middle-class students—nearly always initially and politely resist race, class, and especially gender analyses of the problems of computer culture. The biology majors will deny sexism in the culture of science and they will reject science as culture. The English majors will acquiesce to the existence of racism, but argue that it is on the verge of being overcome. The computer-science majors will agree that computers are expensive, but they wonder why the lower classes don't just register at the university, so they will have access to the Internet like all the other university people. When I persist with a radical analysis, there are occasional outbursts. But, in truth, we are almost always polite to each other's face. We wear masks of uncertain origins: perhaps of Lower North/Upper South gentility and grace, perhaps of middle-class morality, perhaps of the affability that disguises power and authority in academic institutions. We wear our disguises of professional politesse.

Once a week, I strip off my university clothes in the women's rest room near my office, pull on blue jeans and a T-shirt, and drive to a shelter for battered women in the region where, for several years, I have played evolving and multiple roles: hotline counselor, office worker, caring listener, dishwasher, literacy worker and, always, ethnolinguist incognito.[2]

The shelter women inhabit a world utterly alien to my university students (or what would be if they ever crossed over) and, of course, vice versa.[3] Domestic violence may cut across race and class lines, but resources to escape it do not. The women at the shelter are typically under- or unemployed, lower- or working-class African American and Appalachian women. Many are the same age as my university students—late teens and early twenties—but most shelter women tote babies on their hips, not to mention bruises on their bodies and other visible and invisible wounds from abusive partners. The shelter is a loud and noisy place, oftentimes with children shouting, babies crying, and mothers yelling. The women spend their days not poring over books, but rather poring over want ads in the newspaper—much of the time for jobs they will not get and apartments they cannot afford. Unless there is significant intervention, there will be no university degree in their future. These are women hard from years of struggling with racism, classism, and sexism. They are sometimes fragile from physical and emotional abuse. They are often coping with their own drug and alcohol dependencies. They themselves struggle with issues of racism, classism, and sexism: There are sometimes barely concealed tensions between white and black women. There are not-so-hidden hierarchies of worth and self-esteem based on the availability of or potential for material resources and emotional support, thus independence and a better future. The shelter is a place of frequent outbursts.

Some time ago, I began a literacy or storytelling circle in the shelter. Typically, we clear the dinner dishes from the dining-room table—five women or so—choose a topic, and write and read for one another. We use pads and pencils. There are no *PowerBooks* for general access here.[4] The literacy levels vary among the women and, because most of them want to have their words in my research writing or see their own stories in a book meant for display at the shelter, I sometimes end up recording their words myself. I may write their stories as we talk or I tape and later transcribe. Most often, however, women write their own stories, essays, recipes, and jokes.

It was at one of these literacy sessions that I met Sheila, an African American woman who looked knowingly past my ratty tennis shoes, turned-backwards baseball cap, and holey jeans to my honed literacy skills. Obviously schoolwise, she asked me about my life at the university. Then, in a move I read as an attempt to assume her place as my equal in a setting in which clients do not automatically feel equal to degreed white staff members or volunteers, she told me about her own life at a university some years back, her interest in science and technology, her love for reading and writing and computers.

Outsiders and Insiders:
The Cyborg as Storyteller

During her short stay at the shelter, I spoke to Sheila at length a half-dozen times. She was a natural storyteller; yet, she was often tired and was secretly suffering from chemical withdrawal. She liked my attention but, for reasons that surely had to do with hidden rules of acceptance among particular peers in the shelter community, she did not want to write by herself in front of the other women. Like me, she was perhaps traveling incognito.[5] We removed ourselves to private corners where she told me her stories. I took notes. It was an appropriate teacher/student relationship. No matter that I was the university professor; she was the teacher. No matter that I was more familiar with the goings-on of the shelter than she was herself; in the drama of domestic violence and poverty, as far as Sheila was concerned, she was the Insider and I was not.

Judging from the cool, curious flicks of her eyes as she read my language, my behaviors, and my body, for Sheila I was an Outsider and a symbol of power. She was alternately a working-class, then unemployed, day laborer, currently homeless. I was the white middle-class woman from academe. I had a stable job, an apartment, a car, a checkbook, and a credit card.[6] At the same time, she had no real idea of my history, my personal identity/ies: my own childhood years growing up in a transitional neighborhood in Detroit—in those dangerous borderlands between all-white and all-black neighborhoods during the years of racial violence, the Detroit riots.[7] In 1967, I watched tanks drive through my neighborhood, groups of black men angrily roam the streets, rocks crash through our house windows, as my mother and siblings huddled in the living room, afraid. Sheila did not know anything about the years I myself spent struggling for financial and emotional independence while I studied during the day at a university on the northern plains and worked at night for minimum wage at the local hospital and nursing home. She could not know the chilling effect my French professor had on me when she tried to discourage me from applying for graduate school because a serious scholar needed to be a person "of leisure" and "of some financial means." Nor could Sheila know about sexism at the university:

a place where women faculty and students often whisper in the hallways about the latest incident in the local gender wars.

Admittedly, in the beginning, Sheila was just a symbol to me: the down-and-out homeless woman. She was also the extraordinary symbol of the power and indomitability of women. This was a romantic, unrealistic, and so perhaps classist and racist view many white and black middle-class feminists have of working-class African American women. In the end, Sheila became much more than a symbol, she became an icon: the cyborg woman.

A *cyborg,* as Haraway would have it, is the one who holds incompatible things together (1991, 149). That was Sheila. Later, I was to learn that the term described as well, if not better, her daughter LaShawnla. The cyborg—half-human/half-machine—was originally begotten in science fiction[8]; now, of course, in the age of technology, the age of artificial prostheses, the cyborg lives. In social and literary theory, it functions as the metaphor or the embodiment of the fictions we see as the social constructions of identities. Identity is not one sure and forever, consistent and constant, construct. Dismantle-able and rearrange-able, neither is the cyborg. Like human identity itself, the cyborg is a composite of differences, opposites, and partialities. As such, it is a rejection of the essentialist or binary modes of thinking of both modernism and early feminism. The cyborg is also emblematic of the boundary transgressions and fusions necessary to an emancipatory politic in a hegemonic androcentric world. The self, often viewed as "fragmented" in the postmodern world, survives and thrives—indeed, finds connection and unity—only in the interdependence of multiple differences: in oneself or in relation to others (Hewitt 1993, 139; Haraway 1991, 151). The shifting, changing, and realigning so natural to the cyborg of science fiction becomes a survival strategy to those with a postmodern cyborg politic. The strategy takes the shape of temporary alliances, ever-changing affinity groups. This is a point to which I will return shortly.

If there were ever a "celebration of human nature as an interdependence of multiple differences," the cyborg—a fascinating and sometimes horribly awesome creature—is it. Johnson captures for me one of the meanings of the cyborg metaphor. She writes:

> All persons are constituted by a number of anthropological constants, essential elements that are intrinsic to their identity. These include bodiliness and, hence, sex and race; relation to the earth, other persons, and social groupings; economic, political, and cultural location; and the like. These constants mutually condition one another, and in their endless combinations are constitutive of the humanity of every person. (1992, 155)

To my mind, Sheila was the quintessential cyborg: the Audre Lorde of *Zami* (1982) with access to computer technology instead of just a rickety typewriter.

In the brief time our lives intersected, it was good for me to know Sheila; perhaps it is not too presumptuous to believe it may have been good for her to know me and my students. I do know, with a fairly reasonable degree of certainty, that Sheila thought deliberately about my students as she told me stories for them. And she *moved* them. The story of her life distressed them. Her drug overdose on her last day in the shelter made them burst with anger. I would like to tell you about this and several other stories of outbursting: angry performances in public spaces.

First, at the risk of sounding callous, I'd like to suggest to you now, and explain to you later, that these moves, shifts, and changes effected between Sheila and my students were made possible by communications technology. What happened between the shelter and university was a kind of electronically facilitated *infidel heteroglossia:* the rerouting of stories from Outsiders to Insiders. Both Sheila and I were invested in this process. It was the reason I sat with pencil poised and it was the reason she gave me her time.

Sheila and LaShawnla

So I will tell you Sheila's story. The story is already an interpretation, of course. The embedded language of cyborgs represents *diglossia,* a mix of languages resulting from our engagement in different worlds. It is what happened when our languages collided. But Sheila looked over this story and said: Yes, it's like this. She wanted no changes. She knew you would read this story and I believe she knew, perhaps better than anyone, the significance of the code-switching. She gave her story as a gift to me and to my students, and she gives it now to you.[9]

Cyborg Women Birthing

Sheila is a thirty-eight-year-old African American woman and she works construction. On the night we met, she is wearing a striped spaghetti shirt and jeans. She has beautiful muscular arms. She is strong, wiry, thin. Her hair is cropped short and her face is lined. It has a masculine strength; the lines make it so. They emanate out from the corners of her eyes. And her eyes are friendly. She smiles easily and she has quiet confidence. She is very beautiful.

Sheila has a daughter named LaShawnla. The name is the same at the beginning and the end. This is important to Sheila. Shawn is the name of a man Sheila once worked with in an office. He wanted Sheila to name her baby after him. She liked him, so she did. They were never lovers. He was just an ugly Irish man, but they talked sometimes.

LaShawnla is a cyborg. She likes science and she likes computers. She can live with contradictions. She reads physics and chemistry as a hobby! LaShawnla does physics for a hobby like other people do the television. In these areas, she is mostly self-taught. Read, read all the time when other kids are outside running.

Sometimes LaShawnla wants to be a physicist. Even more, she wants to be a veterinarian because she likes animals. In fact, she likes animals more than she likes people. Animals, they ain't dumb like most people think. They don't give you grief, girl. They make a fuss sometimes and you can treat 'em.

LaShawnla studied Greek on her own just so she can study medicine. Believe it: She kept a diary in Greek, and when Sheila found it, she said, "Okay, girl, you go right ahead." Codes work for LaShawnla and Sheila does not insist on decryption.

When LaShawnla was in high school, Sheila had to "motivate" the teachers. They assumed girls didn't like science or computers. They did not encourage her. Girls, of course, do not do well in science. Girls don't "do" computers. Sheila says she had to motivate her daughter's teachers to teach and take care of her daughter. And why not? Sheila thinks it was important to keep her daughter's mind "totally expanding. You can't be narrowing your mind." She did not want her daughter to be another "statistic."

So, since LaShawnla was in the ninth grade, Sheila "groomed" her for Wilberforce, a university in the southwestern part of Ohio. It is the first black university. It has a retention rate, says Sheila, of "ninety-nine percent" and "there's only one white teacher." [10] This is good because "white men teachers cannot motivate black girls." The black teachers motivate the students. And you can't pay your way through the university. You have be accepted.

LaShawnla does Sheila proud. Where did she learn to like physics? How did she get the idea to go to college? Sheila knew about the black university because she went there herself. LaShawnla likes science and computers because Sheila does. The ideas were passed from Sheila's mother to Sheila to Sheila's daughter. LaShawnla's father had nothing to do with this because Sheila left him when LaShawnla was two years old. Sheila taught her how to think for herself, be independent, and not to whine. To think for herself. Sheila's mother does not worry about Sheila and Sheila does not worry about LaShawnla. They were raised to take care of themselves.

For some time, Sheila worked in physical therapy. She took care of elderly people. She did "body movement therapy." But even though she got a degree in physical therapy, she works construction because she could not get a good job. The money she made was subsistence. She likes construction. Once she was in the local newspaper in a story about building the Ronald Reagan Highway. Construction is good for you because it keeps you strong and in shape. It is important to take care of your body, to know your body.

Anyway, now she makes decent money, but the physical labor does hurt her body sometimes. She could use physical therapy herself now! Unfortunately, she is in the shelter now because all she gets is physical abuse from her unemployed spouse. He is forever frustrated because he can't get good work.

How could Sheila be expected to know LaShawnla's body too? When she finally noticed how often LaShawnla was going to the bathroom, she asked. LaShawnla was two weeks from full term. Abortions are okay in the first month or two, but not after. So LaShawnla had the baby and she gave it up for adoption. It is good to make the right decisions and this was the right decision. Sheila also had given up a boy baby for adoption once. You have to make the right decisions. You have to have common sense.

And LaShawnla is strung out on crack. The reason: She got pregnant in her second year at the university and she had to drop out. She lost her scholarships. The baby was given over to an adoption agency and LaShawnla never did recover. There's time.

The Icon: Woman in the Machine

After Sheila's story was on paper the way she wanted it, her story was scanned onto my Usenet newsgroup on the university VAX system.[11] My electronic-literacy students read it. Then, over a period of several weeks, they logged onto the Internet and wrote back to Sheila. The students were sometimes poignant in their concern, sometimes pathetic in their naiveté. Despite the fact that my students had prepared, at least schoolwise, for this nevertheless chance interaction—that is, they already had read the feminist critiques of technology and already had talked online and in class about the problems of computer access and discrimination against women and the lower classes—subsequent responses to Sheila at the shelter made it clear that the middle-class university students were actually the sheltered ones.

Before I illustrate this, I'd like you to notice that by encoding her story electronically and dispatching it across the Internet, Sheila transformed herself into an icon, an offering, a site marked for and by the yearnings or illusions of others. Even before this moment, as I've suggested previously, both Sheila and her daughter were two cyborg women: composites of contraries, contradictions, differences. Black women who liked computers! Girls who liked science! On-line, Sheila became a fiction to whom students responded with a range of responses; yet, she was a fiction in a way different from paper fictions. To her, they had to respond directly: in first-to-second person. They had to write to her, interact with her. They were no longer dealing with theory, but rather with a real person obviously struggling with the sociopolitical oppressions upon which the comforts of their (and my) middle-class life depend.

I would like to share some of these responses with you to illustrate the heterogeneity of responses: the kinds of fictions and types of dictions my students created to cope with the story of Sheila and her daughter. These responses, although excerpted and thematicized, are listed serially, as they appeared on the newsgroup.

First of all, there were replies of politeness and genuine concern born of goodwill and utter naiveté. *Don't worry, Sheila, all will be well: courage.* The white middle-class students who tried to interact with her on these grounds used Sheila's story to reaffirm their own faith in progress; after all, women could learn about science and technology if they wanted. Sheila and LaShawnla simply had had bad luck. But they had the know-how to recover. Just do it, these writers seemed to say:

Lori: Your lives are both more complicated now and they are more difficult. But because of the strength both of you have, you can somehow make it work. You always have. You only have to reassure yourselves of that.

Emma: The fact of the matter is that sometimes we make mistakes. Man or woman, black or white. We *all* make mistakes. But it seems to me that you have refused to blame men or white people for things they are not solely responsible for, and continued to push and stretch until you have shaped a life you are willing to take responsibility for. There are enough men and white people even who blame everyone else and use this as an excuse to give up. Yes, we encounter violence and oppression in sometimes subtle ways, but I thank you that you have not just given up and let others "win."

Tara: Your daughter has the ability to use computers and science as a way to improve herself instead of being forced to remain in a demeaning and possible health-risking environment.

In a similar vein, some of the messages [12] were simple, somewhat thoughtless, cyborg celebrations:

258053 (Female): LaShawnla is not your baby anymore, but a full-grown woman who is now a cyborg of the twentieth century.

887654 (Male): You are both redefining the accepted roles of women in our society. In the anonymous life of cyberspace, no specific roles are required. Anyone can jump onto the computer waves and dialogue with other people. They come from all corners of the world and they represent different lifestyles, backgrounds, cultures, ideologies, and religions. Some people specify their social makeup, but many people prefer to remain "androgynous," if you will. In this manner, women can explore any frontier that their heart desires. They are no longer relegated to certain acceptable positions within our culture. You and your daughter have become the cyborgs we are studying [by] pushing the boundaries [and] entering traditionally male-dominated fields. Keep up what you are doing—you may feel like you're just affecting the two of you, but it seems to me that everything you have done has been a service to women (and to men, indirectly). Thank you.

Mike: LaShawnla is the next step in the development of the cyborg. In cyberspace, there are no preset ideologies that must be conformed to (much like the way you have gone through life).

Meg: A [cyborg] does not mean a woman who has lost her femininity and desires to be a woman in a negative way. You show that a cyborg is a pioneer, and someone to be revered.

Some of the student responses were even more explicit in their denial of the inequitable and unfair socioeconomic situation in which Sheila and her daughter—and even the students—found themselves:

Jan: I'm a science major and I have concentrated on biology and chemistry, and thus far in my education, I do not believe that I have been treated differently because I am a woman.

Jeff: If you can inspire LaShawnla to be as courageous as you are, it won't matter so much if things don't change. Maybe things will be better for LaShawnla's daughter.

Leah: LaShawnla, who is different and exceptional, has been shuffled back into a deck filled with the mediocre and the average.

Perhaps embarrassed by their own privileged lifestyles or simply self-centered, some students were, to a degree, at a loss for words:

Tess: Thank you for sharing your story and opening my eyes a little wider. It was a risk on your part that I truly appreciate. I'm sorry that I can't write more . . . but somehow it doesn't seem appropriate.

Emma: This is one of the toughest assignments I've ever been given [i.e., to write to Sheila]. I stared at the computer screen and erased what I'd written three times or more. And still . . . it was unsatisfactory. I simply can't . . . wish her good luck like I've done. I won't be able to sleep easy for weeks now. What I would do with this story if the assignment was to finish it for her . . . and give it a happy ending.

A more generous interpretation of the reactions of Leah, Tess, and Emma perhaps is that the promise of progress is beginning to break down for them, though they cannot fully analyze or articulate their senses or intuitions of what may be "wrong" with Sheila's situation.

Finally, there was a kind of response I often see in the shelter between shelter women themselves. Uttered by a middle-class student with everything apparently going her way, it can only be characterized as pity:

Lori: I wish you all the luck in the world and . . . please know we are pulling for you and praying for you.

Outburst 1: Iconoclasm / The Electronic Body as the Site for Struggle

For all their naiveté, most of the students were moved by Sheila; yet, not all the reactions were polite. There were outbursts. The anger surfaced in these two posts:

Cary: I feel really awkward writing to you because I've never even met you.

213550 (Male): Laushaunla [sic] is smart enough to know what she did and the consequences. She is even strong enough to deal with them.

Normally an involved participant, a disaffected Cary became completely disengaged; in contrast, 213550 was actively hostile even on the Internet; that is, in a very public forum to which anyone had access and where a reader could meditate at length on the written word. Pushed to think and rethink the story, other students responded in class with less restraint. Their spoken words, directed at me and one another, would vanish as they were uttered. They could back-channel, qualify, disclaim. In class, they did not have to directly address Sheila or address her "permanently" in writing. Intentionally or not, these students excavated Sheila's story to justify classist, racist prejudices. Why couldn't Sheila and her daughter rise to their challenges—escape, study, work, dream? In this conflictive discourse, Sheila's battered body became the site of struggle over the meaning of race, class, and gender. Battle lines were drawn in class about her willingness to surmount her life struggles and all the students took sides.

For those students who could decode the languages of racism, classism, and sexism, however, Sheila's body was the site at which it became manifestly obvious how personal struggle and social injustice melded into one politic—an undemocratic politic necessary to redress with concerted social action. This is the moment when words become oppositional cyborg writing: language that exposes androcentric oppression and constructs alternative consciousness. Brandon struck cyborgian irony when he wrote to Sheila:

> **Brandon:** Maybe the last thing you need is a bunch of smart-ass college students talking about your life. From what Carol told us, you take pretty good care of your own and you've been doing it your whole life. . . . Maybe I don't have any right to talk. I'm a man, I'm a white man, and I've never been a father, never broken my back for years on end working to support the ones I love. I hear your story and feel guilty, lucky, stirred up inside, and inspired. For some reason, though, I know your daughter is the future. . . . If all of these pretty letters tell you anything, let them tell you that the only way we can save ourselves is to help each other.

Respected by one and all for his forthrightness, both in this newsgroup entry and in class conversations, Brandon realized that the way out of our moral morass, our involvement and implication in the social injustices embodied by Sheila and her daughter, was to drop the artifices of our middle-class lives and forge connections, seek political unities, across the chasms of classism, racism, and sexism (cf. Haraway 1991, 157).

Outburst 2: Electronic Suicide/Existential Suicide

Sheila herself was proud to see her story in print and to post it online. You could see it on her face as she read and reread the words. Yet, I nervously waited for her spoken approval and, as I waited, I was reminded of other women I've known at the shelter who insist on getting their stories into the women's book: There is a power to literacy understood with pure clarity by people who move in not-so-highly literate worlds as the world of schools and universities. They know that words in writing, even electronic writing, have staying power, so they must matter.

Later, in the privacy of her own room, Sheila put the story and the students' writings to her in an envelope, addressed it to her daughter, and mailed it. She made some phone calls and talked to the shelter staff. She continued with the business of her life, her problems, her possibilities. The normal rhythms of shelter life moved on. Babies cried, women argued. Then, at some point, for reasons only Sheila knows, or maybe not, she closed the door of her room, laid down on her bed, and overdosed on drugs. She was hustled out of the shelter by a white-jacketed emergency medical team.

Was it the ultimate outburst? Was it an outburst related to shelter life? To a vision of a life of poverty or the remembrance of a life of abuse? Was it related to the story? The students? Was it postmodern anxiety? Fatigue? The seeming hopelessness of it all? Horrified, I spoke to woman after woman in the shelter. Why did Sheila do this? What was Sheila thinking? How could Sheila do this? What was bothering Sheila? Did anyone know there was something bothering Sheila? I looked for the clue that would decode what looked like the meaninglessness of it all and perhaps exonerate me as a contributing factor.

Outburst overlapped outburst. The shelter staff—at the time, mostly young white social workers and students, some of whom rarely crossed the line from the white space of the office to the space of color in the house—were livid. They were angry at Sheila for bringing illicit drugs into the shelter. The ambulance sirens and the medics who rushed up to Sheila's room had scared the children. Sheila had signed a lease for an apartment of her own and the staff had just made arrangements for donated, second-third-fourth-hand furniture to be delivered. Why a "suicide attempt"—as they put it—now?

It was the other shelter women who stopped this refrain from echoing in my own thoughts. Renaming the sequence of events, in yet another act of retelling, they—to the number—told me it was no suicide attempt. Certainly, it had nothing to do with the story. *Girl, you make too much of yourself!* In some renditions, it was shelter life. Too much! In most renditions, it was Sheila herself. Sheila was simply tired and she just wanted some sleep. She was tired of children crying and mothers yelling. She wanted to rest. She took too many pills, prescribed pills. It was an accident. In yet other renditions, it was just for fun, some fleeting happiness, to get high, for a thrill. Sheila had been drugging for years. This time, something went awry.

Unable or unwilling to deal with ambiguities, some staff members insisted on their own interpretation, their own retelling or reinvention, of events. They insisted on their own languages of social work, public assistance, and federal funding. It fit the binaries of middle-class mentality: success or failure, good or bad, winning or losing, fighting or surrendering, sane or crazy, life or death. No matter what anyone privately thought, there were no other public interpretations officially possible.

All interpretations were the embodiments of desires, of course. Everyone had a stake in retelling Sheila's story. Naturally, the shelter staff needed to reaffirm its own effectiveness and to reestablish acceptable rules for behavior in the house. The shelter women needed to maintain solidarity with one another and to divert staff suspicion from the women's privacy and lives. The psychiatric staff surely needed to fulfill its function by finding and attending to mentally disturbed persons. My students and I had to believe that the act of storytelling was not self-destructive.

For days I waited for Sheila. She had been taken to the emergency psychiatric ward at a nearby public hospital and, as at the shelter itself, there was an elaborate screening system to keep friends and family out. Several weeks later, I learned Sheila had been discharged from the hospital. Then she disappeared in the maze of crisis centers and social services. I never saw her again.

Outburst 3: Iconoclasm or Violent Electronic Encounters

When the students learned of the turn of events, the unpredictable and—for Christian and modern capitalist mentalities—the sacrilegious, irreverent turn of events in Sheila's "story," they were silent. Then they were depressed. At first, when we saw each other in the small school hallways, we made lifeless signs of recognition to one another. In class, we talked. The depression turned to anger. Sheila had given up: an affront to the narrative of progress so important to our middle-class mentalities. One student, Mattie, tried to strike a balance between goodwill, hope, and critical consciousness, but her anger was apparent. She couldn't imagine a world without hope:

> **Mattie:** Most of the women in our class hold a very optimistic attitude, which I share [about the possibilities for a world without discrimination such as experienced by Sheila]. I think it is vital to cherish hope and optimism in the face of reality. I have come to define my perception of optimism as having a vision of hope while being firmly grounded in reality.

Neither Mattie nor most of the other students could imagine themselves acting as Sheila had acted. They would not accept the overdose as an accident or miscalculation, let alone a sequence of events with its own logic and coherence, apparent in ways inaccessible to the moral imaginations of people who take jobs, apartments, cars, and checkbooks for granted. There were other loud outbursts in class as the students tried to make sense of the turn of events. Then the topic died.

Outburst 4: The Professionals

In my own effort to make sense of the events, I've spoken endlessly to family, friends, and colleagues about Sheila. While taking elaborate measures to ensure that Sheila's real identity can never be known, I've told and retold the story. I set aspects of the story forth in that weird mode hovering between spoken and written discourse that academics call the conference paper. In this setting too—the professional conference—there were outbursts. One Asian woman I recall at a conference harangued me about the ethics of making available the private life of African American Sheila for the public scrutiny of white students. As I listened to the Asian woman's anger reverberate across the seemingly great divide between us, I recalled the paper struggles between white feminists and black womanists of the last decade. I recalled an angry outburst I saw once at a women's-studies conference during which African feminists argued vehemently with African American feminists about white American feminists' participation in the issue of African clitoridectomies or—depending on your view of transgressing cultural divides in the interest of human rights—female genital mutilation. I recalled the endless self-critiques of white postmodern feminist ethnographers who seek to avoid a rhetoric of colonization as they cast their scholarly gaze to the third worlds that, unfortunately, support and thus help to constitute our first worlds. How to avoid or at least lessen the reductionism, essentialism, racism, ventriloquism? How to avoid cynicism?

With the Asian woman, I argued back. As Haraway puts it: "Representation depends on possession of a passive resource, namely, the silent object" (1992, 313). Sheila was no silent object. She coauthored the discourse. Sheila's voice co-created the narrative. She freely chose to initiate the electronic conversations. Why this attempt by academics to silence her story or shield her words? And, yes, she was an icon. I had chosen the word, then as now, with great deliberation. Her electronic body was an icon, a chimera, a mosaic, a hybrid. It dispersed across the Internet and interfaced with other electronic bodies in an unlikely discourse (Haraway 1991, 163). Scattered across the Internet, Sheila's electronic body—that is, her own narrative construct—became arranged and rearranged in the multitude of readings by *Others:* whites, African Americans, Asians, Africans, and Native Americans; or lower-, middle-, and upper-class users; or female and male; or northerners and southerners; or northern-hemisphere and southern-hemisphere users. Indeed, the angry Asian woman who accused me of "using" Sheila was using her too. Representation is unavoidable, even self-representation. Rhetoric is unavoidable, inevitable, inescapable.

The multitude of interpretations of Sheila's story, her "suicide," and her disappearance can go on endlessly. This is a never-ending story. Whatever your own interpretation, you have to agree to one thing: Sheila's course of action from the beginning to the end was the absolute rejection of an identity constituted simply and solely by another's desire (Haraway 1991, 159). From the decision to study physics to the decision to go to sleep, Sheila was acting in ways unpredictable and unbeholden to *Others*' expectations. She continually thought and did the unthinkable with a responsible agency she could articulate and define: Resist the white schoolteachers because they do not know how to teach black children; study physics no matter how useless the school counselor says it is to a black girl's future; leave the man you love because, when he needs to reaffirm his masculine power in the midst of his own ineffectual life struggles, he can only speak with his fists; give away a son and a grandson because they cannot fit into a viable strategy for survival. Sheila was beholden to no one.

More Outbursts On/Off the Internet

The particular outbursts that make up Sheila's story are just some among the many I've witnessed in my traversals of the academic/community divide. On either side of the divide, women rage. We should be listening. To angry shelter women who rage and to the incredulous university students who hear them, the outbursts have meanings and purposes perhaps too numerous, ambiguous, and important to be clearly defined. What tangled stories are behind the words of these shelter women?

> **Kerri:** I will never marry again.

> **Myrtis:** I am tired of everything. I don't feel as if I'm moving in any direction and as though I have four walls enclosing me. I'm angry because I have no control over my life!

> **Victoria:** What are your hobbies? What is your favorite color? Do you wear condoms? Would you agree to both of us having an AIDS test? Do you have a job? [Written as if to a prospective date, but actually addressed sarcastically to the students.]

Sometimes answers, solutions, and resolutions are forthcoming to outbursts and rages like these and sometimes they are not. Yet, it's not just middle-class white students (or social workers and academics) who blunder, gaff, and injure in response. Jolene is a forty-two-year-old woman with five children. She wrote the following reflections on her birthday card to herself, which she then mailed to her abusive spouse. Later, he responded.

> **Jolene:** Why can't I find an apartment? Why can't I get people to treat every-one the way they would want to be treated? Why can't we have enough food to eat? Drinks for the kids? Why can't I live without the fear of someone jumping [me]? Happy Birthday to me. Happy Birthday to me!

> **Jolene's Spouse:** My blood prasher is still 200/120 varry high most of the time. . . . I know you don't care but this could varry likely kill me. For the childrens sake call this off and come home. I have changed the beneficiary on

my life insurance why should you become rich because you have caused my
death. . . . I am going to sue you for defamation of caricter among other things
[sic].

The response of Jolene's spouse is typical of abusive partners. It is a self-
pitying lament that abruptly shifts into an angry outburst. This time it was ineffectual. Much to her spouse's dismay, Jolene would not reappear on cue. But
Jolene, Sheila, and cyborg women like them also refuse to "disappear on cue"
(Haraway 1991, 177). Online and on paper, their stories continue to circulate
and, for whatever reasons and from whatever standpoint, their stories anger
us all.

Cultural Left Activism and Affinity Politics

If these stories were simply acts of telling, perhaps they would not be worth the
effort of retelling. I have learned that many people, including social workers,
students, and academics, have outbursts when poor and marginalized women
speak up. I would like to believe that the stories—the acts of telling—became
acts of doing. Critical teachers build their pedagogies of praxis on the hope of
such transformations. It is true: It is impossible to measure just how the shelter
women's stories affected my students or how my students affect shelter women.
Most likely, some students were not much affected. Yet, across the seminar and
my other courses, some students were moved to action. Two young women vol-
unteered at local women's shelters. Another student began to talk at local high
schools about sexism and other issues of concern to young women. Along with
other women on campus and motivated by many reasons, two of the students
began to organize a student-activist women's group on campus. A few students
became regular contributors to feminist listservs and bulletin boards. There
they engaged in frequently heated dialogue with both antifeminist and feminist
women and men.

There were other instances of *infidel heteroglossia* originating in electronic
connection. A young militant student walked in a "Take Back the Night" action.
She walked with religious women from an intercommunity peace and justice
organization, nuns and laywomen who are Choice supporters and who use electronic literacy to mobilize grassroots support for social action around a variety
of women's issues. Such are the odd and unlikely couplings of postmodern cyborg
activism. Most of these actions I've described are modest but, in a conservative
environment, it takes courage to draw attention to oneself with even such small
steps. Certainly, I make no causality claims in the aforementioned actions. I
make no personal pitches for direct cause-and-effect relations. The worlds of
motives, influences, rationales, and reasons are too complex in the postmodern
world. Yet, I still believe in epiphanies: chance insights, sudden awakenings.

In acts of calculation, however, and using the tools of technology to strategize, a team of educators in the Ohio Valley has been organizing a social-change

educators network, SCENE, which concerns itself with social issues including domestic violence and sexism in the schools, workplace, and community. The goal is to form coalitions between university and community educators and between activists and community people, such as domestic-violence survivors: cultural workers all who merge in joint social-justice ventures in popular education. The group networks with larger political units, such as NAAPAE (the North American Alliance for Popular and Adult Education).[13] In this way, we hope to counter the political isolation so common in conservative environments and to create social change in the community. SCENE is in its embryonic stage and we struggle with issues common to all nascent grassroots community organizations. Yet, we are hopeful and heterogeneous: We seek the membership of both genders and all ages, sexual orientations, occupations, races, and ethnicities. In our newsletter and in our activities, we focus on women's issues and community issues based on cyborg strategies as affinity, not identity, politics.

SCENE tries to take advantage of the potential of technology. The organizers consciously strategize technology-facilitated relations as our hopeful activity, as our utopian undertaking, in a period and place of right-wing, conservative, individual-oriented politics. We see our task as coalition-building around issues, many of which come to light through technology. We watch the television *and* the Internet for information; we collaboratively compose online with the use of networking software; we keep in contact through both the telephone and the keyboard; we sustain the network through the electronic lines. The point is that we use technology to our advantage; we do not avoid it like many progressive activists.

In our utopian dreaming, one of our goals is to create a supportive space for women like Sheila and LaShawnla. We envision it as an action-oriented space beyond the type of sustenance-only space often provided by social services, public shelters, and church organizations. Instead, we see it as a space in which the leadership skills and political strengths of young women and men in the community are actively developed—a place in which critical action derives from local and personally meaningful political themes of significance. What projects could Sheila imagine and carry out in such an environment? As Haraway would have it, this is about "a possible politics of articulation rather than representation" (Haraway 1992, 311).

As a member of such a network—to an even greater degree than what she did achieve—Sheila would become a new discursive subject/object, articulating herself in relationship to other individuals and organized groups (Haraway 1992, 310). Sheila's authority and the authority of women like her would derive not from an ontological status, but rather from constitutive social relationships facilitated by technology. In an effort to help create this space, one of my first activities was to search for funding to install networked computers in the shelter so women like Sheila can have more direct (instead of mediated or limited) electronic access to other women on the information superhighway and in social-action networks like the one I envision for my own area.

By way of concluding and to return to the litany of names I've chosen for this essay that I elaborated on in the introduction—study, tale, polemic, border-traversing—I'd like to remind you that my essay is not primarily about improvement. Certainly, this is not a narrative about progress, though, in this postmodern age and as a progressive educator, I myself am holding out for utopian dreaming. Furthermore, this essay is not about permanence. Sheila has physically vanished. The seminar is over and all the participants are gone. Primarily, this essay is about a series of interruptions, outbursts, and interventions. It is about electronic communication and the interruption of communication because, whenever the stories of the marginalized get told to the middle class, the homogeneity of experience of lives gets interrupted. This is "a fissure in the ideology of the sameness, wholeness, unity of life in America" (Haraway 1991, 164–7).

Still, my story has been about the kind of learning I wish to sponsor as a woman in academe. I want my electronic-literacy students—indeed, all of my students—to know about the problems of representation and a politics of articulation. I want them to understand the politics of writing and writing as politics. I want them and the women in the shelter to see the potential of writing as weaving, networking, affinity, and social action. As a form of situated knowledge, this kind of writing is iconoclastic, irreverent, and against the perfect code (Haraway 1991, 247). Like all matters of representation and interpretation, it cannot be absolutely controlled, contained, canonized, or curbed. In the context of monodimensional and unilinear academic creeds, literary canons, and institutional codes, it is about anarchy. It is postmodern literacy, radical intertextuality, the voices of others bursting out of the margins. As such, this is writing as outburst and I support it.

Endnotes

1. I acknowledge the influence of Haraway as a *guide figure*—as she herself calls the persons who influence her own work. Building on Bakhtin s notion of *heteroglossia* (1981), *infidel heteroglossia* is the generative phrase that Haraway (one of the most important socialist-feminist theorists of our time) develops in *A Cyborg Manifesto* (1991). I also gratefully acknowledge the contributions of all my teachers in this study: most of all, Sheila and, through her words, her daughter LaShawnla. I thank the members of my electronic-literacy seminar, the staff of the shelter, and the women who live there. Finally, I gained much from suggestions from my editors and readers.

2. To be clear, the students and shelter women described in this essay were voluntary, informed participants in my research activities, willing to share their experience and words for scholarly purposes. All names are pseudonyms. I mean to suggest here that I do not highly advertise or "play up" my role as a linguist or an ethnographer of language and literacy, especially to avoid causing embarrassment to anyone who may feel their language practices (or their life situations, for that matter) are inferior. This is a typical (and methodological) problem for English teachers, linguists, and anthropologists. Instead, I try to minimize any perception of my role by others as an "expert" and I try to maintain the role of student/learner in the shelter and in school. To do so, I must

continually strive to sustain attitudes of humility, solidarity, and sincerity with the other human beings. I do so imperfectly, no doubt. The process is the challenge of a lifetime, surely, and not just confined to my professional encounters. In contrast to my choices regarding presentation of self, I often see social workers and other professionals who make the most of their professional roles, and I see the sometimes subtle, sometimes overtly hostile reactions of shelter residents to them.

3. I do not wish to imply that these worlds were mutually exclusive in any absolute sense. Each semester I meet university women who have withstood domestic or sexual violence. More rarely, I meet (mostly nontraditional) students struggling to pay rent and private-school tuition. On occasion, I've met women at the shelter with degrees from colleges, universities, and technical schools. More recently than the semester described in this essay, my students engage in service learning in the shelter. (More on this phase of my shelter/school border-crossing efforts later.)

4. More recently than the phase of my shelter research described in this essay, I bring my own laptop that, as a middle-class academic, I can afford. I also have been given, by a donor, a computer for the shelter women to use. My university has provided Internet access. At the time of the events described in this essay—my third year in the shelter—there were no computers.

5. Clearly, however, Sheila did not have the option of stuffing her identity, like a wad of clothes, into a satchel. Unlike me, she was trapped at the moment, maybe permanently, in a situation of abuse, poverty, and discrimination. What I mean to highlight here is the shifting, partial, and contradictory natures of both our identities.

Over my years in the shelter, I have learned that some women choose not to write in our sessions for a variety of reasons: from the secret shame of illiteracy, to fatigue, to forms of resistance against white middle-class "social-worker types." In this case, my sense was that Sheila did not want to appear too cooperative in front of a group of shelter women unusually resistant to the idea of writing.

6. A Note on Class: One of my points throughout this chapter is that, although we have a tendency to use them as if they were, the labels *working-class* and *middle-class* are not quite absolute or fixed. The labels mask the complexity of social, economic, and cultural issues. *Class* denotes a relationship to labor and production. In this matter, and at different times in our lives, Sheila and I inhabited some common spaces—even though we were both making some (erroneous) assumptions about one another when we first met. Whatever our family histories or cultures, at times we had both been unemployed, underemployed, and employed at well-paying jobs. Interestingly, although Sheila self-identified as a decently paid construction worker, at the time of our interview, she actually was unemployed and homeless. Note, in her upcoming story, that she does not make her current employment status clear. I take this to mean she believed her unemployed status was temporary and that she still saw herself as a construction worker.

To return to the previous point, however, social class might be contrasted to social stratification. Social stratification, the hierarchical ordering of social relations, is related to many factors, including occupational status, education, and income. In this realm, Sheila and I looked at one another across a chasm. She inhabited working-class culture and I inhabited middle-class culture. For an enlightening, if sometimes problematic, discussion of homeless women's perceptions of class, see Liebow's *Tell Them Who I Am: The Lives of Homeless Women* (1993, especially pp. 198–199). Liebow follows Kohn (et al., 1990) in his distinction of class and social stratification, which I find useful in this particular context with Sheila.

7. The Detroit riots, which lasted seven days (July 23–30, 1967), left five thousand people homeless, two thousand injured, forty-three dead, and five thousand arrested. There were 1,142 fires and 1,700 stores looted. It is recorded—along with the Newark riots—as the worst of the riots erupting in 127 U.S. cities during that volatile time. The Detroit riots followed a police raid on an after-hours club where seventy-three blacks were arrested (Trager 1992, 1009).

8. Haraway points out that the term *cyborg* was originally coined by Clynes and Kline (1960) for the man-machine hybrid they imagined could survive in extraterrestrial environments. (See Gray's *The Cyborg Handbook,* 1995, xv.)

9. Editor Dixon wondered whether Sheila, in fact, gave the story to me and "to us" as a "bomb" (rather than as a "gift"). This observation is exactly on target, pun intended. As I mention later in my essay, Sheila's story incited a number of people to hostile or at least suspicious reactions, including a white feminist, a feminist of color, a nonfeminist male religious counselor, and some of my students. Depending on our own vantage points and the investments we have therein, the story makes all of us suspicious of *something*—including the shelter, shelter staff, shelter women, hospitals, psychiatric workers, men, schools, teachers, students, ethnography, researchers, writing, and representation. As a cultural critic and an iconoclast, Sheila, I'm sure, would be delighted.

10. The statistics reflect Sheila's high regard for the university. To my knowledge, they are not correct.

11. If you are an academic or anyone else with access to networked computers, you know, of course, that a newsgroup is a kind of electronic bulletin board that participants access through their computer terminal. It gives users access to a serial type of electronic writing: the participants can read posted messages and then attach their own messages. Typically, the newsgroups are organized around topics. Our newsgroup had been used all semester to continue conversations about electronic literacy we had begun in class.

Most shelter women have no idea of the meaning of Usenet, although, by now, most Americans have heard of the information superhighway. Unlike Sheila, not everyone wants to use it.

I'd like to point out that, in this essay, I am focusing on the interaction Sheila had with my electronic-literacy students. In actuality, Sheila's story was scanned onto the newsgroups of three of my classes—all of which at some point in the semester were considering various aspects of the androcentric nature of science/technology. In addition to my electronic-literacy seminar, I was teaching two sections of a course on women and violence to peace-studies and women's-studies students.

12. The numbered responses were scripted by students who chose to identify themselves with their computer ID numbers, not their birth names. The numbers, like the names, have been altered to protect student identities.

13. NAAPAE is the North American branch of an international network for organizations engaged in popular and participatory adult-education efforts. Current issues of focus include human rights; literacy; women's, environmental, and indigenous issues; and labor/economic education.

2

Macho in the Killing Zone, or How to Survive Multicultural Reality

Barbara Quevedo Davis

The airport shuttle bounces along the flat road, transporting me across the reliable earth of experience. I am on my way to a conference on multicultural literacies where I'm going to give a talk on the word *machismo* and how this Latino concept is misunderstood when the American-English word *macho* is used in its place.

There have been many changes in the cultural environment where I live in California. A linguistic change I have especially noticed in the last few decades is the adoption into English of the Spanish word *macho*. This new use of *macho* in American culture gives the word a complex semantic life: as an American-English term, it denigrates Latinos; as a traditional Latino word, it simultaneously connotes the sexist nature of men while it defines a strong masculine familial nature. Yet, I am unable to avail myself of this handy word. Am I merely oversensitive to a Spanish word being adopted by English speakers? Some Latinos are much less likely to use *macho* in spontaneous speech or in writing, preferring *machismo* or *machista*. Do other Latinos feel as I do?

As a feminist and a Latina, I decide I am unable to use the word *macho* because, in its Anglo context, it sounds like a racist/sexist taunt. But since my feminism is bicultural, I recognize the positive masculine characteristics inherent in the word *macho,* its rootedness in the Latin concept of *machismo*. Could I be both a feminist and a Latina? Not easily. I am caught in a demilitarized multicultural zone, a DMZ. In this zone, when I am speaking to Anglos and even often to Latinos, I am just one talking head, the volume turned off by an omniscient audience who, noting my ethnicity and femininity, already thinks it

23

knows what I will say. I tell myself it is because my Hispanic and Indian heritage shows so clearly in my face.

I share an American national identity with my audience at this multicultural literacy conference, but this identity is a problematic assumption, something I realize even more fully later. Nevertheless, they are all familiar with the word *macho*. Perhaps that is why the auditorium is almost full. Thus, I begin my talk. I choose a tone and manner of approach unlikely to provoke outbursts, or so I believe.

The word *machismo* refers to masculine behavior when it is assertive, directed, and protective of women and other men. It does have a negative side: drinking, sexual promiscuity, and violence. In the English vernacular, however, *macho*—not a derivative, really, but a simplified alternative of *machismo*—has only a mean, slang face: It implies senseless, aggressive male behavior, domination (especially over women) for the pure pleasure of intimidation—although the power of domination is often more in the sexist's mind than in anyone else's, making him ultimately a ludicrous figure.

When Anglo Americans use *macho*, it slips into a derogatory, pejorative semantic zone, a killing zone of the word's complex Latin meaning, its culture of origin degraded. "In Spanish, *macho* ennobles Latin males. In English, it devalues them . . . the newspaper descriptions of alleged mass murderer Ramon Salcido [as] macho make Hispanics cringe" (Guilbault 1989, 6). The American-English expression *macho* represents to me a kind of masculine egotism that oppresses women, so when men and even women use it lightly in formal settings, I feel its negative meaning has gained the advantage, and that the destructive behavior it traditionally represents has gained an uncritical acceptance.

At a conference for Latinas where I presented a paper on the concept *machismo*, the participants agreed there was a protective, benevolent side to the word *macho*. But I worry that appreciation of *machismo* at its best can be one way of forgetting, even denying, the cruel oppressive side of *machismo*. This cultural dilemma troubles me because I see Anglo Americans poking fun at a problematic cultural practice with their slang use of *macho* and Latinas forced to defend what they might privately feel is largely outdated, damaging behavior. As an American Latina, I am caught in the middle.

Latinas are especially sensitive to the distortion of the word *macho* in English because, rather than confronting sexism, the American use of *macho* reinforces an old stereotype: the violent Latino lover with a submissive mate. This ultimate bad patriarch is a chauvinist or sexist at best, a criminal abuser at worst. In conversation with other Latinas, I find that bilingualism has us asking ourselves whether *machismo* carries the same meaning as *sexism*. Since a yes or no answer cannot get past an emotional knot, we decide the answer is probably—heaven help us—another cultural ambiguity. At a workshop for California Latinas, I gave a talk on the traits of *machismo* and sexist behavior. As part of my investigation, I interviewed three Latinas and one Latino who are civic leaders and educators. I wanted to see what others in leadership positions thought of *machismo*. They all agreed that the word implied the oppression of women, but they acknowledged that the average Latino used *machismo* in ways other than its primary sense as a tendency toward sexism or the oppression of women. In the view of these Latino leaders, there is a constructive side to *machismo* behavior that is not identical to sexism.

Most Latinas are raised in a patriarchal, Roman Catholic tradition. But as contemporary women, heirs of feminism, we find ourselves in a unique situation. Judith Ortiz Cofer described it in a poem that has Latinas "praying in Spanish to an Anglo God," who is of Jewish heritage and hoping that if He is not all powerful, "at least He be bi-lingual" (1994, 225). But the implication is that prayers are part of the problem, not the solution. Subsequently, I have found that the work of sociologist Maxine Baca Zinn (1994) refutes the notion that a rigid cult of aggressive masculinity is the result of Latino cultural heritage. Rather, she attempts to prove that male dominance at an individual level results more predictably from socioeconomic status, which applies to men of all cultures and races.

For all those who have Latin culture as part of their American identity, the wholly negative connotation of *macho* in English is troublesome because it is a classic example of a stereotyping word: a word based on a partial truth but that denies another important truth. In this case, the truth denied is the reality and value of productive male behavior within the family—the behavior commonly valued among Latinos that the Spanish word *machismo* partially denotes. Perhaps this behavior does not have a one-word name in English, which is not to say that men who take quiet yet profound pride in their work and families do not exist in other cultures—they do. But the connection between physical strength, productivity, and family allegiance may not be emphasized to the same extent.

Machismo is distinctly a male physical attractiveness and strength. Some of the personal and behavioral attributes implicit in the word *machismo* cover a semantic area not addressed by the word *sexism*. What bothers me is that non-intellectual, physical appeal should be seen as inherently Latin. It points back to the ravenous Latin lover that I dislike as a stereotype, even though I appreciate the aura of masculine strength projected by it. The appreciation of physical strength and health is a valuable part of Western heritage, and *machismo* contributes to this common heritage. The impulse toward health—that is to say, wholeness of body and spirit, or integrity—is what in fact drives many Latinas and their men to emigrate to the United States. This image of vitality is in opposition to the widely held belief that Latinos are fatalistic. In fact, Latino immigration patterns reveal a people who are far from fatalistic. One scholar makes explicit the connection between *macho* and immigration: "Widespread adoption of *macho* and *machismo* may be ascribed to the [growing] Hispanic cultural presence in the United States" (Sullivan 1993, 220). It is apparently a heightened coast-to-coast awareness of Latinos and their culture—as a result of their increased numbers—that underlies the popular use of *macho.*

From the perspective of my Latin heritage, I find it a struggle to admit that in our increasingly technological world, even the constructive side of *machismo* may be sexist. The usage of *machismo* that persists in Latin America—including Latin American United States—results as much from economic turbulence and political oppression as it does from Latino men clinging to their traditional dominance. Los Angeles is one of the main ports of entry for a swelling wave of Latino immigrants from Mexico and Central America. The newcomers are in large percentage farm workers or *campesinos.* Although often rural laborers, twentieth-century Latinos have been exposed to modern technology that has made them more sophisticated. They come to the United States so they and their families can experience economic well-being. However, not all Latino immigrants are poor rural laborers. Many affluent Latin Americans who would be in the oppressive upper class in their native country are moving out of their homeland, uncomfortable with the resistance that political and social reform has stirred up, and resentful of the excessive economic gains of a few.

It does not matter whether the new immigrant is poor or rich; both must deal with the modern American landscape that is epitomized by Los Angeles. Today's obstacle for the Latino newcomer is as much the impersonality of the American urban landscape as it is Los Angeles itself, the favored port of entry: a city that defeats them, a city that exists as a never-never land of virtual reality, a city located on a nonAmerican yet Americanized media continent. It often comes down to a fight over values.

In the United States, the highest values are seen to be superlative wealth and some sort, any sort, of celebrity status. These may not be universal American cultural values, but they are what greets a huge proportion of newcomers to this country. It is worth noting that pursuing either goal, wealth or celebrity, probably would not lead to that sense of wholeness, integrity, and freedom that many immigrants crave and see as a prime American value in both public and private life. This urban landscape that debilitates private life is the breeding ground for the spread of the word *macho* in English. One instrument of this spread has been the public arena of the arts.

It is in the arts where public and private life meet and often are misunderstood. In Latino theatre in this country, for example, a form of popular drama enjoyed a revival with Luis Valdez's Teatro Campesino, which started in Northern California as part of the civil rights struggles of the late sixties. Valdez aimed to reveal Mexican rural culture to an uninformed and somewhat indifferent Anglo American audience as a means of political protest against the economic oppression of Chicano farm workers. His theatre was by necessity a vaudeville that exaggerated the exploits of the bad versus the good guys. Audiences, however, often misunderstood that the violent men and passive women were not realistic figures representing Latin culture (Broyles 1986). Consequently, the word *macho*—the burly, physical meaning of the word—which expresses the thoughtlessly violent American stereotype and only the negative side of the Spanish word *machismo,* was introduced to a large non-Latino audience.

At the end of the same decade, Anglos picked up on another meaning—a more blissfully physical sense—that emerged in The Village People's hit single, "Macho Macho Man": The recent performance of this song in the gothic spoof *Addams Family Values* (1993) occurs in a scene with Latin sailors outrageously toasting and singing about their own maleness in a simplified refrain of the original macho man song as they flirt with an equally boisterous but unimpressed Marilyn Monroe look-alike. She shows, as do the cheerfully oblivious sailors, that this idea of overwhelming male seductiveness is no more than laughable, narcissistic posturing.

The Village People's intention in performing the song can be seen as a broad gay parody of entrenched and intolerant heterosexuality. Yet, what remains in many viewers' minds, I believe, is not gay criticism but rather the ludicrous refrain of "macho, macho man" as a negative commentary on Latino culture. A problem with this type of comedy in both the song and the movie is that its irony can be easily missed by audiences who leave the theatre mindlessly parroting a phrase like "macho man." In this way, a simplistic label of ridiculous Latin masculinity remains intact.

The aggression that is reduced and parodied in "Macho Man" is referred to more explicitly in other forums. We know that posturing militarism, a recognizable behavior, is widespread and certainly not confined to Latin countries. In reality, many countries in the twentieth century have carried militarism to almost apocalyptic extremes, and it is the United States that has the most powerful military today. Nevertheless, when former Secretary of State Christopher speculated on the *MacNeil/Lehrer News Hour* about the nuclear warheads North Korea might be making, he said, "We don't know their motives. It could be just a *macho* thing. But it's unacceptable" (1994). Was the Secretary implying that American military behavior was unacceptable too? I don't think so. He was suggesting that excessive, unwarranted violence was unacceptable, that it was not American, and that it was so foreign that an English derivative like *militarism* would not do. Instead, the Spanish word *macho,* an American slang word, should characterize North Korea's behavior.

Another example appears in Sullivan's article in the 1983 *Journal of Ideology and Literature.* She quotes President Carter using *macho* to label aggression on the part of a Republican opponent. Apparently, there has not been any change in the last decade. Sullivan goes on to say that "most speakers and writers who use the word appear not to connect them [*macho* and *machismo*] with Hispanic culture" (Sullivan 1993, 219). But it is my contention that *macho* does not serve the intentions of these Anglo American speakers. If our political and intellectual elite wish to point to excessively aggressive behavior—the militarist or sexist—they should not use the word *macho,* unless they specifically wish to target Hispanics, for we surely will be hit.

Related to aggression is stoicism, again seen in *Addams Family Values.* This movie uncovers the phobias Americans have about Latino families. While Gomez and Morticia Addams have taken an Anglo name, they still address each other with Latinate endearments, enduring both insults and joy with expressionless faces in a hilarious, exaggerated version of upper-class Latin stoicism. Their dark but cheerful attachment to anything corpse-like is an ironic comment on the Latin acceptance of death. But somehow this parody merely exaggerates *macho*'s negative sense for me and never does modify the word's sexist connotation.

The Village People's original hit song "Macho Man" produced a silly everyday alternative for referring to someone as a sexist. (Perhaps the 1970s term *chauvinist* sounded too remote and esoteric, while *pig* was too shrill or threatening to apply to the everyday sexist.) English-speaking Americans have taken a certain freedom with the Spanish word *macho,* which reveals the sometimes perplexing blend of familiarity, affection, and ignorance that exists in North America toward Latin culture. So while there was no deliberate conspiracy to demean Latinos, the resulting usage trivialized the cultural pattern of *machismo* and simplified *macho* into a faddish word.

I am not suggesting we ignore or admire cultural attitudes and practices if they harm people; a word may be needed to point to certain masculine behaviors. Certainly, the incorrigible male egotist, both disdainful and envious of female power, is a Latin archetype sometimes shaping the behavior of the real-life Latino. I do not in any way claim that such behavior has vanished from everyday experience, either in Latin America or in this country. But as I have explained, *machismo* allows for broader, more complex implications than the pejorative English slang word *macho.*

We often borrow words from other languages to represent an idea that seemingly cannot be contained within our own; the French *sangfroid,* for example, suggests both a charm and cold-bloodedness for which we do not really have an English word. The German *gestalt* refers to a special pattern of behavior and recognition that does not fit any one English word. But those two examples do not reduce the French or the German people to stereotypes; indeed, they express an admiration for the French and German cultures. In contrast, *macho* suggests depreciation and opposition to Latino culture; it names what is simpleminded aggressive or violent behavior, often directed at women. The fact that there is an English near-equivalent to *macho* (i.e., *sexist*) emphasizes that the use of *macho* might result from unconscious contempt or disapproval on the part of the speaker toward Latin culture. The jocular, casual use of *macho* in everyday English is therefore not innocuous; in fact, it could be considered a bigoted assault on current Latino culture, having a divisive effect on the culture at large, with those Americans not of direct Latino descent disowning that part of their Western heritage every time they say *macho*. The use of *macho* is likewise divisive depending on whether it is delivered by a non-Latino speaker to a Latino listener or vice versa. As it is relayed, it sounds a clash of identity and difference. It defines a stance, a position taken, furthering cultural conflict and misunderstanding.

Of course, any word's meaning can change, moving from a positive to a wholly negative connotation. Feminists have shown us that we can consciously change our word choice or adopt new terms within a relatively brief period: *Ms* for *Mrs.*, for example. Furthermore, we can change the implications or connotations of a word. Hence, *lady* is now an insulting term to many college-educated women, whereas *bitch* might suggest an enviable level of power and sexual freedom. In a Central American and Mexican context, *hembraismo*, a Spanish equivalent of *feminism*, is a political term for women who organize protests against military and governmental oppression. *Hembra*, while it was once the equivalent of prefeminist *bitch*, now also means a strong-willed, courageous woman who fights for loved ones and principles.

Hence, *hembra* has become a term elevating Latin culture. Because *macho* shows no signs of undergoing a similar ameliorating change, might it be possible for English speakers to drop *macho* and stick to the less culturally charged, but no less precise word *sexist?* Or perhaps we all could make the stretch to the three-syllable word *machismo*, using it in its full complexity? Would not such a change show true multicultural literacy because it would avoid unintentional prejudice? I am not saying that we confuse verbal habit with genuine tolerance. Actions speak louder than politically correct words. On the other hand, speech is action. It can shape or distort reality. And there is no more voguish verbal distortion these days than *macho*.

(My talk on *macho* at the multicultural literacies conference ends here. What follows describes what I thought and how I felt during the question-and-answer period after my talk and at the picnic at the end of the conference.)

The conference audience stirs briefly, shifts from side to side. Silence. Then one person speaks up: "You can't keep people from saying *macho.*" A couple of heads nod in agreement. No debate there. No questions.

There is at least one Latino in the mostly Anglo audience. He observes that *macho* is used primarily by Latinos—a word used by men among men. "I wouldn't use it in front of you, Barbara." I am put in my place, a Latina protected and also subordinated by a man. I frown at him and say nothing. Here is an example of the disadvantage of having one culture imprinted on your face and at least one other imprinted on your character and mind. This is the side of *macho* that goes bad for the adult woman like me. I am no longer a Latin girl looking up to a protective, solicitous father. I am an adult woman looking at a sexist.

Still, I feel myself in a time warp: *It is the 1950s. My father, who emigrated from Mexico, has taken us to a county-wide celebration of Independence Day, el 16 de Septiembre, the day we used to celebrate before Cinco de Mayo got popular. One man has stabbed another, who is lying on the ground with a bloody face and arm. My mother, who is not from Mexico, is angry about the knife fight and quickly rounds up all five of us children. My father is summoned from the speech he is giving somewhere else on the fairgrounds. The next thing I remember, he is sitting at my bedside as I do a child's suckle on a blue popsicle. He's saying with concern that he is going to buy us that new thing, a television, so we won't stay out so late in the evenings. There will be no more fiestas or drive-in movies on warm California evenings, no more falling asleep over each other in the big Studebaker after playing in the sand in front of a gigantic movie screen in the twilight.*

This memory defines *machismo* for me, and my father is its positive embodiment. But as the adult woman who has been raised to speak English by her mother and trained in English language and literature at school, I also realize through this memory the limited value of *machismo*. The protective father is outgrown by the adult woman who learns to sustain herself and who feels a certain nostalgia for the very activities her father's action has ended.

The editor of a well-known multicultural composition textbook motions to me with her upraised hand. She is at the back of the auditorium, but she speaks softly, so I have to strain to hear her: "My Chicano students think Richard Rodriguez is a fool. A sellout." Have I heard her right? What does her comment have to do with my talk? I have not mentioned Rodriguez.

Does she think everything Hispanic has to do with a precocious altar boy, a stellar student hungering for memories? A colleague has since suggested to me that this woman was equating Rodriguez with Latino excellence and his excellence with *macho*. Here my bicultural background is a disadvantage, because *macho* as male intellectual excellence is not a concept that readily occurs to a Latina. I imagine the editor who is questioning me assumes I share the claims of her Hispanic students and see Rodriguez only as a political conservative, not appreciating his intellectual talent.

Her tone seems insincere, so I am wary about answering her. Her students, too, may have been wary, telling her what they thought she wanted to hear. They may have known that many Anglos mistakenly assume all Latinos to be politically left-wing or liberal. In fact, the political makeup of the Latino community is complex and, in some states, much more likely to be conservative (to use one of the two popular but inadequate political labels). What she claims as knowledge regarding her students' reactions to Rodriguez is questionable. Perhaps she is only baiting me, hoping I will make some sort of politically incorrect comment that would alienate this academic audience.

My own graduate-school career was lived under the umbrella of an illusion, that the rhetorical triangle was a perversely inverted uterine symbol conceived by men but effectively upturned by feminists. In the seventies, when I was a graduate student, feminists had begun to exert a great deal of influence in academe. But for me, the interest in books had started with Aristotle and

Seneca, precursors of Aquinas, Loyola, and Bacon; Coleridge, Eliot, and Woolf came along much later. My first exposure to spoken public rhetoric was in Spanish. My father translated legal papers into Spanish and interpreted in California and Texas courtrooms.

But at home, instead of his native Spanish, he often used English, the language my mother's New Mexican family had mastered two generations before. English was my mother's language, a domestic and personal language for me, encouraging individual development. When she disagreed with my father, she said so in English. Furthermore, it was the language spoken by clever entertainers on television, like Lucy and Desi, who in my mind spoke Spanish only in ceremonious gatherings off-camera.

The unstructured potential English represented for me was a kind of linguistic promise that persisted through my years of graduate study in literature. Something new always seemed possible in this wonderfully improper language. The revisionist perspective on a male-dominated Western culture that American feminists of the sixties and seventies brought to life seemed to me unsurprising, given my own personal experience that English had always had an anti-establishment character. I shared a good deal of the feminist view of history and culture. Therefore, I expected that an academic audience such as the one at this conference, which was predominantly female, would engage in a healthy discussion about language, that they would critique their cultural bias, just as I have heard such women do in feminist-led discussions where the topic was gender bias in language.

There is a picnic after the last day of talks and workshops at the conference. A light-haired man in his thirties who gave a talk after me gets to be captain of the volleyball team. He does not speak to me and expresses disdain when I wind up on the same team. Although I score points for the team, he says "Bye" loudly and pointedly when I leave the game. Perhaps he did not like my criticism of the American word *macho*, which his sexist behavior suggests is alive and well in his person.

There is only one other Latina at the conference. She is from the University of Denver and her parents live in Mexico. We had been introduced by one of the workshop coordinators. At the beginning of the conference, she tells me she does not know whether she will attend my talk because she already knows what *machismo* is. Yet, she has every reason to trust that my academic credentials and heritage will make my comments reliable, even enlightening. What her tone of voice tells me is that no American woman, brown or white, can tell her anything about Latino culture.

This woman is more immersed in Latin culture than I am because she regularly crosses the border to visit family. My own immediate relatives, on the other hand, have lived in the Southwest for several generations with no political allegiance to Mexico. But like other Latinas who have more recently emigrated to the States, she often feels betrayed or "one-upped" by Americans who criticize Latino culture. Their own cultural egotism is a perverse form of *machismo,* another reason I wish such Latinas would count themselves more loudly as feminists in order to vanquish the *macho.* But at that moment, all I get from my conference Latina is an *Addams Family* stare (and why do I make reference now to that stereotyping movie?). She then turns to talk to another woman to advise her on how to make a soufflé.

But her interlocutor is more interested in barbecue. She is with several other young women who are graduate students, who tell me they liked my talk on *machismo.* They did not know that *machismo* had a positive side. They think *macho* can be a dangerous word because it is a way of denying American aggression, especially militarism, in the way it displaces violence onto Latino culture. We all decide to go out to dinner at a local bar.

I should not forget that it is more than twenty years past the civil rights and feminist revolutions of the 1960s and '70s, and that the DMZ has expanded to include not only women, but also Latinos, Asians, and African Americans, among other ethnic identities of working-, middle-, and upper-class backgrounds. It is not only my bones and brains that matter, but also an entire ancestral and economic history my audience imagines imprinted on my face. Now I am not only my own reality, but also inevitably somebody else's illusion. For how can we possibly know enough about the cultures and histories our diversity requires?

Meanwhile, I have been experiencing reality at its fullest in the new American DMZ, and have been provoked by an irksome Latina into making some of the same stereotypical references encompassed by that despised word whose use I would proscribe.

So I am thinking of the negative side of *machismo* as the conference ends. I return to my original hope: that the English use of the word *macho* will be dropped by informed speakers of both Anglo American and Latino cultures. An alternate but more dangerous solution would be the complete deconstruction of *macho,* which already may be in progress.

Response
Whose Icon?

James Degan

Carol Winkelmann declares that she "still believe[s] in epiphanies: chance insights, sudden awakenings." More power to her, for all serious and conscientious teachers should share her hope for such occasions. Her experimental assignment, which both employs computer technology and directs students toward social issues, is—at first glance—intriguing and admirable. She endeavors to take the class outside the classroom. She asks her students to confront the different and all-too-often untouchable world of poverty and desperation ignored by many Americans. To Winkelmann, the use of computer technology allows—and in her class, mandates—something she calls "border-traversings." Her assignment constitutes an attempt to bridge what she terms the "academic/ community divide." As a "case study," Winkelmann's essay is an innovative but flawed experiment. Its focus is lost between a desire for idealism and the sort of control research scientists expect in a laboratory.

Winkelmann's tone (and focus) wavers between sociopolitical jargon (she describes herself at the outset as a "white middle-class female" with a "postmodern socialist-feminist ethnolinguistic identity") and a more engaging, lyrical narrative voice. At times, it is moving, powerful narrative; at other times, it comes off as undigested polemic. I like Winkelmann's edgy account of her friendship with Sheila, the woman who becomes the compelling, ambiguous, and ultimately elusive center of this essay. Initially, I appreciate the account of her attempts to "engage" the students in her writing seminar to communicate with Sheila, to know and understand her by writing to her on the computer, although the final results are disappointing. There is a good deal of self-searching, even uncomfortable self-scrutiny, in this aspect of the study.

I am less comfortable when Winkelmann describes Sheila as an "icon." Early in the essay, she characterizes Sheila as "just a symbol to me: the down-and-out homeless woman." She acknowledges this impression as a "romantic, unrealistic, and racist view," but while she proceeds to document her evolving relationship with Sheila, by the end of their "collaboration" (i.e., Winkelmann's transcription of Sheila's autobiography and the dissimulation of that text to her students), her description of Sheila as an icon ultimately dehumanizes and manipulates her. To most readers, an icon is a visual image, frozen in time and space, beautiful, but inevitably a remote, lifeless representation of an idea (or ideal). I do not think this is what Winkelmann originally intended to do, but there is a sense of the person becoming an object, primarily for the purposes of research. When Winkelmann equates the icon with something she calls "the cyborg woman," the image she intends us to imagine and accept as a viable identity becomes more problematic and more elusive. She implies as much when she describes the cyborg as "half-human/half-machine."

Winkelmann never satisfactorily articulates exactly what a cyborg woman—or a cyborg *anything*—is. The term itself raises inevitable and perhaps unfortunate echoes of the technological dystopias of Huxley and Orwell. While Winkelmann quotes Haraway, a proponent of cyborg politics, Haraway herself remains inaccessible. Any message she has is congealed in a mix of jargon and polemic. Citations from Haraway do little to illuminate either her philosophy or Winkelmann's pedagogy. What, for instance, does Haraway mean when she celebrates "Cyborg politics [as] . . . the struggle against perfect communication?" I assume Haraway resists the notion of an absolute, monolithic language imposed on everyone, because it would inevitably freeze and codify human experience, emotion, and intellect. In theory, this is fine. In the reality that is pedagogy, however, the theory sounds merely like theory.

Winkelmann's implied desire to "connect" between Sheila and the students in her writing seminar, unfortunately, is undermined by her assiduous insistence on controlling the assignment itself. How ironic that, for all her enthusiasm for the Internet, and thus the implied opportunity for immediate, universal communication—virtual "call and response"—Winkelmann seems intent upon keeping Sheila as distant from her writing students as possible. While this may be merely a reflection of her desire to protect Sheila (but why, then, bring her into the project at all?), it strikes me more as a compulsion to both oversee and interpret the assignment; that is, to predict and then conveniently validate circumstances and evidence implied therein.

In short, Winkelmann wants to have it both ways: her frequent reminders to the reader that she is an "ethnolinguist" weaken her assumed tone of sympathy and support both for Sheila and the writing students. Sheila well may be a potential academic (even an ethnolinguist) in her own right. Her intellectual curiosity, particularly her interest in the sciences, is compelling evidence of this. So is her encouragement of LaShawnla's endeavors in similar areas of study. But we never actually *hear* or *read* Sheila's testimony, except in the transcribed (and, hence, translated) version by Winkelmann, who essentially becomes Sheila's proprietor. Winkelmann's authorial intervention ("[s]o I will tell you Sheila's story") is actually less a concession than an expropriation.

Winkelmann's students are similarly "silenced." While Sheila is "just a symbol," Winkelmann's students are dismissed across the board as "privileged" and "naive." Winkelmann damns them with faint praise in their initial attempts to respond to Sheila. If they were "naive"—I think *uncomfortable* is nearer the mark—it is not so much because they were indifferent, but more that they felt awkward about initiating a dialogue. They had no contact with Sheila other than what was "published" on the computer's "bulletin board" following Winkel-mann's editing.

This is why Winkelmann's "possession" of Sheila and her narrative is so problematic and, ultimately, so flawed. Her insistence on remaining the "care-taker" of Sheila and Sheila's narrative perpetuates (albeit unintentionally) a racist and sexist sense of automatic, assumed rights of property. When she rele-gates Sheila to the status of an icon, Winkelmann invites her students to address a fictional character. Perhaps this is just as well—her students, who linger on the periphery of this essay, seem just as fictitious.

Response
Beyond Stereotypes: Las Latinas Caught Between Linguas y Culturas

Annemarie Pérez

The difficult position of Barbara Quevedo Davis in her essay *"Macho* in the Killing Zone, or How to Survive a Multicultural Reality" is representative of the conflicted position of the Latina feminist. She is caught between protesting the "adoption" or appropriation of the word *macho* as a descriptor of sexist male behavior that signifies, "domination . . . for the pure pleasure of intimidation" across ethnic lines, while simultaneously criticizing and stereotyping Latino men and Latin culture in general. While as a Latina Quevedo Davis attempts to protect *la cultura* from Anglo misrepresentation, as a feminist she also must question *"machismo'*s positive protective face, which, if not identical with sexism, is nonetheless patriarchal." I find this paradox a depressingly apt example of the dual nature of the Latina's marginality. On the one hand, she stands in solidarity with her community; on the other, she must protest that community's oppression of her. The response of her audience indicates that Quevedo Davis' refusal to retreat from her criticism of either Anglo or Latin culture is met by a move by both Latino men and white women to force her out of the speaker's position back into silence.

As members of the larger Latino community, Latinas indeed do feel "our culture of origin degraded" by the adoption of the term *macho* and the word's derogatory use by the externally oppressive Anglo society. While it is true that Latinos, like anyone else, can be sexist, the use of a culturally exclusive term like *macho* to describe *all* male sexist behavior forces the assumption that Latinos are inherently more sexist than men of other cultures—something that Quevedo Davis indicates is not supported by sociological research. Yet the "positive" protective face of *machismo*—which Quevedo Davis illustrates by relating the story of her father—may be fine for protecting children, but is trivializing for an adult woman. Yet, I have often felt (and Quevedo Davis' tone indicates that she has similar concerns) that by urging the resistance of *machismo,* I am not merely criticizing my culture in general, but my father in par-

36

ticular—whose sacrifice and hard work have helped me place myself in a position where, ironically, I am able to write a critique of him.

Given Quevedo Davis' desire to resist mischaracterizations of Latin culture, her description of the role played by Luis Valdez's Teatro Campesino in the origins of the *macho* stereotype is worth revisiting. While it is true that the Teatro performed plays that were often bawdy parodies, Quevedo Davis' comment that Valdez "aimed to reveal Mexican rural culture to an . . . Anglo American audience" misrepresents the mission of the Teatro Campesino. The mission of Valdez's theatre, which began in the late 1960s, was to inform Chicano farm workers of their rights and urge support for the United Farm Workers Union (Kanellos 38). The intention was not to educate Anglos; indeed, Anglos were not even part of the Teatro's audience in its early years. Knowing this, I question Quevedo Davis' explanation that the Teatro helped the term *macho* enter larger popular culture.

When reading Quevedo Davis' essay, I found myself most drawn to the audience responses and nonresponses to her presentation. Several days after I read the essay, in a graduate seminar discussion of *This Bridge Called My Back: Writings by Radical Women of Color* (Moraga and Anzaldúa 1984), I found myself reflecting back to those responses and comparing them to the reactions to the anthology by the (predominantly) white feminists in my class. *Bridge* was "historicized" as "significant but dated" and "theoretically naive." As I sat in silence, trying to find the words to argue for the continued authority of a text—published by a nonuniversity press and edited by untenured women in their twenties—to express individually and collectively the anger of women of color at the American and European feminist movement, I found that I was too afraid to speak for fear of being deemed naive. Before I could object to this condescending judgment of *Bridge,* an Asian American woman defended the text's power, which she felt had allowed her to see herself as both a feminist and an intellectual. I felt so grateful for her courage, but also embarrassed that the "intellectually naive" remark had pushed my own similar opinion on *Bridge* into silence. How had Quevedo Davis responded to the silencing criticism her paper had received? This essay's publication indicates that her reaction was not silence. Her critique of *macho/machismo* thus becomes all the more powerful.

Response
Response-ability
John Schilb

I feel self-conscious about responding to Carol Winkelmann's and Barbara Quevedo Davis' essays for three reasons. First, I fear that in my own few pages, I will fail to honor the considerable range and depth of these essays. So let me say at once that for me, each brings up several important issues and does so with keen awareness of complexity. Second, given these essays' attention to the effects of people's social positions, I fear that I may come across as presumptuous in commenting from mine: that of a white, straight, middle-class man of Anglo-Saxon and Scandinavian descent. Of course, I did not have to read these essays to know that not everyone enjoys my privileges and speaks from such a vantage point. But the essays remind me that I have got to keep my social location in mind if my comments are not to seem merely solipsistic. (I realize they may appear that way anyway!)

The third reason I respond with trepidation is that the two essays are so much *about* responding. Winkelmann recalls how she, her students, and her conference audiences have responded to Sheila, as well as how Sheila herself responded to academics and others in the world around her. Quevedo Davis spends the second half of her essay discussing how members of her audience reacted to her original conference talk. Indeed, in elaborating the title of this volume, editor Dixon defines an *outburst* as "a response to a conflict that expresses a person's orientation to that conflict and to the social and political conditions that underlie it." I would add that rarely do people use the word *outburst* to describe a speech act of their own. Most often, it is a label they give *someone else's* speech act in the process of responding to it. In this respect, *outburst* differs from *coming out,* a term that sounds somewhat similar but is nowadays often used by the person engaged in the speech act it denotes. Worth remarking, too, is that the word *outburst* hardly ever functions as a compliment. When people call some act an outburst, they are usually being negative or neutral. In part, this book as a whole is wonderfully thought-provoking because it asks us to re-evaluate the term. It suggests we can learn much from attempting to see at least some outbursts in a positive light. Defining *writing as outburst* as "the voices of others bursting out of the margins," Winkelmann even ends her particular essay by declaring "I support it." To me, her stand is indeed worth considering. Nevertheless, as she may agree, we should remember that, at present, the word commonly has a less glowing aura.

In her introduction, Dixon notes that "just who is allowed to perform an outburst when, where, and in the company of whom is part of what this volume seeks to determine." These two essays, and presumably the rest of the volume, explore as well the issues of rhetoric, ethics, and politics that inevitably arise in acts of *response*. Who gets to respond? Who is deemed worthy of a response? These questions are similarly important, as are the questions of when, where, and how responses are made.

Further complicating the whole business of response is that, once they are spoken or written, words can travel to various sites, take on different meanings and connotations, and get responded to by people distant from and unappreciative of the original circumstances of their utterance. As Quevedo Davis anecdotally reminds us, even the audience sitting right in front of a speaker can react insensitively to what he or she has just said. At the end of her essay, Quevedo Davis refers to deconstruction and, for a couple of decades now, theorists associated with it have pointed out that words *always* take on what Quevedo Davis calls "a complex semantic life." To have public meaning and significance in the first place, they cannot be tethered to their utterer's original presence; rather, they must risk appropriation and reappropriation.

If anything, contemporary social developments have heightened semantic instability. Winkelmann discusses at length how electronic networks can circulate a text over great distances, making it prone to numerous shifts in interpretation and use. In tracing some of the dynamics between and within the many cultures now inhabiting the United States, Quevedo Davis describes a situation bound to promote *heteroglossia,* including various uses of the word *macho.* As she points out adaptations of this word that especially disturb her, Quevedo Davis also notes the increasing power of the media, now able to take a word and put almost any spin on it they choose. In the specific case of *macho,* examples continue to abound. Think of the recent commercial in which a man stuffs himself from a Doritos bag as he dances to the song "Nacho Man."

Over the years, many people have criticized deconstruction, including numerous feminists and other advocates of social change, who worry that because it stresses the indeterminacy of language, deconstruction undercuts their effort to name and transform oppressive material conditions. How are progressive movements helped when deconstructionists muse about the verbal tensions at work within a metaphor rather than about the forces of capitalism, racism, and sexism that operate within the world at large? To quote from Quevedo Davis' opening sentence, I see these critics of deconstruction as concerned that "the reliable earth of experience" will be overlooked if people get interested in how words and their meanings are subject to various kinds of "transporting." In fact, I can imagine many deconstructionists becoming preoccupied with this very term, because etymologically a metaphor *is* something that "transports" meaning. At any rate, the fears of social activists have not been adequately addressed by deconstruction's chief American advocates, most of them white males comfortably ensconced in academe and out to deconstruct literature alone.

Nevertheless, semantic flux is not necessarily to be decried. Rather than protesting every instance of it, all of us might be better off targeting particular cases that bother us, especially those that enable the powerful to maintain dominance. At the same time, we might strive to recognize ways in which we ourselves might productively appropriate or "transport" words we encounter. After reading Quevedo Davis' essay, I am convinced that the word *macho* has been used in unfortunate ways and should be dropped. Yet, I assume that she is not protesting *all* departures from original meaning. After all, to do so would be to reject basic dynamics of language. Furthermore, it would put the critic at least roughly in league with the English Only movement, as well as other groups that ominously pursue social control through linguistic control.

I have no idea whether Quevedo Davis would like my appropriation of her opening words. Nor am I certain that she means to be ironic with her phrase "the reliable earth of experience," although much of what she proceeds to say complicates it. Her essay shows that a person's "experience" may involve not only numerous settings and audiences, but also shifting self-presentations and self-interpretations, with various aspects of one's identity fading into the background or coming to the fore at any given moment. I am especially struck by the intricacy of thought Quevedo Davis displays as she concludes her reminiscence about her father: "The protective father is outgrown by the adult woman who learns to sustain herself, and who feels a certain nostalgia for the very activities her father's action has ended." Quevedo Davis remembers her father being called away from giving a speech; to be the kind of person who now gives speeches herself, she has developed a nuanced, multilayered view of him. In other words, "the reliable earth of experience" is not all that "reliable," at least if we take *reliable* to mean beyond reinterpretation and rewriting.

At the outset of her essay, Winkelmann also indicates that "experience" may involve "transporting" rather than being opposed to it. Although she lists various elements of her material situation, and carefully delineates the geography of the "borderlands" she inhabits, she mainly discusses the "border-traversings" involved in her interactions with various people, including her students, Sheila, other women at the shelter, and audiences at conferences. As she notes, she is able to cross certain borders because she has access to computer networks; in this respect, concrete experience and the possibility of linguistic "transport" are intimately related. At one moment in her essay, when she is discussing the shelter women's desire to see their stories in print, Winkelmann does appear to share their belief that "words in writing, even electronic writing, have staying power." But I take this statement to mean not that linguistic meaning is fixed, but rather that words cannot go anywhere unless they survive in the first place by being recorded in some form. Besides, in the spirit of Haraway, Winkelmann calls for "an *infidel heteroglossia:* a multitude of multitudes of perspectives on life, a multitude of Other-minded discursive practices." In various respects, this is "transporting" carried to extremes. Obviously, Winkelmann refuses the academic hermeticism characterizing much deconstruction so far; just as obviously, she rejects the well-regulated linguistic climate dreamed of by many of its opponents. Instead, she hopes for a discourse whose idioms, meanings, procedures, and participants are unlikely to remain in place. More precisely, she would have a discourse continuously open to changes by "the children, the women, the indigenous, and the other silenced, exploited, and poverty-stricken populations on the planet."

Winkelmann's is a stirring vision and, after reading her essay, I find myself sharing it. I especially like the distinction she makes, following Haraway, between *representation* and *articulation*. I take it that a representation model of social action would operate from the premise that a particular person could stand or speak for an entire group. In a project of articulation, on the other hand, people strive to forge provisional alliances in the face of their differences as well as their similarities. The representation model can be associated with metaphor, the figure of similitude, for it assumes that a group is so uniform that a single member can symbolize the rest. Articulation is based on metonymy, the figure of proximity, for it aims to connect people through laborious contacts rather than taking commonality for granted.

As Winkelmann indicates, her student Brandon's message to Sheila nicely exemplifies this model. I hesitate to judge how the various members of the class responded to Sheila, mostly because I myself have not been faced with having to decide what to say to her. But I do admire Brandon's sentiments, and not only (I hope!) because he is a fellow white male. Rather, I agree with the agenda he begins to outline: "Maybe the last thing you need is a bunch of smart-ass college students talking about your life. . . . If all of these pretty letters tell you anything, let them tell you that the only way we can save ourselves is to help each other."

Much as I like Winkelmann's essay, I do have a reservation about one of her main points. I appreciate her distinction between viewing Sheila as a symbol and viewing her as an icon. Clearly, this is a distinction between treating someone as a stereotype (the representation model) and treating her as a person with multiple dimensions and affinities. Furthermore, along with Winkelmann, I am excited by Haraway's notion of the cyborg woman, finding this concept a promising avenue for socialist-feminist inquiry. Yet, I am more leery than Winkelmann about taking the cyborg woman as *the* prototype of the future and regarding Sheila as her embodiment. I am always nervous when any concept threatens to become what Burke (1969, 355) calls a *God term,* leaving people unable to sense its possible limitations and explore better alternatives. Insisting that Sheila is a cyborg, I think, does risk making her a symbol rather than an icon. Besides, to sanction the reign of a master concept is to discourage the *heteroglossia* that Haraway and Winkelmann otherwise promote. Ironically, to permit the dynamic, multifarious universe they see emblematized by the cyborg woman, they may have to resist deifying (and thus reifying) the figure herself.

As I read Dixon's remarks about outbursts and saw in these two essays some examples of them, I kept thinking about a speech by Audre Lorde that I was privileged to hear. Entitled "The Uses of Anger: Women Responding to Racism," it was Lorde's keynote address at the 1981 National Women's Studies Association Convention, a meeting devoted entirely to racism. The speech subsequently was published in a volume of Lorde's prose, *Sister Outsider: Essays and Speeches*. In effect, Lorde was suggesting a way for white women to interpret so-called outbursts by women of color. "Anger is loaded with information and energy," she pointed out. "Every woman has a well-stocked arsenal of anger potentially useful against those oppressions, personal and institutional, which brought that anger into being" (1984, 127). Furthermore, she said, "If I speak to you in anger, at least I have spoken to you: I have not put a gun to your head and shot you down in the street; I have not looked at your bleeding sister's body and asked, 'What did she do to deserve it?' This was the reaction of two white women to Mary Church Terrell's telling of the lynching of a pregnant black woman whose baby was then torn from her body" (130).

Years after she first made them, Lorde's observations remain cogent and especially pertinent to the matter of outbursts. Back then, the audience for her speech was certainly electrified by it, as I can personally attest. Yet, interestingly enough, the speech itself was interrupted by an outburst of sorts. It came near the beginning, as Lorde was enumerating various examples of white female insensitivity to women of color. One was as follows: "I wheel my two-year-old daughter in a shopping cart through a supermarket in Eastchester in 1967, and a little white girl riding in her mother's cart calls out excitedly, 'Oh, look, Mommy, a baby maid! . . . '" (126). I am not sure how Lorde wanted or expected her listeners to respond to her anecdote. But she was clearly disconcerted when several audience members laughed, including me. At the time, I thought we simply were amused by the girl's astonishing naiveté. Lorde thought otherwise. I cannot remember what she said then and there in response to our outburst; in the published version of her speech, however, she wrote the following: "And so, fifteen years later, at a conference on racism, you can still find that story humorous. But I hear your laughter is full of terror and dis-ease" (126).

I now think Lorde's diagnosis was right, or at least worth pondering. But I recall that day in order to make three more general points. First, an outburst is not necessarily a blatant display of anger. It can even involve laughter, albeit laughter that perhaps reflects "terror and dis-ease." Second, outbursts that disconcert one party or another can occur even among people who supposedly share a political ideology—in this case, the NWSA conference participants. Third, outbursts are often oral events that will not survive as educational resources unless they are noted and commented upon in print. Fortunately, Lorde did decide to write about this one, and the book you are reading analyzes several others.

I want to conclude by noting that, as one of the very few men attending the 1981 NWSA conference, I often felt uncomfortable. At first, I worried that the women there would constantly confront me, verbally attacking me as the enemy. But soon I found that, if anything, they were indifferent to me. My discomfort came from being ignored. Upon reflection, I realized that this in itself was an educational experience. Many of us white males, I suspect, go through life expecting we will be asked for our responses. Furthermore, many of us also expect that we will be responded to. Both expectations indicate the social centrality we have long enjoyed and now simply have got to surrender. As I try to feel my own way through that process, I thank Winkelmann and Quevedo Davis for pointing out to me things that I must consider. I thank Dixon, too, for inviting me to respond.

Inter-view One
Reading Conflict in English Studies

Kathleen Dixon

Winkelmann has given us some clues as to how she reads the outbursts produced by the shelter woman Sheila and Winkelmann's "middle-class" undergraduate students. But how can we understand the outbursts that appear in Degan's response to her essay?

Degan particularly dislikes Winkelmann's use of the term *icon*, which, he says, "dehumanizes and manipulates" Sheila. He does not like Winkelmann's use of Haraway's theory of the cyborg: "half human, half machine," nor does he appreciate Haraway's language, which he describes as "jargon." He opposes "theory" to something he calls "reality"; he believes that Winkelmann's self-epithet "ethnolinguist" works against a "tone" of "sympathy." Both Sheila and Winkelmann's students are "fictitious" and "controlled" by Winkelmann; Degan would prefer "immediate" communication between Sheila and the students.

Standing in-between, I read this outburst as the response of a humanist literary critic—with perhaps a bit of the New Critical—to the work of deconstruction. Everything about Degan's criticism betrays a belief in something understood as "human." A "human" can and must be addressed as an educated layman—without use of "jargon." And that human must be free of control by other humans, a position that I would describe as liberal or maybe even libertarian. Degan's own prose is carefully crafted and as free of jargon as he requires of others' prose.

My use of the word *betrays* itself betrays my own sympathies. Although I have found and still do find humanism, liberalism, New Criticism—indeed, the much-maligned Western epistemologies!—beautiful and useful, I am aware of how they privilege the sensibilities of certain humans over other humans. Work like Haraway's carries out this critique. But even some forms of humanism and liberalism, which once existed more harmoniously, now seem at odds. An economically defined liberalism rules the day, even in academe. State legislatures, boards of higher education, and academic administrators have begun to control faculty, administrative policies, and curriculum by means of theories antithetical to both Winkelmann's and Degan's values.

I refer, of course, to the new Corporate Academe, defined by such directives as Total Quality Management. In the lexicon of corporate theory, faculty are "deliverers of services" and students are not so much "humans" as "consumers" who are to be satisfied with the "product" they are purchasing. Because "education" or, God forbid, "wisdom" might be difficult to view as a product, I conclude that in corporate theory, students are buying a degree, a certificate for entry into "the workplace"—provided their anticipated job has not been downsized out of existence. Will the new Academic Marketplace have any use for Winkelmann's cyborg or Degan's human? Borrowing Schilb's invocation of Burke's "God term," one might wonder if, instead of God, we can see ourselves as incorporated into the body of Late Capitalism, lurching this way and that as the great Leviathan seizes upon the next profit opportunity.

But, as Schilb warns, the God term is better left alone. My monstrous fantasy, however, does point to a limitation of humanism, which often seems ill-equipped to trace the movements of power. For that, certain contemporary theories, such as those cited by Winkelmann and Schilb, lead us to political analyses effective in today's world.

What remains important to note is that all of the authors represented in Part I have been educated as liberals and humanists. Deconstruction, as an opposition to humanism, depends on it as any response depends on that to which it responds. But might we move beyond Winkelmann's (and Haraway's) "polemic," which so often implies an Us-versus-Them orientation? My fingers work some of the same keys I hit over and over again in high-school typing class: "Now is the time for all good (men) liberal arts faculty to come to the aid of their (country) college." I have reworked the old commonplace to show in part how history both works against and with those who are trying to forge community. Community must be reimagined and reworked continually. Nor will its maintenance be in any way possible without recognizing its fractures and fragmentations. We will have to learn what a postmodern "community" might be, and do so in the process of putting it together. At this moment, I rather like Wells' rendering of community-making in her *College Composition and Communication* essay, where she declares that groups with common concerns can enter into community without their thoughts being in all ways congruent (1996). Her neighborhood, composed of people of several racial and class backgrounds, focused on its common concern—crime—working out its conflicts in light of that topic.

Which brings me to the implied outburst of Quevedo Davis' essay. Here, again, I see the influence of deconstruction. One can form whatever conclusions one wishes about whether Quevedo Davis has presented persuasively a case for academic self-censorship. I was originally struck by the reception of the paper at a multicultural literacy conference, which I, necessarily, remember differently than Quevedo Davis does. In my memory, the largely white audience deconstructed the essay, joyfully tossing about the word that Quevedo

Davis had asked Anglos not to use at all. Her plea was couched in the language of argumentation, of rationality—but, at bottom, the request made to her Anglo peers arose out of her pain and that of other Latinas. The audience made no acknowledgment of any need for the delicacy of feeling that Pérez demonstrates in her response. Maybe they ought not to have. Perhaps a response to the argument (offered as a deconstruction) is all that mattered. But academics have accepted other, similar arguments before and, as a result, have engaged in self-censorship. *Chairman* has become *chair;* there are some words, like the infamous *n*-word, that we rarely if ever use. So why not do as Quevedo Davis asks and avoid her *m*-word?

After witnessing the reception of Quevedo Davis' conference paper, I have begun wondering what would have happened if proposals for nonsexist language had been made in the ambiance of deconstruction, an intellectual and affective environment described by Jameson as postmodern (1991)? The *euphoria* (Jameson's term) of a playfulness that can never be grounded might seem more plausible than a grounded moralism at this historical juncture, the period of Late or Multinational Capitalism. But our Western past suggests that an either/or scenario is not the only possibility for the future. Somehow, out of the seemingly mismatched fabrics of humanism (originally associated with the noble/man) and democracy (originally intended for only a minority of white men), some moralists made arguments for just the kind of sensitivity Quevedo Davis seeks. Winkelmann, Degan, Pérez, and Schilb would seem capable of providing the kind of audience for which Quevedo Davis was hoping. It would be of the greatest usefulness to inquire into what might constitute this proposed community. Which parts of the "human" or the "cyborg" need to be brought to the fore for such a community to come together, now and again, at critical moments?

Part Two

Classroom Conflicts

3

Revisiting White Feminist Authority, or Gang Life in the University Classroom

Kathleen Dixon

The title is tongue-in-cheek. Many urban anthropologists are studying inner-city gangs these days, so I figured we could use a term that might signify some of the detrimental aspects of social groupings, and apply it to a place we usually think of as gang-free. I will be applying it to white middle-class women and men, and that, too, will throw a wrench into the connotation machine.

I want to bring theory into talk about *the personal*. So often in my women's-studies classes, women want to tell their stories—frequently stories of tribulation and victimization. The stories I am offering are similar in that they are stories of conflict in the classroom. I understand these conflicts as having arisen from differences, especially power differences, among the students and teachers. But these are not simple stories of victimization. When these vignettes of the classroom are taken together, they give a picture of oppression and its dialectical opposite, empowerment, as something enormously complex. Power relations shift from group to group; sometimes groups of men "gang up" on a woman; sometimes "gangs" of white women go after other white women; sometimes white women group together to act against a woman of color. (Because of the racial demographics at my school, it would be unusual for women of color to "gang up" against anyone.) I would like to do here what I try to do in my classroom, though not always successfully; that is, to get women (and men) to go beyond the confessional or testimonial moment to see how their stories are instances of larger social tendencies.

To do so, I will invoke the term *narrative,* alternating it freely with the more colloquial term, *story.* Post-structuralist theorists and critics make use of *narrative* as a technical term, which differs from the way compositionists use it to mean a form or mode of writing or speaking. *Narrative* to a post-structuralist (sometimes referred to as *meta-narrative;* see Schilb's reference to Lyotard in his essay in *Contending with Words* [1991, 174]) is a function of discourse. *Discourse* (the reference for this word is usually to Foucault; see Clifford's essay in *Contending with Words* [1991]) is the whole of all the power relations inherent in (what we compositionists might call, after Berthoff [1981]) "the making of meaning."

I am well aware that post-structuralism tries the patience of those who love "stories" told or written by "real people" about "real people's lives." But while continuing to tell stories myself, I must insist that none of us has direct access to "real life"; indeed, stories are mainly what we use to make sense of our lives. Our existence, in other words, is mediated by stories. And those stories that we may feel to be self-invented are, in large part, stories that we have received from others, from institutions, from history—from discourse.

Nonetheless, people's "ownership" of "their" stories is important. Colonialism is partly the history of who gets to tell which story. Even if no story can be shown to be the "right" one or the "real" one, it cannot be doubted that people's experiences emerge through their material existence and relations to others. These relations are perhaps infinitely variable. In a democracy, many would argue, everyone's perspective is important. It has seemed to many of us that justice would be better served and learning greatly enhanced if the public arena could be filled with perspectives previously excluded from it. To some extent, this has happened. Yet, the outcome was not as glorious as some of us might have envisioned. The victim narratives that now suffuse the airwaves through television and radio talk shows, and women's-studies and composition classes (to name a few places with which I am familiar), vastly and dangerously simplify the power relations that they represent. Good thinking, good writing, and effective political action are the most obvious victims of the victim narratives now being circulated. We will need to find another method in addition to that which divides people into classes of oppressor and oppressed in order to analyze the outbursts that this essay and this book record. I believe that we will find the post-structuralist notion of *discourse* to be of use.

Discourse is a purposefully murky term, carrying (for me, at least) a sense of a mysterious and pervasive power, operating through institutions and individuals, through their symbol-systems (i.e., their rhetorics, their narratives), as well as the material structures of civilized/colonialized life. If we see that our individually created "stories" are taken in large part from the meta-narratives of discourse, we may feel somewhat cheated of our empowerment. I would argue otherwise: If there is any possibility of empowerment, for us or our students, it will be owed to our capacities to deconstruct our "selves" and the "stories" of which "we" are made and which we make. Narratives of race, gender, and class—to name three large categories of meta- or master narratives—have a grip on us such that we have trouble recognizing them, much less breaking their hold. Or, if we cannot break their hold, maybe "we" (i.e., we who are both oppressors *and* oppressed, in varying ways) can engage in purposeful redeployment of these "master" narratives such that the question may become: Just who *is* the "master" here?

The simple act of terming stories *narratives,* then, puts us in the realm of theorizing, which, to my mind, is nothing more than saying, "We are now adopting a conscious method for selecting and interpreting the classroom stories we will encounter in this essay." In interpreting some of the classroom scenarios that follow, I sometimes feel fairly confident about identifying the larger narratives that might be shaping the scenarios. At other times, I only hazard guesses or may offer fragments of narratives that are as yet unfamiliar to me.

As I do this, I invoke an elementary distinction in feminist theory: public performance—public discourse—historically has been the province of men (and sometimes and in some ways, only of certain privileged men). Therefore, we might say the public is masculine; the personal or the private often has been the province of women, and therefore, is feminine. *Masculine* and *feminine* also denote subject positions—that is, they indicate *places* a person might occupy in power relations defined by gender. Generally speaking, the masculine has been used to denote a position of superior power with respect to the feminine. Yet, at this historical moment, white women with middle-class values have made enormous gains within certain areas of academe; so, too, has feminism. Feminists should congratulate themselves for getting these results from their political work.

However, the victory—for me, at least—tastes bittersweet. Women, it must be acknowledged, can do terrible things to other women. Women must be superhuman supportive Mothers, or they are Evil Witches—that is still how one of the feminine meta-narratives goes, and it circulates even among us enlightened ones, us feminist women. These gendered narratives also interact with narratives of race and class, as well as narratives of liberal political ideology (e.g., everyone is equal, we are all free, anyone who works hard can get ahead). Although politically active people within and outside of academe are questioning, altering, or making new uses of these narratives, none of us can exactly escape them.

So, we must not proceed too hastily. Yes, there are more women in academe, especially more white women with middle-class values. Now we must alter our theories and our uses of theory to accommodate that change, and we must consider: What new forms will those old narratives take? Now that certain women, too, are contributors to discourse in academe (at the same time they are shaped by it, of course), what is happening? The public is no longer so overwhelmingly the domain of men. Now some women, at least, have power—the power to act as decision-makers in the public sphere. This means necessarily that they have power over others, women and men. Is this power a *feminine* one because those in power are women, or a *masculine* one because power-as-gendered is masculine? Knowing the characteristics of power and how it operates remains important; being aware of how our naming affects outcomes of meaning and action is equally important.

Thus, I find myself continually reconsidering my words. *Is* academe—all of it—in the *public sphere?* What gives that term its meaning? Classrooms, for example, may be—by state law or university policy—"open to the public," but that does not mean that communities do not form there that are quite different from those of the courtroom or the halls of Congress. As more women, more people of color, more first-generation college students enter academe, the old conventions about what the public sphere might be are changing.

The pervasiveness of common narratives, the continual shifting of power relations among people, and the differential but yet overlapping gendered domains of the public and private apply to the classroom vignettes that follow. These classrooms are mainly but not wholly occupied by white students with middle-class values. Most of the students described are Upper Midwesterners, an especially homogeneous group, the kind of people satirized by Garrison Keillor. The reader should keep class, race, and region in mind, for considerations of gender differences cannot be made without these other categories of difference.

There is but one more bit of introductory business to mention before the stories, a brief retelling of how I got involved in analyzing pedagogical relationships. I acted as a participant-observer of my own student-teacher writing conferences. My early excitement over my relationship with one of the men, Dave, grew into a typology of student-teacher relationships. Our relationship progressed in a predictable and academically successful fashion, such that I termed it an *Apprentice relationship.* It was not only academically successful, but also emotionally satisfying for us both. Among its many pleasurable qualities was what I called *repartee,* our ability to intellectually prod and poke each other and to joke together.

Most of my relationships with women fit into a category I called *Student-Teacher,* and they were not nearly as exciting to me. Taking my cue from the students (or so I thought at the time—and still do, to some extent), I played a more dutiful Teacher role to their more dutiful Student roles. These women got the work done, but frequently wanted to do something a little different, something that sometimes did not fit into my notions—or, even more often, the university's notions—of what ordinarily constituted such things as argument or analysis. For example, for an analysis assignment, Dave had chosen to analyze the lyrics of a John Lennon song and was able to make use of a genre we might call *music criticism* to direct him in his writing; I, too, was directed by the genre as I read his piece. In contrast, Elizabeth's attempts to analyze her roommate kept getting frustrated by outside forces and, ultimately, by the two of us together. Neither of us knew what, in academic terms, she was doing, although both of us were attracted to it. Nonetheless, over the course of a term, our relationship did not develop in the smooth linear fashion that Dave's and mine did;

it seemed to consist of a series of frustrations and complications. It was not fun or exciting. Thus, I began to theorize about something called *female disruption* (Dixon 1995, 1997).

In a recent article, "The Teacher's Breasts," Gallop refers to the disruption male students can cause in a utopian women's-studies classroom. Gallop is rereading a piece from what she calls "the best-known collection of essays on feminist teaching" (1995, 79), *Gendered Subjects*. The 1985 essay that Gallop revisits is written by Helene Keyssar and entitled, "Staging the Feminist Classroom." Keyssar's feminist drama teacher believes she ought to be using her authority in a nurturing fashion, but the play-within-the-classroom "play" calls for a feminist teacher who acts as a "bad girl" (according to Gallop), becoming sexually involved with a female student and then, at a crucial point in the story, kissing a male student. The male student in the play, a "real" student in Keyssar's classroom, grabs the teacher's breasts at this point in the story because, as he says, "No man would do otherwise" (1995, 84). Whereupon the entire class is thrown into a kind of crisis, emerging finally with what Keyssar offers as new knowledge. As Gallop puts it, "Once they recognize that he is a man, he is able to 'play' a student" (1995, 96). Gallop seems to further the knowledge. "Can a man be a student or, to the extent he is a man, is he only always playing a student, a fiction that is belied whenever he shows he is really a man? Is the student role itself, finally if only ever implicitly, gendered female?" (85)

It seems clear from Gallop's retelling of Keyssar's story that—even? especially?—women's-studies classrooms offer male students the potential to enact their manhood. Indeed, it may be that masculine disruption—wherein men take their pleasure, whether sexual or humorous (as with Dave's jokes)— is normative. Perhaps we teachers ought to expect this to happen and plan for it. Women teachers and professors, as well as men, enjoy their male students for this reason, and that includes feminist teachers, like me, and perhaps even Keyssar—certainly Gallop. (Many researchers have noted the phenomenon of female teachers enjoying male students more than females. See Best [1983]; Russell [1986]; and Stanworth [1987], to name a few observers of gendering in the classroom.) The problem might seem to be that many women students would be reduced to observers in this equation, passive participants in other people's pleasure. And yet, somewhere off center stage, they may not be so passive.

In her article, "Passing Notes and Telling Jokes," Canaan describes a middle-school classroom she observed in white suburbia (1990). She notes how guys rank guys and how girls rank girls, according to social class—and how guys and girls have agreed to inhabit the utterly separate domains of the public and private, or what I call *the personal*. The guys liked to grab the floor from the teacher, primarily through "telling jokes"—actual jokes or just smart remarks. They did this to win the right to public speech and to get the admiration of the teacher, the boys of high rank, the boys of all other ranks, and the girls of high rank (did the girls of low rank even exist to them, I wonder?)—

and, of course, they did this to have fun. However, high-rank boys would not put up with low-rank boys telling jokes. They would not laugh and would put the boys down. Girls did not attempt this game. They engaged in another form of ranking: passing notes. Girls passed notes to other girls, high-rank to high-rank, and so on. High-rank girls put down other girls for the way they dressed and for their lack of social graces; in other words, they were policing each other for good white middle-class feminine values. Boys did not pass notes. In each case, there was an articulation of excellence: of male excellence in public performance and female excellence in dress and manners. Both were being trained—were training themselves—for their differently gendered futures relative to white bourgeois society.

So, you see, while the guys are publicly performing, the girls are privately performing—or perhaps, performing within a space that is somewhere between public and private. It is that border realm that we want to keep in mind as we hear the stories.

Undergrad Guy Gangs

The guys sat on one side of the room, the women on the other. I forced them to notice this in my introductory composition class, day after day. I forced them to notice how it was the case that the entire class paid attention to the guys whenever they spoke to the whole group, usually laughing and joking as they spoke, but that only the other women paid attention to the women, who often seemed more tentative (e.g., speaking more softly) and rarely joked. The class— both sides of the room—agreed with me. By mid-semester, they were even trying to change their self-selected seating patterns. But they could not seem to change the attention problem. When the women talked, the guys whispered their jokes to each other, maintaining what I call a *guy gang;* after a while, even the women who had previously tried to address the whole group turned to the other women to talk. Their seating patterns had made sense, I could see. While seated together with other women (and later, among the more receptive men, too), the women had someone to listen to them. Otherwise, women could only successfully address the whole group if I used my authority to the maximum to keep the men quiet. I did the best I could to use joking to all of our benefit, but it could only stretch so far. This problem with young guy gangs is deep-seated.

An even worse scenario occurred in Reading Popular Culture, a cultural-studies course I had invented to further young people's abilities to "read" their own lives better, so the kind of thing that happened in my composition class would be less likely to happen. I wanted students to be aware of how people are social and political animals: that they belong to groups—many groups simultaneously—and that they get their identities mainly from these groups; that all groups constitute themselves and contend for power within and around something called a "dominant culture." I designed the class so that we could study ourselves as representatives of "popular culture," which might sometimes mean we were part of a dominant group and sometimes not. And, of course, the *we* was a fragmented one.

The class was deliberately provocative. I listened to them as they formed groups to work on group projects on topics of their own choice. One group had opted for some topic in contemporary pop music. One of the two black women was in that group, and I heard her mention Queen Latifah. But later, there was no mention of Queen Latifah; rather, white male rock stars took the stage. Of course. (And this was a group that contained a guy who had earlier proclaimed to the class that feminist men were "wimps.") So I went out and purchased a videotape called "Sisters in the Name of Rap" and asked the class to watch it and respond.

Most did not like it, for reasons we decided were probably partly related to the hold that their cultures had on them, together with their lack of knowledge of rap culture. But there was definite gender criticism of Queen Latifah and Yo-Yo, another woman rapper. Among other criticisms, some of the younger guys thought Queen Latifah "dressed like a man," which raised the ire of many women, older and younger, who said they would sooner dress in a suit like Latifah's than in the sexy getup Yo-Yo wore. In fact, some younger women called her a "slut," which aggravated a couple of brave young women who said Yo-Yo had a right to dress sexily if she wanted to and not expect to be called a slut or get raped by a guy. But, mainly it was clear to me that the women rappers were taking some pressure.

So I next played Billy Idol's video, "Rock the Cradle of Love." Perhaps I should warn my readers that it is one of the videos shown in Sut Jhally's "Dreamworld," a male feminist's condemnation of MTV music videos. In it, a young woman (some say a too-young woman) goes wild over a Billy Idol video that she plays on the home-entertainment center in a nerdy yuppie man's apartment. As she sheds clothing and dances from room to room, she breaks some of his pretentious artwork, spills red wine on his white dress shirt, and nearly, raunchily, seduces him. Then she packs up and leaves as though nothing happened. The narrative is such that you cannot tell whether this is the nerdy guy's fantasy or what.

As might be anticipated, the same aggressive guys who criticized Queen Latifah liked the Idol video. Some of the young women seemed to like it, too, but they were quieter. Some of the older students, Moral Majority types on both issues, grumbled about the Idol video even more than the rap video. Also, a couple of young feminist women were especially upset by it, and one tried to articulate her concerns. Her arguments were similar to those advanced in "Dreamworld": Women were being used as sex objects, and to this young woman's eyes, the girl in the video was truly a girl—"I think of my little sister when I see this video," she said.

The discussion went on for some time, with four or five of the boisterous guys at one point attacking the young woman. I did not know what to do. Should I intervene? She was a bright young woman; was this experience of defending herself something she needed? And how exactly *could* I help her? The reason I liked the video was that I could see it as a representation of a woman's desire as well as a man's. What if women just refused to accept the victim status? In other words, while the young woman and I were both feminists, we were different kinds of feminists, or feminists with differing views, and—

"What do you think?," the guys demanded. "Do you like this video? Why did you show it?"

I tried to avoid the question for a minute, and then thought, well, why? "Yes, I personally like the video, but. . . . "

The gang of guys heard no more. "That's what I thought: We're right." And they may as well have given each other high-fives, planted the flag on the hill, claimed their victory before the stunned audience. There was no hope on that day or the following days of getting them to reflect on what they had done or why they had done it: It did not matter, they had won. They had captured me for their side in their game of adolescent male rivalry. But their denunciations of the young feminist woman were bitter and mean; they made it clear that she had never been seen as a worthy player in the game.

I had not even *wanted* to play the game this time, but they got me.

And there is a reason that I could play—even if unwillingly—and she could not. I had a power that the young feminist woman did not have. I was a professor, a professional, the giver of grades in this college classroom. I easily could be made to count for something, she could just as easily be laid low (nor probably was it incidental that she was not a fashion model; she was overweight and not conventionally pretty). In my rather privileged world, most of my colleagues at least must pay lip service to feminism. Men rarely victimize me these days (maybe because the ones I see most often are my students), and I do not generally fear them *as men*. On the other hand, I have often felt the need to defend the right to my desire, partly on account of my lesbianism. The feminists and the Moral Majority were singing what sounded like the same song to me: censorship, sexual intolerance. I could not support that. At the same time, I was completely unwilling to raise the specter of lesbianism in this classroom of the rural Upper Midwest.

So when push came to shove, it was the young heterosexual—or so I deduced—feminist woman alone, and it was trench warfare—or worse, because no one would help her, no women, no men. The feminist teacher, too, was alone, smarting from the experience of having had her own classroom hijacked.

Now, then, what narratives were operating to create the scene described previously? Clearly, I have made use of metaphors and images to call up certain narratives. The young men planting the flag and giving each other high-fives might be the men in the famous statue of Iwo Jima or they might be boys playing "King of the Hill." In either case, a narrative of masculinity earned through war or warlike aggression is being enacted. I use the line "take their pleasure" consciously, knowing that it might implicate that narrative of masculinity in the crime of rape. Indeed, we might say that a symbolic rape occurred—of the young feminist woman by the gang of guys, observed and enabled by the rest of us, within a context set by both academe and the mass media (i.e., the Billy Idol video).

Engaging in war and warlike actions is the ultimate claim to rights to public space, we might say. Historically, women have not often engaged in war, nor have they enjoyed the rights to the public spaces. In the Western world's not-too-distant past, the woman-in-public was the *Public Woman,* seen to be engaging in the oldest profession. Although supportive of sexual liberation and, therefore, opposed to the Moral Majority element in the classroom, the gang of guys might have shared with them this narrative of the Public Woman. The young woman in the video might be seen by them to fulfill this role of a woman, even though that was not at all how I saw her. I had wished to argue that this woman could be the subject rather than the object of the video and, therefore, the subject of her own desires rather than only the object of men's—or, given my affinity for post-structuralist theory, she could control at least as well as a man the negotiations between sexual subject and object. But my argument never had a chance in this classroom. Instead, the young feminist woman, linked in an odd way to the Moral Majority, was probably also wanting to put forward an argument for another kind of woman-in-public—a woman with rights to act, speak, and be heard respectfully—and as she attempted the argument, was herself attacked. The gang of guys could have confronted one of the middle-aged Moral Majority men, but they did not. This is why I suggest their participation in a narrative of gendered aggression; they meted out the punishment that is properly due a woman of her kind.

Ong (1981) theorizes that Western academe was masculine and is now feminine. For two millennia, it excluded women and made use of the masculine propensity for *contest,* effectively harnessing for academe the power of the rule-governed aggression practiced on the battlefield and in the sports arena. Ong focused particularly on oral disputation as an aggressive component of academe. For him, the decline in the practice of conducting oral defenses of one's scholarship exemplifies the movement in academe from masculine to feminine.

Certainly Ong's theory squares with the fact of greatly increasing numbers of women entering academe during the past hundred years. My classroom was composed of approximately thirty students, with at least as many women as men. But the feminine in academe, whatever it might be, did not rule. I myself wanted a classroom discourse that would be neither private (like gossip) nor public (like the rhetoric of Ong's ancient academe), but rather both in dialogical relation, where various languages might speak playfully to and through one another. Various notions of masculine and feminine, private and public, could interanimate one another. We could, at times, stand back and behold the play—so went my ideal. But by conducting a freewheeling classroom discussion among this group of students, I opened the classroom not to the masculine academe Ong refers to, where credentialed older male scholars discipline their younger male apprentices. Rather, it was a postmodern variety, where anxious young men devoid of a male master enact the rules of mock battle upon a public territory they feel they have a right to claim as their own, even as that claim increasingly feels hollow.

Grad Girl Gangs

This scenario treats a graduate class, and you can see how deeply I am invested in this one. I view graduate courses differently than undergraduate courses, as places where I can take some of my pleasure in being an intellectual. And yet, reflection on this vignette shows that, unlike the guys of the previous story, I am perhaps not aggressive enough in making claims to my own rights to pleasure in public spaces.

Our graduate seminar's topic was Cultural Studies, Ethnography and Pedagogy. This title was wide-ranging partly in reflection of my interests, but mostly to attract the greatest number of students; I myself could have been happy with a course called Composition and Cultural Studies. Composition occupies a delicate position in our English department and across the university, as is the case on most campuses. Those of us who claim it as a specialty must take special care to note the audience before which we make our self-representation. And, for reasons that I well understand, composition has suffered damage as a specialty of (feminine) "helpers," who give guidance to (feminine and masculine) colleagues and students about "the writing process." In short, I felt that "composition" would not have accorded my graduate course the intellectual status that I wished for it. I was hopeful that intellectual activity might not be always and only a masculine preserve.

I was not aware then of all the intricacies described previously as I launched the cultural-studies course. But I did know that there was a great deal that I knew, which the students did not, and that much of my cultural-studies knowledge was contextual and intertextual. The actual texts chosen for the course would reference some of the contexts within which I believed careful and responsible readers would place the texts. I wanted the students to become those careful and responsible readers, but I also wanted them to make use of the texts to inform "readings" of their own lives and of our lives together in the classroom. However, I did not know how far critical texts already had been pushed toward the margins of the classroom by certain circumstances; for example, the increasing irrelevance of critique in our popular political culture. For me, the texts were objects of love and I wanted them to occupy as central a position as possible. They were difficult texts and it was an ambitious course. But I had always had faith in the power of intellectual discourse and the abilities of students to participate in it.

Many of these were second-year master's or first-year doctoral students. There were five female and three male graduate students, as well as one female professor, whom I had invited to audit the course. "Professor X," as we will call her, knew a great deal about Marxism and feminist psychoanalytic theory, and clearly represented a substantial resource for the class. She was widely read beyond that and unusually generous in her estimation of people and their capacities. The class represented to her an opportunity to learn more about a new area of study. As the departmental chair, busy with administrative duties, she looked forward to being an intellectual interacting with other intellectuals. And she was my friend. What a boon, I thought, to have her there.

But our happy vision was not to be. By the last month of the term, one of the female graduate students snarled loudly in the general direction of Professor X that she was sick of hearing about "that Marxist garbage!"

"Well, *that's* a mature argument!" Professor X snarled back. On that day, she left the class and never returned.

I still do not know exactly how it happened. The class was a demanding one. I expected students at least to be willing to try out a number of current critical theories. In addition, there was the demand that all of us theorizers also make practical application of our ideas — in politics (as feminists and cultural-studies practitioners do; several students avowed interest in this), in the field (as ethnographers do; one sociology student was doing ethnographic research), in the classroom (as teachers do; most of these graduate students were also teachers). Two of the men — who remained quiet throughout — and one of the women were superior students, by my standards. The others — and this included four of five women — seemed poorly read, generally, and uninterested in the course texts except as points of departure for their own autobiographies. Instead of putting their energy into analyzing the texts as cultural-studies inquiry into a complex contemporary world, instead of reading closely as a New Critic might do, they put the focus on themselves and their own responses, a way of reading that I now see as fairly common in English courses — common enough in our department, where a simplified form of reader-response theory often governs class discussions — often enough in my own classrooms of this era. These graduate students had themselves become the texts, as had Keyssar's students acting out the feminist play in *Gendered Subjects,* except that the extemporaneous "script" was apparently not available to the students *as* script despite my attempts to make it so.

Confusions abounded in this postmodern classroom. How was this a "graduate English class"? We were reading several texts from several disciplines — or, more accurately, from several areas of study. Students were attracted to the course from various identity positions. Those identities "worn" by Professor X and I were surely multiple: theorists in a variety of areas, practitioners of various pedagogic and political activities, middle-aged women. A few of the women represented themselves to us all (and to me alone, outside of class) as feminists. They knew that I considered myself a feminist. But this same identification hardly bound us to one another for very long. Professor X and I both were persuaded by feminist psychoanalytic criticism and poststructuralism. To three of the five women in the class, "feminism" was second-wave feminism; to one woman in the course, "feminism" required the denunciation of men as male chauvinist pigs, which was for me unpleasantly reminiscent of an older feminist rhetoric. Indeed, when one of them rattled off a good list of feminist titles for one of the other women to read, she named nothing that had been published after 1979. These three women declared most of the texts—*all* of the male-authored texts—unaccomplished because they, the students, found them to be difficult reading. I do not recall whether "academic discourse" had begun its now painful circulation among certain faculty and students in our department. Placing oneself in opposition to "academic discourse"—within the English department, this has often meant opposition to theory—has constituted a bond among some expressivist faculty in composition, students and lecturers in creative writing, and students and faculty in women's studies. In retrospect, I see how certain forms of cultural studies and ethnographic work can appeal readily to those whose primary interest is narrative as a "natural" art. Perhaps I was even trying to address those interests and bring them to what I view as a more self-reflexive relation for which theory proves especially useful. But I might have anticipated resistance to such a move, knowing as I did the widespread feminist doctrine that Theory Is Inherently Male and Patriarchal.

To those three women, add a fourth, who did not present herself as a feminist but rather as a historian (because she had an undergraduate history degree). She condemned the entire educational ethnography, *Ways with Words* by Heath (1983), because Student D (as we will call her) was certain there was more to be said about the history of mill strikes than Heath mentioned in her brief introduction. "But the book is primarily an ethnography of the contemporary setting!" I exclaimed. "The history is there for a basic orientation."

"But as a historian," Student D countered, "I'm lost. I don't think she has any credibility."

Student D liked to represent herself as a no-nonsense, get-to-the-point individual with the further suggestion that she was working-class, or at least someone with vast experience in the working world. Since Professor X and I both considered our upbringings to be working class, we might have shared this identity with Student D. But we felt that our working-class backgrounds led us to appreciate theory—even the most "impractical" theory—all the more, because intense intellectual activity was what we feared would be unavailable to us were we to continue in the paths of our parents. Indeed, Student D's evocation of the world of work combined with her rapid rejection of the texts for the course recalled the pain of class struggles for us, of working hard and being denied some of the most important fruits of our labor and the objects of our love. When the class discussed Williams' (1983) definition of *culture*, Professor X narrated an autobiographical story to counter the one she was "reading" in the women students' quick rejection of the class texts. It was about her youthful eagerness to experience the very "culture" popularly held to be "elite," and about her awkward entry into such "culture." Professor X and I had deliberately sought the kind of disciplining that academe offered us; we not only accepted it, but took pleasure in it.

Such stories illustrated and created the working-class intellectual identity Professor X and I shared. We wanted respect for our accomplishments, but, even more, for the accomplishments and intellectual activities of scholars and artists generally. Yet, we had to admit (when she and I discussed this course much later), we had been among the generation of scholars who had questioned profoundly many of the established practices of academe. The kind of "graduate English course" this was, then, could be regarded as unclear or open to question and redefinition. Having fractured some previous incarnations of academe, we might well have expected our students to fracture ours. But what these students seemed to be going after was the *continuity* of academic values that our work, we felt, upheld. The problem was that the attempts by the students to wrest control of the classroom from us were not resulting in work that we considered intellectual. I am not even sure the students would have considered it so (*intellectual* was not a word they tended to use). It was outrageous and depressing, from our shared perspective as intellectuals, to have Williams' and Professor X's learned Marxism reduced to "garbage" or Heath's much-admired book rejected by a provincial and simplistic reading of the preface. We were not accorded the courtesy that academics often bestow to one another and certainly not the kind of respect we had shown our own professors. This we might have borne had we understood the students to be offering up some interesting intellectual opposition; if such was there, we could not divine it.

Yet, how does one (if one is a graduate student) negotiate one's identity under the exceedingly complicated circumstances of postmodern academe? If Student D's claim to working-class identity were to be honored—indeed, were it to be offered to the class as a whole—the question of how to act, how to pull together a usable identity from one's previous life experiences that might work in this postmodern classroom might pose a struggle itself. The students needed to find something in their past that would correspond to something in these difficult texts and practices (themselves multiple), in the company of two women who both were and were not authorities (Professor X was a student for the moment; I was an authority who usually offered up more questions than answers), in an English course and at a university, both of which already had been deconstructed by academe and the mass media (the political correctness battles meant to taint intellectuals of Professor X's and my ilk were just then being reported in the news magazines) before these students ever set foot there.

Add to all this the marginalized status of any intellectual work that transpires in North Dakota. There is, for instance, a great deal of literary activity in and around Grand Forks that is not very highly remunerated. A number of doctoral students are attracted to the university because of its option of a "creative" dissertation in English. Not a few of these remain skeptical about the usefulness of criticism and theory; ironically, the more popular criticism and theory becomes in academe, the more unappealing it may seem to people who self-consciously pursue the identity of marginalized romantic poet.

Furthermore, Professor X and I were both women. Did our gender and our gendering of ourselves through our appearance or behavior help to mark this classroom site as one more private than public or at least confused in its orientation? Perhaps these students had in some sense fended off criticism and evaluation of themselves (as one could suppose anxious graduate students might do, even more than usual in this unsettling postmodern context) by harshly criticizing the texts I had chosen (and then, later, criticizing Professor X) and by replacing the texts of the class with their performative identities. Were they hoping to make of this class a place apart from their more public struggles in the postmodern world, a place of leisure rather than work? A place properly presided over by women? (Some say graduate-school applications rise as employment opportunities dwindle, and they are doing so now.) When the "English" classroom is deconstructed, is it merely a place of play among the elites? For the one performing a working-class identity, was our classroom hopelessly impractical? If the elites themselves have been taken down a peg, who is to say what the nature of the play should be?

Professor X described my teaching style as "a kind of temperamental phenomenology." I typically began class by posing reader-response questions to the students and wove together each unfolding session by connecting text with student comments. The pedagogy itself was an intellectual exercise, one that might well have seemed student-centered, because inquiry was directed or at least made to relate to the students' self-positioning as I understood it. Yet, the brashest of the women students, Student C, one time said she had felt "trampled upon" by me. Student C knew of my Elizabeth and Dave study and made opportune use of it. To one of the quiet, bright young men in our class, she said, "You got an A because you have a penis!"

During the fateful session before Professor X stomped out of class, I attempted to lead a discussion on, yes, a piece of Marxist-informed cultural studies criticism of the popular children's book, *Peter Pan*. The discussion that followed was not reminiscent of any experience I had ever had in a graduate classroom, although it did recall some undergraduate women's-studies classes in which I have participated. Class discussion (dominated, as usual, by the women) had begun to enact one of the central points of the article. One effect of capitalist ideology, according to the author, was that the consumption of mass-produced objects like children's literature could come to seem like an individual person's comforts, something like fetishes. In particular, children's literature could comfort by keeping the adult readers to whom they were really directed ever young (and ever uncritical of capitalist consumption), just like Peter Pan.

Instead of talking about the article, the women began talking about their favorite children's literature. And they kept talking about it. "How much did you pay for your *Peter Pan*?" I remember one asking. "I keep mine next to my bed at night," and so on. This seemed like the perfect teachable moment. I intervened. "This is really interesting. Take a look at the text, page 418, middle of the page." I read it aloud. "The publication of *Peter Pan in Kensington Garden,* therefore, had very little to do with a child reader. Rather, it illustrates just how far the child had become one of the chief fantasies—object of desire and investment—of the turn-of-the-century publishing trade. Thus, its publication has been taken to show that children were now considered 'worthy of loveliness, not to say aesthetic luxury'—as if they could assimilate into themselves, render innocent (again), the more glaring commercial realities of the trade" (Rose 1991, 418).

I spoke. "Right now, you were all just enacting this text. Do you remember when so and so said . . . ," and I tried once again to link their conversation with the ideas of the text. What followed was not excitement at this novel idea. What followed was silence. Then, they went on to talk more about children's literature.

Out of this class, I believe, came the complaint from some women graduate students: We have no women professors to mentor us! Meanwhile, some of us women faculty grumbled, they do not want us to be intellects, but rather mothers and therapists.

A partial explanation for what happened in this class plays off Gallop's story of the man impersonating a student. What if I, the teacher, in this narrative have been impersonating Socrates, the prototype of a certain sort of revered masculine teacher. Let us say, somewhat reductively, that my primary goal had been to discipline myself and my students to the texts, the initial "temperamental" or reader-response questions acting as a seductive way into that disciplining. Let us imagine that the women in this class—who clearly want my attention—do *not* impersonate Phaedrus, but instead some other feminine character, one who gives chase. For as I sift through memories of all the difficulties I have had with women students, from Elizabeth to the women in this graduate course to others, I think I see a common pattern. "They flee from me," I want to say, in joking reference to the poem all English-literature majors used to memorize. Sometimes they may be fleeing in fear of being "caught" by me—caught unable to answer for themselves, as Socrates might say, caught not knowing the "right" answer.

But sometimes they also seem to give chase for the fun of it, deliberately chiming in (during class discussion, say) with a non sequitur. In one recent upper division/graduate level Rhetoric of Popular Culture class, some of us were excitedly engaged in comparing notes on the "text": a discussion we had all taken part in during the last class session with our guest, the newly appointed Youth Coordinator of the City of Grand Forks. We had been reading written texts on postmodernism and youth culture, Gaines' *Teenage Wasteland* among them (1990). *Text* was a critical term for us (as it was not for the cultural-studies graduate course), one we had built for half a semester, reading Brummett's (1994) introduction to the study of popular culture and Bakhtin's (1986) "Speech Genres." A very bright theory-oriented man and I were probably the most vocal; we were frequently in sync during class discussions. Suddenly, one of the women broke in: "Did anybody notice her [the Youth Coordinator's] wooden leg?" Shocked silence followed, then an eruption of laughter in women's voices. The class, led now by the women students, was compelled to ascertain whether our guest had indeed worn a wooden leg. She had, they decided (the male theory student and I being agnostic on the subject). Naturally, such an outburst became a running joke among the class—my apologies for the possible pun on locomotion—and the young woman who had turned class discussion around did not let us forget it. She would tease the male theory student—and possibly, indirectly, me—by reminding him that he was so "out of it" he did not even notice the wooden leg.

Perhaps it is partly because I like this young woman very much; because I think she is bright and accomplished (I wrote on a paper, "excellent, if quirky, analysis"); because her fear of theory (so she confessed) did not lead to wholesale rejection, but rather to constant messings about; because she attempted to get my attention in ways that I find both likable and frustrating; because, in short, I find her more charming than the women of the cultural-studies graduate class—perhaps for these reasons, I am able to believe that her derailing of class discussion had some critical merit. It was, after all, a feminist theorist, Irigaray (1985a), who pointed out Socrates' infatuation with the (paternal) ideal, at the expense of the (maternal) body. Her reading of Plato's myth of the cave ends when the philosopher voluntarily quits the brilliant ambiance of the ideal for his pedagogical work among the unenlightened ones in the dark cave/womb. This section is entitled, "The Vengeance of Children Freed from Their Chains."

> Imagine then that someone, not for pedagogic reasons this time, but moved rather by other political goals, or by a perverse desire for entertainment, rouses these prisoners who have been freed of their chains at the very moment that the philosopher, still a little lost in his idealities, has sat down among them, in his old place. Don't you think that if they "catch the offender, they would put him to death? No question, he said." All that remains to be known is whether what they caught was not already dead: the poor present of an effigied copula. And whether in this fight they did anything but tear themselves apart. Making blood flow from their wounds, blood that still recalls a very ancient relationship with the mother. Repeating a murder that has probably already taken place. Mimicking once again in that gesture what Plato was already writing, Socrates already telling. "No question, they would put him to death." It had long been inscribed—surely in the conditional tense of a myth—in their memories. (364)

Reading Irigaray reading Plato—and by this means, reading the texts woven by my students and me—I waver in my identifications. The body, the maternal, the material, theory, politics. None of the versions of my discomfort releases me from wondering what it means that intellectual authority may have been torn asunder by us all.

Undergrad Girl Gangs

Native American students comprise the largest racial minority on campus, about four percent of the University of North Dakota's student population of about twelve thousand. If there is one Indian student in class, she or he is usually the only one. Fewer than one percent of the students are of African American descent (University of North Dakota, 1992).

Because there is a big emphasis on group work in my lower-division, undergraduate popular-culture class, students' relationships to each other are perhaps more important than is usually the case. Each small group has to work together for most of the semester on a large-scale project, culminating in a written report and an oral presentation. Many students have found this method appealing. However, as I think theoretically, I note that small groups are likely to fall within that category I described previously as in between public and private. This is a domain within which many women feel comfortable. Ordinarily, one might think, this is what we want: for women, especially the many quiet Upper Midwestern women, to feel comfortable in the classroom.

Andie, a Turtle Mountain *metis* (a term denoting a mixed Cree/Ojibway/French ancestry), became part of an all-woman small group in this pop-culture class. By the time the groups formed, she already had missed a few classes and had been late for class frequently. She had explained to me that she was having difficulty with her child-care arrangements. She spoke of the reservation in such a way that I was not certain whether she might not, at least on occasion, be commuting from Turtle Mountain itself, a good four hours from our campus.

I made it a point to greet Andie whenever I could, because I was fairly certain the students—mostly white—would not make her welcome. I visited Andie's group, which was animated, while she was quiet. When the group was trying to decide which cultural theme or artifact it wanted to focus its research on, I mentioned *Powwow Highway,* a film based on a book by David Seals, who is Native American. The others in the group seemed "out of it." They did not know what to light on and could not seem to get involved in my talk about the film. I did not know if they were confused or uninterested, but did notice that Andie was excluded. Andie and I turned to one another and talked a little about it.

In the end, the group decided to do research on Malcolm X. This seems partly to have been because one of the white women had done a report on Malcolm X in high school and because the group of mostly white women had been impressed by its own ignorance about black culture during our earlier segment on rap music. During the oral presentation, the white women emphasized the more accommodating Malcolm X, the man who had returned from Mecca with a vision of racial harmony. Meanwhile, the white men in the classroom audience repeatedly and hotly took issue with the earlier Malcolm X, of the "blue-eyed devils" speeches, depicted in video clips shown by the presenters. The group of women presenters could not muster a response to the men, so I made one, letting them know what I found admirable in Malcolm X—including the humor that was missing from the video clips, which I also read into such phrases as "blue-eyed devils." Andie was absent for the presentation. Later, she did show up for class and we worked out a project she could do on her own. It was a topic on Native American oral history, and she drew upon local sources from the Turtle Mountain reservation. It was a good paper.

Sandy, another woman of color from Andie's group, who called herself biracial, part black, part white, had also been quiet in the group. During the entire Malcolm X presentation, Sandy remained quiet, and seemed almost physically to distance herself from the group. Later—at the end of the term, in fact—I found a one-page sheet in my mailbox from Sandy, apparently to be shared with future popular-culture classes, for greater understanding and less criticism of people of color. She had pointed to the white students' criticism of Malcolm X after her group's presentation. This plea for understanding was something that I realized was just as much for me as for the students. I now know that I have to use my authority even more prominently in this class, which already has been designed to ferret out people's prejudices. I have got to theorize groups better and I need to lay out more ground rules for the whole class, particularly with regard to racial difference. Recently, I have begun to offer the option of working alone whenever I introduce long-term group work. Such a choice by any student who feels marginalized may lead to a stronger bond with me than with the rest of the class—which is certainly preferable to the complete alienation of a student of color.

What I think happened in the women's small group was the white women's inculcation of white middle-class feminine values. It is a cultural imperative for many white women to keep peace in the family, where *home* is the hardworking man's solace in a troubling world (much like the *Peter Pan* books as studied by Rose). Thus, I make a partial reading of these women's support of Malcolm X as their domestication of him. When the "real men" of the classroom kicked up a ruckus, these women retreated. However, these same women were not necessarily unwilling to criticize. In the small group's written report to me, under the required section on group dynamics, most of the white women literally wrote Andie off. A couple misspelled Sandy's name. Andie—whenever she *was* mentioned—was described, basically, as a slacker who did not attend meetings outside of class. True enough, no doubt. Yet, these young white women seemed to have no notion of how their group might have affected Andie; indeed, they were rather haughty in making their pronouncements. This I do not fully condemn. They picked up on my desire to make students responsible for their work, including group work. What *responsible, work,* and *group* might mean in the context of our multiracial class—even what that context was—had not been problematized. For a group whose topic was Malcolm X, there was more than a little irony in the disappearance of Andie and near-disappearance of Sandy.

4

Essays That Never Were: Deaf Identity and Resistance in the Mainstream Classroom

Jacqueline Anderson

"Do you want to hear a joke," she signed. While I recognized her question as an attempt to shift attention away from her paper, an essay that we were revising together, I too was ready for a break, so I shook my head affirmatively and settled back to watch her hands, face, and lips. The joke she told was one I already knew; indeed, it had been circulating in the Deaf community for years. And each time I heard it, there were two things about it that troubled me.

"Three handicappers, a paraplegic, a blind person, and a Deaf person, were going to a meeting," she began. "They were in an accident and died. When they buried the paraplegic, his friends threw his wheelchair into the grave on top of the coffin, covered it with dirt, and left. When they buried the blind person, his friends threw his cane on top of the coffin, covered it with dirt, and left. When they buried the Deaf person, his friends threw his interpreter on top of the coffin, covered him with dirt, and left."

The first thing about the joke that bothered me was that it equates the kind of mechanical assistance provided handicappers who are blind or paralyzed (i.e., a cane or a wheelchair) with the personal and humane assistance offered by an interpreter. At the same time, in a more subtle way, the joke underscores a major flaw in the public's perception of the handicapping conditions referred to in the joke. The handicaps associated with blind people and paraplegics is one of mobility; the handicap associated with Deaf people is one of communicative ability.

The second thing that worried me—as it was meant to—was that like many Deaf jokes, this one had hearing people as the brunt of its humor (Anderson 1991). More specifically, it assailed interpreters—hearing people who spend

66

their lives helping the Deaf bridge the gap between the Deaf and hearing worlds. Significantly, I—a hearing woman—was told the joke as I was assisting a Deaf woman revise a paper that she needed to hand in to a hearing teacher. By telling the joke, the Deaf writer had placed unanticipated strain on our collaboration because, as we proceeded with our work, I continued to wonder how she felt about me and my efforts to assist her. Did she think my attempts at assistance reflected negatively on her abilities as a thinker and communicator?

This was not the first time I had experienced ambiguity and uncertainty while working with a Deaf student. The more I learned about deafness and Deaf culture, the more questions I had: Were the dynamics of the Deaf/hearing *cultural* dyad negatively influencing the student/teacher relationship? Was I trying to nudge my Deaf students into an academic world that they found undesirable and that was not willing to make way for them or their culture? What kinds of assumptions could I make about Deaf attempts to write English? And by assisting Deaf learners to write academic English, was I estranging them from their native signed language in a way they found offensive? Even more specifically, I was forced to consider whether Deaf expressions of anger, like those embedded in the joke, were occurring in my classes without my noticing them or recognizing their implications.

Deaf students first began matriculating at the university where I teach during the 1970s. Because of an increased demand for higher education on the part of both mainstream and minority students across the country, the special schools created for Deaf students (Gallaudet University and the National Technical Institute for the Deaf, to name two) could not accommodate all those seeking admission. Because our school had a Sign Language Studies department to educate future interpreters for the Deaf, it seemed appropriate for the institution to recruit Deaf students. Here they not only would be able to obtain a liberal arts education (at that time, most postsecondary programs for the Deaf were vocational/technical), but also would be surrounded on campus by other members of the Deaf community and by hearing American Sign Language (ASL) users with whom they could communicate and socialize.

Deaf students from the Upper Midwest and Ontario responded enthusiastically to the recruitment attempts, and by 1980 the university had one of the largest mainstreamed Deaf populations of any liberal arts college. More importantly, because the university had on-staff experts in the language and culture of the Deaf community, a total communication environment was created for its Deaf population. This meant that Deaf students would be provided with interpreters fluent in ASL who also knew signed English and who knew how to translate technical vocabulary for which there were no signs in ASL. Initially, the faculty at large was prepared for teaching Deaf students, albeit in a cursory way, through a series of faculty workshops. Additionally, some of the university's administrators and faculty took an introductory ASL course. The workshops offered the faculty a general background on Deaf culture (Deaf people are not "dumb," speech is just difficult for them); ASL (it is a legitimate language with is own rules, not a signed approximation of English); and appropriate educational practice (never speak with your back to Deaf students, as when writing on the board). Over time, however, as new faculty were hired, these workshops were not repeated and the newly hired met their first Deaf students without preparation. I was one of these instructors, and for me the experience was perplexing.

My first contact with Deaf learners came in 1984 in a first-year composition class. As an instructor, I had always assumed that my students would be able to keep up with the reading I assigned, produce essays that were organized in recognizable ways, and write an English that was reasonably free of errors. Because of my background in composition, I understood the writing process, and I tended to be more tolerant of grammatical errors than many of my colleagues in other disciplines. Yet, initially, the writing of Deaf students violated all of my expectations and seemed to defy all of my teaching skills.

The institution had attempted to minimize difficulties for both hearing instructors and Deaf students by providing remedial classes in English; by encouraging Deaf students to utilize the university's Center for Personalized Instruction, where they could receive tutoring; and by ensuring that competent interpreters and notetakers were available to assist them. Yet, not surprisingly, their difficulties with reading and writing persisted. Our institution was not alone in its experience. Researching the Deaf postsecondary experience, Crandall (1982) found that even after remediation, the texts of Deaf college students were only about seventy percent comprehensible to their hearing instructors, and Fisher (1982) concluded that Deaf students' "knowledge of English differs a great deal from the knowledge a native speaker would have" (12).

Yet, despite their difficulties with language, the Deaf students at our university rarely complained directly to their hearing instructors about classroom content or procedures. This should not have surprised me. Deaf students, members of a minority culture, who reach college level after matriculating in mainstream hearing institutions have become quite expert at hiding their feelings from their hearing teachers and peers. They are certainly capable of lashing out when upset with the teaching; in fact, they feel quite free to issue complaints and make insulting remarks about instructors to the interpreter when they assume the instructor does not understand sign. They regularly create unflattering name signs for offending teachers. When bored or upset with the content of a lecture, they will close their eyes or stop watching the interpreter. But the actual, in-class outburst of a Deaf college student, an outburst that will stop the instructor and disturb the conduct of the class, appears quite rare. This appearance, like so many others, I suspected, was misleading. My supposition was that just as hearing teachers regularly misunderstood and/or ignored what Deaf students were doing when they signed to an interpreter during a lecture, so hearing teachers might well be misunderstanding or ignoring other Deaf student outbursts addressed directly to them—but hidden in a joke, existing in divergently patterned English, or lurking in statements added onto assignments.

It was particularly their divergently patterned English essays that intrigued me. As a linguist, I knew that marked but patterned differences in generic texts such as essays, letters, or journal entries did not happen by accident. If the differences were patterned consistently across texts, then the differences were very likely to be culturally conditioned and needed to be explored if the reasons for their being were to be understood. Although linguists accept that there are "slips of the pen" analogous to "slips of the tongue" and call such slips "mistakes," they generally maintain that patterned deviations from standard forms of language are not perceived as errors by their language-users; rather, the deviant forms are fulfilling a function.

Discourse, inside the classroom and out, is patterned culturally in its norms, forms, and codes. When the cultural patterns of those communicating are not shared, particularly when one communicant is operating from a situation of power and the other from a position of subordination, mispatterning can lead to misunderstanding, and misunderstanding to perplexity and hostility. Communication under such conditions is called *asynchronous*. Elements leading to asynchronous communication can include the way a message is encoded, the employment of unfamiliar formulas, and thematization of information.

Anger expressed within the context of a shared culture is, in most instances, *synchronous*. That is, it is verbally and/or kinesthetically recognized as anger, although its cause may not be perceived immediately. It is understood because it *both conforms to and disrupts*. What it conforms to is the discourse rules for an angry interchange within a specific culture; what it disrupts is an interactional structure governing the discourse rules for *conversation* or *classroom lecture* or some other discourse genre with which both participants are acquainted and in which both participants are engaged. An inappropriate remark is regarded as inappropriate by both the sender and receiver only if both share the same cultural conditioning. Similarly, an anonymous note or angry letter is interactionally dynamic only if the parties involved are aware of why notes might be both angry and anonymous.

Deaf students code their cultural identity differently than hearing people do because they are members of a different culture (or subculture). The National Center for Health Statistics (NCHS) of the U.S. Department of Health and Human Services estimates that there are approximately twenty million Deaf or hearing-impaired persons (8.6 percent of the total population) in the United States. Of these, about 2,309,000 are of college age, eighteen to thirty-four years old (NCHS 1994). Because there is no legal definition of *deafness,* what the word means depends on who is using it. Audiologists measure deafness in terms of decibel levels perceived by the ears; the NCHS describes it as the "inability to hear and understand any speech unaided." But within the Deaf community, *deafness* is a political term based on linguistic preference. Individuals who consider Sign their first language, regardless of the degree of hearing loss, usually prefer to call themselves *Deaf* and typically are active in Deaf culture. Individuals who have an oral language preference, regardless of the degree of hearing loss, typically call themselves *hearing-impaired,* generally strive to be as hearing-like as possible, and usually are more involved with the hearing rather than the Deaf culture.

Although language, specifically the use of ASL, is the key identifying feature of the members of the Deaf culture, it is not the only one. As with all cultures, members share attitudes and beliefs. Deaf culture also encompasses the lives Deaf people lead—"their art and performances, their everyday talk, their shared myths, and the lessons they teach one another" (Padden and Humphries 1988, 1). But unlike other cultures, most people are not born into the Deaf culture; they attain Deaf identity by their usage of and allegiance to ASL. And, unlike other cultures, Deaf culture is a culture most Deaf people do not share with their parents or families because more than ninety percent of Deaf children are born to hearing parents.

Misconceptions about Deaf individuals, their culture, and their abilities have persisted through the centuries. Writing more than two millennia ago, Aristotle asserted, "Those who are born Deaf all become senseless and incapable of reason"; Lucretius rhymed, "To instruct the Deaf, no art could ever reach/No care improve, and no wisdom teach." Time and research have done little to dispel these views. At the beginning of the twentieth century, Pinter and Patterson (1916) analyzed a series of national studies charting the reading achievement of Deaf students. They found that the median scores of Deaf learners of all ages consistently fell below those of eight-year-old hearing children. Sixty years later, Quigley and his companions (1976) reported that at eighteen years of age, most Deaf students had considerable difficulty understanding syntactic structures that were used in beginning reading books; these same students also had problems comprehending and using English verb and noun inflections, determiners, and auxiliary verbs. Other researchers added that Deaf individuals typically could not understand or create relative clauses, nominals, complements, and similar linguistic structures associated with adult written language (Babbini and Quigley 1970; Quigley et al. 1976). Even when Deaf students wrote sentences in what appeared to be standard English during their grammar classes, studies showed that they did not necessarily know what these sentences meant nor how to use the sentential components appropriately in other contexts (Wilbur et al. 1975, 1976; Wilbur and Quigley 1975).

The problems that Deaf students have interpreting and producing written language—which is an encoding of oral language—have been well chronicled (see Anderson [1993] or Scouten [1984] for a full discussion). Why these problems persist even after Deaf students are given intensive training in English over the course of their scholastic careers is hard to explain. The simple answer is that it is almost impossible for a person who has never heard an oral language to reproduce that language with a native-like fluency; hence, an oral language is not an appropriate choice as a first language for a Deaf person. A complete answer is much more complex.

Only a relatively small percentage of Deaf children are exposed to a language whose modality is accessible to them (i.e., available to them through the sense of sight) during those years when language acquisition takes place in hearing youngsters. Hence, many Deaf individuals reach school without a first language (e.g., ASL) on which to base their study of a second language (i.e., English or another oral language).

Although deafness can be diagnosed shortly after birth, it often goes unrecognized until the child is two or even older when he or she repeatedly fails to respond to verbal and other sounds. It is then that parents first seek professional help from doctors and audiologists. Because most hearing-impaired youngsters have some residual hearing, the specialists consulted usually suggest that the young child be fitted for hearing aids and begin immediate training in speech recognition and production so that he or she might navigate successfully in the hearing world. This is what the hearing professionals desire; this is what the hearing parents desire. Rarely, however, does this happen.

Individuals who are prelingually Deaf—that is, born deaf or deafened at an age prior to language acquisition—must rely on sight to assist them in their acquisition of language. When they are born into a Deaf clan or family, they are surrounded by Sign—a visual language—from the moment of their birth and acquire language the same way that hearing children do: through constant, natural communicative interaction. Deaf children of Deaf parents, then, have a first language, which can be used to instruct them in English, a language that is lexically, semantically, and syntactically different from ASL.

Deaf children of hearing parents are not so fortunate. Because their parents and siblings do not know Sign, they must often wait until they are in school before they are exposed to a language they are capable of learning. If they are placed in a mainstream educational institution rather than a school for the Deaf or a school with a Deaf program—a school in which the emphasis is on orality rather than Sign—they may graduate semilingual, knowing neither ASL nor English. Such students typically pick up at least a pidgin Sign from other Deaf children on the playground or on school buses (Covington 1980).

Schooling in an inaccessible language, however, is not the only problem facing Deaf students. Liben (1978) has shown that Deaf children of hearing parents regularly experience quantitative and qualitative reductions in communication with adults. That is, their parents communicate with them less often than they do with their hearing offspring and do so in "primitive, homemade gestures and nonverbal" signs (205). Hearing adults and older siblings, she goes on to note, rarely provide Deaf youngsters with the names of objects or ways to describe the world around them. Similarly, Deaf children are not exposed to the sounds that fill the life of hearing children and help prepare them for reading and writing in their native language. Conversations between adults, television shows, children shouting in the backyard—these are not accessible to Deaf children. Hence, the pragmatic aspects of language (e.g., when to say "thank you," how to take turns, how to use politeness formulas) also are closed to Deaf youngsters.

Therefore, when Deaf children of hearing parents are enrolled in oral or speechreading programs, they have no context in which they can ground the lessons they are being taught, no sounds that they can recognize from the ambient noise that has surrounded them from birth. Speechreading for Deaf children is rarely successful because it is based on incomprehensible and incomplete information. Additionally, only about forty percent of the phonemes in English are easily distinguishable on the face and lips. The English words *pet* and *bet*, for example, look exactly the same on the lips when articulated. They are distinguished by the process of "voicing," which can be felt by placing one's fingers on the throat during articulation of a word. Because voicing is not visually available to a speechreader, a speechreader must rely on context cues to distinguish between word pairs like *came* and *game*, or *touch* and *Dutch*. But, it is estimated, even the most facile speechreader (one who can hear English) can decipher only about half of what is said in dyadic conversations and approximately five percent of what is said in group exchanges (Liben 1978).

If speechreading English poses problems for Deaf children, reading and writing are almost insurmountable challenges because both processes are based on a knowledge of the sound system and lexicon of an oral/aural language. Hearing children bring to reading and writing a fairly complete language system; that is, by the time they begin reading and writing, they are well acquainted with the phonology (sounds), morphology (meaning units), lexicon, syntax, and pragmatics of English. Furthermore, they themselves are proficient language users. Orally trained Deaf children are not. They cannot dissect words into their component sounds, a skill essential for reading. They have not mastered the phonologic-to-orthographic transformation rules that make comprehension and production of written English possible for hearing people. Hearing children who can be taught to transform spelled letters into sounds usually can be taught to read. Deaf children, on the other hand, do not have a fully functioning sensory system that allows them to map sounds onto printed signs.

Conrad (1979) maintained that, as a result of early oralism, many Deaf youngsters enter school not realizing that objects, people, and feelings have names; they do not know that things can be referred to when not immediately present; nor do they possess any way of revealing the past or projecting into the future. Reflecting on the efforts of his grade-school teachers to instruct him in English, one of my Deaf college students told me, "I felt it was fun, but I did not know that what the people were doing was using language." It is little wonder, then, that studies conducted at Gallaudet University have indicated that grammatical errors persist in the writing of Deaf people throughout their lives (Kelly 1989, 22).

Although one might expect Deaf students' problems with English to diminish as they advance up the educational ladder, this does not happen. The language of higher education relies on complicated rules of semantics and pragmatics, rules involving the understanding of indexicals, beliefs, expectations, and intentions of a given speaker or writer in a given situation or text. It involves the interpretation not only of such items as deictics and ellipses, but also every communicative aspect of language use "not analyzable as literal meaning" (Morgan and Green 1980, 113). Hearing-impaired individuals tend to learn *the rules* of English rather than acquire *the language itself* because what they are taught—over and over throughout their education—are the rules: syntactic, morphological, and phonological. Language has been presented to them as linearly patterned and literal in meaning. The result of this instructional emphasis on rule-governedness is familiar to every instructor of Deaf students: they tend to approach all texts literally. Indeed, Blackwell and his colleagues have noted, "either something is literal or it is absurd and thus regarded as insignificant" by Deaf learners (1978, 138). Often they disregard descriptive or figurative language as incomprehensible. Texts that convey meaning indirectly and words that do not carry their dictionary definitions are indecipherable to the Deaf student just as such texts in a foreign language typically are to a beginning hearing student. Because most college texts use both grammatical and descriptive metaphors extensively, college reading and writing pose interpretive difficulties for Deaf students that cannot be imagined or forestalled by hearing instructors who, like all hearing users of language, take metaphorical usage for granted.

Yet, Deaf students are not mentally incompetent; they score just as highly as hearing students on nonverbal tests of ability. When exposed to a signed language from birth, they not only approximate hearing children in language development (they actually exceed hearing children very slightly during their early years), but they also are subsequently able to learn reading and writing of oral languages with more fluency than Deaf children trained through oral methodologies (Bonvillian et al. 1985; McIntire 1977; Prinz and Prinz 1979; Schlesinger and Meadow 1972).

Deaf students, both those who sign and those who are oral, are somewhat less likely to graduate from high school than hearing students (NCHS 1994). But of those who complete their secondary programs, Deaf individuals enter institutions of higher education at the same rate as hearing students do. The problem is that, as a result of Public Law 94–142, a significant number of the Deaf students entering colleges have been in a mainstream (i.e., oral) environment for much of their educational career, and, as Evans (1982) has shown, oral teaching methodologies have left more than thirty percent of these same Deaf high-school graduates illiterate and sixty percent reading at a fifth-grade level or below.

Of course, early educational mainstreaming was never seen as a viable solution to the English language difficulties of the hearing-impaired by members of the Deaf community. Like most decisions affecting their lives, the decision to mainstream the hearing handicapped was made by hearing people. The communication barriers that a hearing environment imposes on Deaf learners are severe even when interpreters and notetakers are provided by the educational institutions they attend (and this is by no means a universal provision). Unable to hear their teachers or classmates; unable to voice their opinions, ask their questions, or participate in discussions without the mediation of a hearing interpreter; unable to comprehend the grammar and metaphorical language of their textbooks, Deaf students regularly find education in the mainstream—while important for future employment—troublesome and sometimes useless. In particular, they find teacher emphasis on error correction of their texts perplexing.

As Levine (1981) pointed out, Deaf persons are constantly on the alert to detect unfavorable reactions to their use of English. But, because of teacher correction patterns, English language errors in spelling and grammar tend to be highlighted whenever Deaf students hand in a paper. These surface-level errors are so salient and so easily marked that it is not surprising that they are the focus of many (sometimes all) teacher-suggested revisions. Yet, even when Deaf students correct all the errors red-penciled onto their papers, their texts frequently are still difficult to read. Hence, when it comes to reading and writing English, Deaf students are constantly having placed before them what they did wrong rather than what they did right.

Unfortunately, some of the things they do "wrong" in English are considered "all right" in ASL. For example, whereas both English and ASL have multiple ways of showing plurality, they are not the same ways. In the English clause "the three girls are going," plural markers are carried by the first four words; in ASL, the correct form would be "three girl go," one plural being sufficient to mark the clause for number. Also pertinent to the clause quoted, ASL does not use definite or indefinite articles as markers of nouns as English does.

The classroom implications of this kind of linguistic confusion—called *interference* by linguists—are difficult to gauge. Clearly, many teachers are frustrated because they expect college students to read, write, and understand academic prose at a twelfth-grade or better level. Similarly, many Deaf students are frustrated because they do not understand what they are doing wrong or how to correct it; at times, even the suggestions made by their teachers make no sense to them. Their sense of frustration, often hidden from their classroom instructors, surfaces in the literacy narratives I have them write at the beginning of the introductory composition classes I teach. Two examples, with the original spelling, grammar, and punctuation maintained, give a flavor of their attitudes toward English and the corrections they receive. One young woman writes: "I hate English because my feeling that I always lousy writing and difficult to read." The second asserts:

> ... grammar was one of my worst enemies. The reason why that is I become frustrate trying to understand grammar and all the different type of sentence. ... When I talk or write, some of the hearing person tell that I have a problem. That upset me. English is very important to me because I want other

to understand me. It really bother me and make me frustrated if someone does not understand me.

It was the joke of a student, thrown into a tutoring session, that started me thinking about possible Deaf resentment of hearing teachers. Passages like the preceding, found in Deaf students' literacy narratives, confirmed my feelings that Deaf students must be experiencing anger and frustration in the classroom. It was my background in functional linguistics that compelled me to examine those passages in Deaf student essays that angered and frustrated me most, those passages when Deaf students allowed an essay to die by refusing to continue writing. I knew that if I was feeling anger, it might well be because I was reacting to anger—even if that anger was not immediately perceivable.

Written texts, like oral texts, are expected by their readers to "hang together" in patterned ways. These patterns, besides encoding content, also present the writer's views *and* a view of the writer for evaluation. Teachers, in responding to the informational content of texts, simultaneously judge the writers of those same texts to be "smart," "lazy," "creative," or "ill-prepared" on the basis of the kind(s) of coding they find in the texts. This judging takes place whether the text is a written essay on "The Life of a Cell," an exam response on "The Effects of the American Revolutionary War on the Economy of the Colonies," or a face-to-face interview on the first draft of a paper. What is getting communicated during each discursive moment, then, is more than informational content—it is also an image of the sender. In this sense, academic essays can be said to possess multiple contents: contents that convey information, contents that convey a writer's attitude toward the contents, and contents that convey a view of the writer as student.

The study of the various (meta)levels on which a text makes meaning is the object of *systemic-functional linguistics.* Systemic-functional grammar is anchored in the clause or clause complex. Although the clause can be studied at several levels, the level of theme, embedded in what systemicists call the *textual metafunction,* is productive in demonstrating how writers code both explicit and implicit meaning. If Deaf students were using the structures of English to code their frustrations, to issue their outbursts, then a study of theme should reveal whether and how this was being accomplished. Such a study also should show why such anger—if present—was being misinterpreted by me and other hearing teachers.

My theory was that structural deviance in Deaf student writing was patterned and, more specifically, patterned to accomplish two purposes that I see as essential to an outburst: (1) explanation or expansion of a personal stance; and (2) the interruption and/or alteration of a discursive pattern. To test the idea, I decided to look at several problem texts written during an activity that I strongly suspected students might have a reason to resent. The essays were composed during a special tutoring session arranged for thirteen Deaf students enrolled in an introduction to the humanities class. This class is taught several times each academic year, and class size is large: between 125 and 200 students. Because of the size of the class, and because the class is team-taught in a large lecture hall, the students have little opportunity to interact on a personal level with their teachers: four instructors, one each from the disciplines of literature, art, music, and history.

Throughout the course, instructors emphasize several questions that the College of Arts and Humanities has identified as being central to the study of texts in the humanities: What does it mean to be human? Is one way of life better than another? To what extent are we responsible for the decisions we make? What values should guide our lives? As the course progresses, students are asked to consider how the authors (and artists and composers) of the works they are studying might have answered these questions or how various characters in the narrative and historical works they are assigned to read have addressed these issues. The four humanities questions also appear on both the mid-term and final exams to elicit two student essays, which count for fifty percent of each test grade. In answering the essay questions, students are expected to refer to salient quotes, episodes, passages, or visual elements from appropriate works.

Because the Deaf students taking the introductory humanities course historically have performed more poorly on the essay portion of the test than the hearing students, the instructors arranged for a special session during which the Deaf students could "practice" answer-writing and obtain feedback before taking their final exam. This mandatory tutoring session cut into the Deaf students' free time and required the reading of an extra book. During the tutoring session, the students received instruction concerning the organization of their essays and were given examples of the kinds of evidence they needed to provide in their essays. Finally, the Deaf students were asked to write, under time constraints, an essay such as might be required on their exam. While eight of the essays the Deaf students wrote were structurally very much like essays written by hearing students (i.e., they had an introduction that referred to the question asked, a body that offered arguments supporting the stances of their writers, and a recognizable conclusion), five—all written by orally trained Deaf writers—were markedly different.

Texts A, B, and C in the following table are the complete texts of the practice essays of three Deaf students whose responses deviated significantly from what was expected by the teachers who set up the tutorial. The prompt the Deaf writers were given asked them to locate the values that guided the lives of Steinbeck's characters in his novel, *The Pearl*. The student texts in the table are divided into their constituent clauses and each clause is separated into its theme, rheme, and N-rheme, elements that are explained later. The students' grammar, spelling, and punctuation remain unchanged.

One of the basic tenets of systemic-functional linguistics is that the various units of the clause derive their meaning in at least three ways: intratextually,

	Clause	Theme	Rheme	N-Rheme
Text A	1	I	read	the chapter
	2	and I	am not enjoying	to read the kind of book.
	3	At night Kino	wake up,	
	4	and there	were stars shone out there.	
	5	Roosters and pigs	made	any noise
	6	while people	were sleeping	
	7	His wife Juana	lay	beside him on the mat.
Text B	1	I	wasn't interested	about it
	2	because I	don't like	to read "The Pearl" book.
	3	I	tried best	to write the sentence.
	4	The woman	don't understand	the husband.
	5	She	have	big problem of the child and something else,
	6	because she	never remember	seeing them.
	7	Closing when her husband was awakened, she	has	her eye reflected the star.
	8	She	always look	at him.
Text C	1	I	readed	the Pearl book for eight page.
	2	When I	readed	it,
	3	I	not do understand	a little
	4	but I	some understand.	
	5	it	's	because it's not make sense.
	6	I	think	it's a little hard to reading for me.

contextually, and heterotextually. They derive their meanings *intratextually* when they are examined for their distribution of information, which is done subsequently. They derive their meanings *contextually* because the discourses of a community operate in predictable ways. When two students who have a class together but do not know each other outside the classroom meet in the corridor, the greeting, "Hi! How are you?" is never taken as the opening move of a long conversation in which one person will describe his or her existential problems to the other. The discourse patterns of life in the United States tell the participants that in this type of encounter, a simple formulaic response is in order. The context influences the text. If the same two participants had been paired together by an instructor to work on a project, the context would shift, and the same opening move by one student might be interpreted by the second to mean that an accounting of time and effort spent on their mutual project was in order. Knowing when "Fine. How about you?" is suitable and when "Awful. Let me tell you about the troubles I had in the library!" is acceptable is part of what linguists mean when they talk about *communicative competence.* To be a competent communicator, one must master the discourse patterns appropriate to various contexts in which one might find oneself.

The context of the three text excerpts cited previously—a tutoring session—was predicated on a specific academic/community assumption: the Deaf members of a predominantly hearing university community must learn how to write papers that sound like papers written by their hearing peers. Hearing instructors across the university expect papers to have a recognizable beginning, middle, and end. They expect certain kinds of evidence to be offered; they are looking for overtly or subtly stated and developed stances or theses. Indeed, so important are these textual behaviors to the faculty at the institution where I teach that they are stated in the institutional objectives that flow from the university's mission statement. The four humanities instructors conducting the introductory course also agreed that student essays should exhibit an identifiable global structure, adhere to recognized syntactic rules of English, offer citations appropriate to the domain of literature, and address the theme of *values.*

Also relevant to the production of these three essays was the element of *heterotextuality:* that the instructors—all hearing—had familiarity not only with similar papers written by hearing students in previous sections of the class, but also with essays written about Steinbeck by hearing scholars in academic journals and books. Additionally, each hearing teacher had in mind how he or she might respond to the essay prompt, and the literature teacher of the team had provided a sample essay response to be used as a benchmark in the evaluation of student responses. The context, then, in which student papers were produced and read was highly structured and strongly heterotextual. The academic structure—and the worldview that initiated the structure—is shared (although unequally) by those who are acculturated into academe. A major facet of the structuring of academe is the interplay of multiple texts (i.e., heterotextuality). In short, in the university classroom, if a student wishes to be considered a scholar, he or she must sound something like the scholars with whom the instructors are familiar.

In terms of academic essays, the genre or activity formation of expository writing demands that certain kinds of things be done in a recognized order. Longacre, in his 1983 book *The Grammar of Discourse,* studied how written texts of various genres tend to be arranged. He called the units of organization *syntagmemes* and the subunits *tagmemes.* An expository essay of the kind demanded in this tutorial session would start with an *introductory* syntagmeme, which would consist of two mandatory and one optional tagmemes. The tagmemes are the *preliminary,* in which the general nature or goal of the discourse is presented; the *text,* which states the topic sentence, research question, or writer's stance; and the optional *background,* where information salient to the general topic or question is given (see Anderson [1991] for further discussion of tagmemic analysis of academic texts).

Texts A, B, and C, in their opening syntagmemes, violate the expectations of most academic readers by not following the expository pattern for prose in English. While academic essays allow for many optional moves in beginning a paper, a statement of purpose is needed somewhere toward the beginning of the text; readers expect to have some idea why the text is being written in the first place. In a book, the statement might occur somewhere in the introductory chapter or essay. In an article, it might occur several pages or paragraphs into the text. In a short essay, it needs to occur fairly rapidly—within the first few sentences or paragraphs.

In each of the three essays quoted previously, the writer begins with a personal statement about her (all three essays were written by women) attempts to read the book under discussion. In none of the three openings is there a statement of goal or purpose. In none of the three is there reference to the question asked by the instructor. None contain the writer's stance on the content of the book, although two of the essays begin to present some background information. In structure, then, the three essays written by the Deaf students fail to include the two mandatory tagmemes of the *introductory* passage of an academic essay that most academic readers would expect them to contain.

Furthermore, the background information that the writers present is not connected to the topic of the question; in all three essays, background is confined to a chronological recitation of events, rather than used as evidence to support an opinion required by the question asked: What *are* the values that seem to be guiding the lives of Steinbeck's characters? The Deaf writers are clearly not doing what is expected of them: They are not performing like most hearing students would perform; not responding like most hearing teachers would expect them to respond; and not sounding like most hearing scholars who have written on the topic. However, they are doing what several other Deaf writers answering the same prompt are doing. In doing it, I contend, they are linguistically exposing the irritation they feel at having to read a book that they had not chosen, and about having to attend a tutoring session (no matter how well intentioned by its organizers) that implied they were incompetent.

The anger of the Deaf students becomes more clear when the *thematic structure* of the three texts is examined. The thematic structure of a text is related to the flow of information. In English, the ordinary or unmarked thematic progression of the clause is theme, rheme, and optional N-rheme. Simply, the *theme* of an English clause consists of those elements that begin the clause or clause complex. Its purpose is to signal "that with which the clause is concerned"; it is the "point of departure of the message" of the clause (Halliday 1985, 38). The *rheme* of the clause is what is being said about the theme. Typically, the implications of the theme of any clause can be recovered either from previous information in the text or from information shared by the writer and readers of the text. The theme of the clause, therefore, usually contains information that is *given* or *known*. The *rheme* of the clause contains information that is presented by the writer as *new* (although, in linguistic analysis, the terms *given* and *new* more appropriately apply to spoken texts than to written texts). New information is that which the writer considers "newsworthy" or worthy of emphasis. Of course, English—or any language—is more complex than this simple distinction implies. *New* information can be presented first in a clause; that which is treated as *given* may not always be recoverable or shared by the writer and readers. But when texts produced by experienced writers are examined, the *given-new* progression is quite consistent across clauses (Clark and Haviland 1977; Danes 1974; Firbas 1966; Witte 1983). It leads to communicative efficiency.

Because of its theme/rheme structure, the clause in English is said to have *endfocus*. That is, because new information tends to occur at the end of the clause, readers concentrate on endings. Writers also concentrate on endings, placing what they want their readers to remember at the end of their clauses. Until recently, the final constituent of the clause (i.e., that which followed the verb and its modifiers)—considered maximally communicative by readers and writers—was not identified by a separate name. It was simply described as an element of the rheme, although it served a critical ideational function in texts. Linguist Fries suggested that this element be called the *N-rheme* (1995), and defined it as the element of the clause that "contains the newsworthy information; information that is in focus in that message" (3). Furthermore, Fries contended that as a result of the communicative dynamism that they possess, "the N-rhemes are likely to contain information that is directly relevant to the goals of the text or the text segment" (3). The theme, although it is fronted and thus does call attention to itself, is "less relevant to the goals and purposes of the text or text segment" (4).

When the themes of the Deaf student texts are examined, it is readily seen that ten of the twenty-two clauses "front," or place initially, the writer through the use of the personal pronoun *I*. Linguistically, this fronting of the self serves several purposes. First, in using the self as the starting point of the message unit, the writers are reminding the reader of the texts, an instructor, that *who* they are—their skills and their differences—*ought to be given*. In most cases, indeed, this would not have to be stated. But since hearing instructors regularly expect Deaf students to perform like hearing students, the writers apparently find it necessary to front their identity in the *introductory* syntagmeme of the text. They do this by choice and, in so doing, affirm that from their perspective, self-identity is more salient than the topic provided by the essay prompt.

Of course, it may be argued, many proficient personal-essay writers front the self in their texts. That is the purpose or function of the *personal* essay. In fact, in recent years, for a variety of reasons, expository essays such as the ones in this book have become more narrative in nature. As such, they have focused, in part, on the observations and feelings and reflections of their writers. There are several important differences, however, between what is happening in Texts A, B, and C and what happens in personal and narrative expository essays. First, the Deaf writers of A, B, and C were responding to a prompt that required specific information of its respondents. That information needed to be extracted from a text read by the essay writers. Yet, the information called for never gets inserted into Texts A, B, and C and certainly never gets thematized. Second, answers to essay questions are a specific genre of prose, and thus are generically different from either the personal or narrative expository essay. Essay-question responses of the sort dealt with herein are short; their theme is selected by someone other than the writer; and they call for the defense of a specific point of view. Third, essay-question responses are obligatory in nature and are meant to ascertain the familiarity of their writers with terminology associated with a restricted body of knowledge; in this case, with the language of literary criticism. They are tests. Personal essays and narrative expository essays are not tests; their agendas are more in the control of their writers than of outside agents.

But the personal aspect of the student essays is instructive for a very important reason: the "I" of the texts is *agentive;* that is, the students are presenting themselves as being in control of their conduct. They "read" but do "not enjoy"; they "read" but are "not interested"; they "read" but do "not like"; they "read" but do "not understand." Although within the context of the class and the essay quiz, they are subjected to the language of a hearing author and hearing instructors, they are not passive. For them, the cognitive domain of the writing test is in opposition to the affective domain of their existence as students. Hence, they choose to make their own kind of meaning in which the interpretive idiom of the classroom plays no part. They do not begin their essays by referring to the text under consideration, *The Pearl,* as they might be expected to do. Books like *The Pearl* are not a *given* to them. The domain of the (con)text is not one they share with the instructor or their hearing peers.

Additionally, by thematizing themselves, the writers are shifting the grounds of the communicative context from the written text to the personal subject—one of the key purposes that I identified for an outburst. The instructor who reads their texts will find his or her reading brought to a halt. The writers, in effect, are rewriting the assignment, connecting themselves to the testing situation in ways that are exceptional. They are, in effect, canceling out the essay question and providing an alternative discourse that allows them to do what they cannot do during class time: object to the hearing bias of the mainstream classroom. Essays, as Mann and Thompson (1987) point out, consist of hierarchically related segments or chunks in which the first segment presents a problem and the second chunk presents a solution. The Deaf writers whose texts are examined herein thematize the Deaf self as the problem for which there is no solution in the hearing classroom; hence, no solution in the text. The essays they write do not work because the (con)texts on which those essays are based do not work for Deaf readers.

Finally, in effective essays of any sort, the themes of the various clause complexes ought to be connected in some way (Halliday and Hasan 1976). One important way that texts in English are connected is by transitions, which surface the logical relations existing between the various segments of the essay or between the various clauses in a clause complex. The most common place for such transitions to occur is in the theme of the clause. When connective material does occur at the beginning of a clause, it is referred to as the *structural theme,* and precedes the *topical theme,* which corresponds to the subject of the sentence. Although several of the clauses that begin the Deaf students' papers do have connective material (i.e., "and" [A:21]; "because" [B:2]; "When" [C:21]; "but" [C:41]), in none of these instances does the structural material connect the self of the writer (i.e., the *topical theme*) with the subject of the essay. In Texts A and B, a major disjuncture occurs between the writer's expression of dissatisfaction with the novel assignment and her discussion of the book. In Text C, the writer widens the chasm between self and the novel by not even considering the content of the book.

Frustration and anger are equally obvious when the rhemes and N-rhemes of the student texts are examined. The verbal elements of the rhemes in the clauses thematizing the student writers tend toward *mental processes* (Halliday 1985); that is, they emphasize the affective or cognitive state of the writer. Of the ten clauses having "I" as a subject, six stress the writers' mental attitudes (i.e., "am not enjoying" [A:21]; "I wasn't interested" [B:1]; "don't like" [B:21]; "not do understand" [C:2]; "some understand" [C:41]; "think" [C:61]). Of these six, four are expressive of negative mental states, one qualifies the mental state to allow for some understanding, and one introduces a second clause that is negative in nature. The remaining four verbs are all *behavioral* (Halliday 1985); that is, they encode the writers' conscious attempts to complete an action—in this case, an academic event (i.e., "read" [A:1]; "tried best to write" [B:3]; "readed" [C:1, C:2]). If one of the purposes of an outburst is to define or expand reasons for personal dissatisfaction, then the student writers are using this essay-writing practice session to enact their anger and dissatisfaction with the nature of mainstream classroom discourse. They do not like it, enjoy it, or understand it.

Lest there be any doubt as to the nature of their frustration, the Deaf writers have saved the end of the clause—the N-rheme—for elaborating on the reason for their dissatisfaction. In those clauses that thematize the writers, the N-rheme invariably refers to the book being discussed. If, as Fries suggests, the N-rheme "indicates the *point* of the sentence as message; what one is trying to say" ([emphasis added] 1995, 14), then these writers are saying that reading the book (i.e., "the chapter" [A:ll]; "to read the kind of book" [A:21]; "about it [the book]" [B:ll]; "to read *The Pearl* book" [B:2]; "the Pearl book for eight page" [C:l]; "it [the book]" [C:2]; "a little [of the book]" [C:3]; "because it's not make sense" [C:5]; "it's a little hard to reading for me" [C:61]) is the cause of their anger and frustration. This anger and frustration—unrecognized, unacknowledged, and unmediated by understanding hearing faculty—can lead to even more overt linguistic demonstrations of dissatisfaction, such as those expressed by the two other Deaf students whose papers did not follow standard academic essay practices.

The textual anger of the two remaining Deaf students whose papers deviated markedly from the norm is more perceptually salient than the three quoted previously. Both of these writers stopped their essays abruptly after beginning to write about the novel they had read. Both of their essays start by attempting to follow the pattern of an expository *introductory* syntagmeme and then, at the point where a reader might reasonably expect a statement of purpose or the stance of the writer, the Deaf writers insert an overt statement of irritation, after which they write no more. Their texts are as follows:

> **Text D:** The star shone and the day. The beautiful's Day. The brush house was in the tuna chump. Kino wake up and He opened his eye, looked the window. The outside's lightening a day. The birds flied and sitting on the phone. This book is too hard for me.

> **Text E:** Kino heard the waves from the beach and listened the sound music. Then he needed to wrap his blanket to keep him warm. Juana had a fire with throwing spears of light through the chinks and brought it out to the door. Kino's brother and his fat wife brought 4 children to Kino's house. Juana's baby looked sick and they should ask their doctor for help so doctor can check for the baby. I don't like this book use alot of new words, some like old boring words.

In these two abbreviated essays, the writers begin to do what Mann and Thompson (1987) suggest writers do in expository writing: They state their problem. But it is not a problem for which they have an answer, so that segment remains absent from their texts. Individuals who are without power in the classroom are not allowed answers that deviate from the norm. Nor are they allowed to pose questions not sanctioned by the (con)text created by the instructors. What they can do is attempt to change the conditions of discourse. They can register an outburst, even if it results in a lowered grade and continued misunderstanding.

I have found in my own life that when helplessness and resentment become intolerable, they find a way to express themselves, to burst through the careful layers of civility I use to conceal them. Although I find such outbursts (whether I am the initiator or receiver) disquieting and uncomfortable, they appear to me to be productive. They allow me to call attention to or expand upon some feeling or belief that is important to me. And they give me some modicum of power by allowing me to disrupt the governing social activity in which the outburst occurs in order to change the nature of its discourse (i.e., what gets talked about, by whom, in what ways). If this is true for me as a hearing woman with access to the privileges and discourse patterns of academe, how much more so must it be true for those whose place in academe is more tenuous and whose discourse is more divergent.

In academic settings, specific discourse patterns—written and spoken—and the activity formations of which they are a part (e.g., lecturing) embody most of the meaning that gets made. Not only do instructors teach from notes (hastily jotted or carefully word-processed), but they also assign readings, encourage debate of scholarly articles, select speakers, evaluate student-generated papers, comment on discussions and responses, and plan essay tests and assignments. In all of these activities, authority and meaning get played out in language. Through language—used or mediated by the instructor—favor is bestowed or withheld, information is imparted or challenged, identity is defined or negated. The textual, to quote Lemke, "in the broad sense of all the meanings we make, whether in words or by deeds, is deeply political" (1995, 1). In the mainstream classroom, it is also deeply auditory. For those with hearing impairments, therefore, entrance into the mainstream classroom has not meant linguistic equality. As Cohen noted, "even among the brightest [Deaf] students, English remains to some degree unnatural, like foreign territory" (1994, 153). Clearly, this is reason for anger.

The genesis of anger, as Scheler said, is a pervasive feeling of impotence and inferiority in dealing with others (1961, 46). The more powerless a person feels, the greater the anger at the conditions causing the helplessness and the greater the inner tension for the person experiencing the emotion as he or she strives to present an outward pose of satisfaction and understanding. Often incensed about being excluded from those processes of communication essential in the hearing classroom, while simultaneously being reminded that the academic institution is going through a great deal of trouble and expense to accommodate their needs, Deaf students are led to believe—in ways both overt and subtle—that complaint is neither appropriate nor appreciated. Given an institutional system whose discourse is constantly that of the other," Deaf students—like many other minority students—are placed in an atmosphere where frustration is a constant companion.

If the outbursts of Deaf and other minority students do not follow the conventions of hearing academic discourse that teachers have come to expect, I would suggest it is not because they are failing to occur, but rather because they are being misinterpreted *solely* as evidence of other kinds of things: most notably lack of linguistic competence, failure to study adequately, or an inability to cope with workload and content at the college level. This single-cause fallacy tends to mute the Deaf student outburst, making it more comfortable for the instructor who then never has to decide *if* workload and content might be unfair, *if* poor linguistic competence is the result of poor pedagogy, *if* textual difficulties have made the task of studying impossible for some students.

Using a systemic-functional approach to analyze those texts of Deaf students that deviated from the norm of expository writing helped to clarify for me, as a reader of such texts, the various purposes the texts were serving. That the deviant texts were patterned became obvious. That the student writers of the texts were doing more than demonstrating an inability to function in academe became equally apparent.

Because Deaf students are minority members of the mainstream classroom, majority teachers may not always be able to orient their texts appropriately. Instead of reading minority-student texts *in terms of* majority-student texts, we who teach should see minority-student texts as *standing against* majority texts. Deaf students—indeed, all minority students—regularly select to thematize viewpoints that differ from those who represent the mainstream. When they select an approach that is not familiar—particularly when they have just been told *how* they are *expected* to write an essay so that it conforms to majority patterns— then their texts, I suggest, can be read as outbursts, as acts contesting existing social relations in the classroom.

However, I have no intention of painting teachers as uncaring and unsympathetic. The instructors of the humanities course described previously, for example, were very sensitive to student differences and desirous of student success; otherwise, they would not have arranged for special tutoring sessions for those students who were in danger of failing the course. The problem is that the discourse patterns of teachers and of the mainstream classroom—like all patterns in our lives—are persistent; they were created over the long term and tend to endure for a long time. We still, I would note, pay attention to what authors such as Aristotle, Longinus, and Cicero have had to say about writing, if only to disagree with it.

As Makler said, "Teachers and students are quintessentially interdependent knowers" (1991, 29). But when they lack essential understanding of each other and of each other's discourse, that interdependence will be strained and possibly unproductive. The solution to the problems of students who are uncomfortable with the educational institution's expectations ought not to be found in failure or transfer to another institution. It should rest in a genuine attempt to listen, unpack, discuss, and act upon what the other is saying. We all, teachers and students, seek understanding. We all, teachers and students, wish to grow in wisdom and understanding. The more culturally different we are, the more we need to negotiate our language through language.

Of all the semiotic systems that human beings have at their disposal for the making of meaning, language offers the most semantic choices and, thus, is most likely to be misinterpreted. When members of a minority group select from a series of linguistic and textual options specific choices that contrast with selections made by members of the majority, and when those apparently deviant choices are regular or patterned within the minority group, then the selection must be regarded as political, as Lemke contests (1995). That is, the selection—whether a joke, an essay, or another kind of text—needs to be viewed as an attempt to disrupt the social activity of the mainstream and to present and expand a minority viewpoint. By choosing to read such linguistically deviant texts in terms of dominant discourse patterns, we as teachers are ignoring *texts that are* in order to read *essays that never were*. When this happens, the classroom cannot be safe for multiculturalism, no matter how much we protest that it is.

5

A Captivity Narrative: Indians, Mixedbloods, and "White" Academe

Scott Lyons

For Jared, Dakota storyteller, and Landon, Michif poet (ages seventeen and eighteen)

"Do I look like a rice-eating rabbit-hunter to you? No, I am not a Chippewa, but I'm not white, either—I am Michif, a Metis [mixedblood]."

A Turtle Mountain graduate
student

"Those Michifs aren't real Indians. You know why? They talk too much."

A Devil's Lake Dakota elder

"Turn 'em into taxpayers."

A white director of a largely
Indian educational program

Captive Audiences

Captivity narratives, one of America's oldest literary genres, were enormously popular texts for white, reading Americans in a young nation: exciting Colonial tales of bravery and guile, savagery and civilization, godly triumph over pagan evil in a newfound, rapidly developing, Manifestly Destined "white" society. In many ways, they were the perfect metaphoric vehicle for popular nation-building sentiments. Narratives like Rowlandson's (1985) seventeenth-century story, untouched by the as-yet-to-come (and not very Puritan) romantic concept of the noble savage, were filled with anti-Indian bile; to Rowlandson and her readers, Indians were "wolves," "hellhounds," and "ravenous beasts." If Rowlandson's vitriol seems somewhat understandable considering her rabid fear of Indians, alien epistemology, her child's death, and generally all-around unpleasant time with her hosts, the ravenously vitriolic consumption of her text by readers attests to the symbolic power of literature in early American constructions of both nation and race. Rowlandson's readers got a close-up view of Indian savagery, viciousness, and pagan—even demonic—identity. Her story, thrilling and entertaining to white readers as it no doubt was in its time, also served as further psychocultural justification for the continuation of policies of colonization, war, and genocide, a bloody history whose genealogy reverberates in the lives of Indian people today, including those of my own family, friends, teachers, and students.

While Indians in Rowlandson's time and beyond were both captives and narrators in much greater number than were whites, they produced no literary genre we call *captivity narratives.* By no means am I trying to reclaim the term now. On the contrary, I want to invoke the signifier as an ironic metaphor multiplicitous in its meanings, as stories open to revision. Indian students are multiply interpellated by a variety of contradictory discourses—ironic narratives of race, subjectivity, history, and learning—which at times can feel constraining (and which at times are), but also can be viewed as strengths, sites of possibility, intersections of difference that might work against the confinements of racism, poverty, and cultural genocide. I would like to exchange narratives of captivity for captivating narratives: for me, those narratives are stories of hope. Because this work is the work of stories, I am also interested in the kinds of popular imagination that might be—and doubtless are—formed by their reception. If Rowlandson's readers had their emergent racism (and, for that matter, their very notions of *race* and *nation*) spurred on by her narrative, what views of academe, or "society," or race, or politics, or even their own identities will my students take from the stories they wrote, read, saw, and contributed to in my class? How will their narratives be read (and, consequently, told and retold) by teachers, both Indian and non-Indian? What would it mean to revise the narratives of captivity that govern the discourses, material conditions, and lived experiences of people all across the educational spectrum—and beyond?

In the stories we tell, we translate lived experience into narrative; conversely, we rely on narratives to live our lives, make sense of our worlds, engage in production, relate to others, and construct and assert our identities. Is language then, as Nietzsche suggested, a prison-house, narrative captivity? Or is language intrinsically liberating, sites of continual creation, what Vizenor calls "ecstatic strategies" of creating reality and "original eruptions of time" (1984, 7)? Or are the moves dialectical? To my mixedblood mind, the stories of Indian students are clearly *heteroglossic*—produced against, within, and in tandem with the grand narratives of contemporary American life and culture: race and racism, intelligence and learning, literacy and orality, success and failure, them and us. The voice of the Other is continually present in discourse, as Bakhtin (1981) said it would be, and often those voices conflict. There is reinscribed contact made in every heteroglossic utterance; in America, this contact is (among other things) between cultures and races. Each time we speak or write, the history of this contact is quietly (and sometimes not so quietly) stirring. There is a European in every Indian and an Indian in every "white"—each relationship positioned differently—and the two are not together by choice. It is this kind of *contact heteroglossia* that has been repressed by educators and theorists for centuries, and that Indian students not only know, but also use daily—we can all learn from them in this regard.

From the Enlightenment thinking professed by so many educators (emphasizing belief in Western progress, faith in reason, and valorization of the individual) to the nationalist, at times nativist, sentiments expressed by some Indian activists, most discourse on Indian education wants to downplay the dialogism of student language and thought in lieu of more monologic tones (and tomes); either way, arguments are frequently made, overtly or not, for the teaching of Our Culture, Our Language, Our Dialect, Our Nation(s).[1] One of the many casualties of this sort of thinking is the *mixedblood,* a term I use to refer to humans, texts, language, and consciousness emphasizing duality-as-wholeness. Thus, one point of this essay is to mystify somewhat popular notions of what people mean by the term *Indian* (and, consequently, *white*). And yet, another casualty of the Enlightenment (and an understandable precursor to Indian nationalism or separatism) is a late twentieth-century America in which Indian people endure the poorest quality of life in this country; where one thousand more Native American people die each year than would be expected if they were living in the same conditions as white America; and where, in fact, if reservation conditions existed throughout the total population of this country, 150,000 more Americans would die each year. In other words, America is a racist, white-supremacist nation. So another point of this essay is to *clarify* the material consequences of racial signification, to ruminate on some of the reasons why it is not only hard to be an Indian in academe, and in America at large, but also to read and be read as one (or as not one). The mixedblood metaphor is meant to be *re-visionary,* not to erase (*de-race*) material bodies.

The story of the mixedblood is one that has fluctuated historically in this country between comedy and tragedy. Comedy: My Michif friend makes fun of my "Sioux nose"; my Polish American friend makes fun of my "Roman nose." I appreciate both insults but do not have two noses. Then again, I do. Tragedy: In the United States, discourse on mixedbloods has oscillated between nasty rumors of miscegenation and racialist scientific "fact," on the one hand (see Telford [1932] and Garth and Smith [1937] for research on North Dakota Indians' and mixedbloods' "intelligence" and psychology), and a mutual fascination with hybridity and both romantic and revisionary literary fictions (from the punished "mixing" in *The Last of the Mohicans* to mixedbloodedness as dominant and powerful theme in Native American literature) on the other. Today, the mixedblood is being reclaimed as both problem and solution. In my story, *mixedblood* signifies both material bodies and discourse, *identity* and thinking, *race* and subjectivity: the moral of this story will be that these binaries do not hold.

Anzaldúa's *new mestiza* learns to cope in multiple worlds, none of which lay claim to her multiple identity, and to none of which she can devote complete, monolithic allegiance herself. Anzaldúa's *mestiza* is continually caught in a conflict of boundaries:

> In perceiving conflicting information and points of view, she is subjected to a swamping of her psychological borders. She has discovered that she can't hold concepts or ideas in rigid boundaries. The borders and walls that are supposed to keep undesirable ideas out are entrenched habits and patterns of behavior; these habits and patterns are the enemy within. (1987, 79)

The "borders and walls" are both *hers* and *not hers* and, in patrolling her interior boundaries, she finds herself imprisoned: both captive and guard, both "brown" and "white." Yet, this logic of the borderlands also offers a release from its own captivity, one possible only through a flexibility of thought:

> Rigidity means death. Only by remaining flexible is she able to stretch the psyche horizontally and vertically. *La Mestiza* constantly has to shift out of habitual formations; from convergent thinking, analytical reasoning that tends to use rationality to move toward a single goal (a Western mode), to divergent thinking . . . one that includes rather than excludes. (1987, 79)

The mixedblood is mobile (yet excluded) and flexible (yet caught). *La mestiza's* multiplicity of "race," language, and culture—in a land and time both hostile and welcoming, attacking and defending—both imprisons and releases her continually against backdrops both discursive and material. In a culture of *convergent thinking,* she must choose her allegiances carefully, all the while being aware of the impossibility of doing so in exclusive fashion: "Being tricultural, monolingual, bilingual, or multilingual, speaking a patois, and in a state of perpetual transition, the *mestiza* faces the dilemma of the mixed breed, which collectivity does the daughter of a dark-skinned mother listen to?" (1987, 78). Mixedblood subjectivity can feel like—is—schizophrenia, for the dominant culture wants its subjects to be one, not many. Anzaldúa's project is about showing the value of such a subjectivity in an age that requires divergent thinking, in a land caught in a crisis of multiplicity.

People of *visible* or otherwise *authenticated* mixed-race backgrounds are not the only ones who experience this crisis. On the contrary, recent work in psychoanalytic, phenomenological, and especially feminist theories has contributed much to our understandings of multiple subjectivities, raising questions about discourse, power, essentialism, and the body. Among the most interesting and controversial is the work of Irigaray, whose symbolics of the female body—a multiple erogenous entity devalued and repressed in a phallocentric culture of "one"—allows her to theorize a feminine subjectivity of "difference" that works on both discursive and bodily material levels. She has been attacked as essentialist for this work (see Moi [1985] and Silverman [1988] for the critiques; Gallop [1988] and Whitford [1986] for the defenses). I find useful her bodily symbolics, which posits a relationship (although I would say not a causal one) between material and discursive experiences of "reality": a body made into discourse and vice versa. Irigaray's thematics of the female body—a desiring body harboring multiple sites of pleasure—focuses on the fluidity, mucosity, and porousness of boundaries, a functioning at odds with a culture based on the unity of male phallic desire. In opposition to a masculine discourse limited to terms of positivity and absence, feminine discourse can create a "sort of expanding universe to which no limits could be fixed and which would not be incoherent nonetheless," the sensation *"of never being simply one"* (Irigaray 1985b, 31; her emphasis). Indulging in feminine discourse, she acknowledges, might "involve *a new prison,* a new cloister, built of [women's] own accord" (my emphasis, 33), a bodily/discursive confinement reminiscent of Anzaldúa's ("racial"/cultural) dilemma in the borderlands.

At once (in) a sort of prison *and* (with) a promise of freedom, *la mestiza* (i.e., feminine mixedblood) ultimately works "to break down the subject-object duality that keeps her a prisoner and to show in the flesh and through the images in her work how duality is transcended" (1985b, 80). Mixedblood is not a *race* (although often treated as one), nor even a definable *subject position* (although different *mixedbloods* can compare their different experiences). Mixedbloods are racially designated beings who both resist and perform "racializing," divergent thinkers resisting convergence. They are fluid, porous, mobile—and schizophrenic, cloistered, captive. Their captivities are both *theirs* and *not theirs,* both material and discursive. Mixedbloods can operate in the dominant culture and make it home in time for dinner. They can transculturate and/or assimilate the mainstream. And they know both sides of the story; they *are* both sides of the story. They are the *story.*

Mixedblood narratives are not only heroic narratives of liberation from captivity or dualistic declarations of war, but also porous stories about both captivity and release. In that sense, they are truly ironic, playful, infuriating, and hopeful, substituting for the prison neither the asylum nor the battlefield, but rather a different language. The mixedblood narratives that follow are an attempt to figure out what that might mean.

Fish Out of Water

The fish in the tank was definitely a captive.

It was "Eelpout Days" in Walker, Minnesota, and the local elementary school was as excited and self-promoting as were the local businesses and townspeople. The annual week-long winter festival—featuring an ice-fishing tournament, parties, parades, and numerous storewide sales—takes as its playful neototemic symbol the eelpout, a large, scavenging roughfish usually unpalatable to tourists, anglers, and fish connoisseurs. To actively hunt and celebrate it for one week out of the year is a testament to the ironic humor (and savvy business sense) of white northern Minnesotans during the coldest time of year. The school got in on the fun by challenging the entire student body to read a certain number of books by a deadline; if they succeeded (which they did), the principal would assemble the students during the festival week and kiss a real live eelpout, a testament of its own (albeit a surrealistic one) to the sacrificial differences between educators and businesspeople in these times. (If you have ever seen an eelpout, let alone kissed one, you will understand just how committed to literacy the principal was.)

This was 1992, the Colombian quintcenteniary, and the school district in this predominantly white border town on the Leech Lake Chippewa[2] reservation had just changed its sports nickname from "Warriors" to "Wolves," an initiative made in response not only to the Minnesota Department of Education, but also to the protests of Indian parents served by the school. Indian students at this public school are a noticeable minority, a "problem" in the eyes of some teachers and administrators, and the focus of much attention and discussion by educators, social service workers, parent committees, and a small coalition of American Indian education programs in the school directed by my Indian father, Dick Lyons, who grew up in the small Anishinabe community of Bena and attended schools not unlike this one himself.

The fish was anxious, splashing and thrashing about in the cramped thirty-two-gallon aquarium, looking out through the glass at the distorted images of wildly cheering elementary students, chuckling teachers, and a nervous principal. My father, in need of some quiet work time, was in his office during the event, only to be interrupted by an urgent request to come immediately to the teachers' lounge. One of his students, a second-grade girl, was extremely upset, kicking and crying, screaming on the floor in both English and Anishinabe. "Awasasi, awasasi!" she repeatedly sobbed. "They're laughing at my brother!" When my dad arrived, he found her with his Indian Education partner, Bob, who had successfully calmed her down. Bob, a traditional Ojibway himself originally from a Canadian reserve, explained to my dad that this traditionally raised girl, a member of the Bullhead clan and, hence, a descendent of roughfish, was humiliated by the wild laughter and jeering going on in the gym. My father agreed with Bob's suggestion that he take her down to the lake and perform a tobacco ceremony asking for forgiveness. After they left, he called the girl's parents, explained what had happened and apologized, then met with the student's teachers and, later, principal to do the kind of mediating work his job often required of him. Nobody was happy with the circumstances, he told me: The non-Indian teachers felt bad but uncomprehending (and, along with that, a little powerless, a little annoyed); the girl's parents were thankful for Bob's actions but spoke in quiet, resigned tones about the insensitivity of the school; and the principal seemed thankful and relieved that the situation was "under control" once again and spoke of the matter no more. The little girl finished her outburst, Bob took her to the lake and then home, my dad went back to his office, kids and teachers returned to their classroom, and the eelpout was placed back into its aquarium before making its final trip to the taxidermist, where it was killed, stuffed, and eventually put on display as a trophy.

Another Fish — Stanley — writes about "interpretive communities": social groups and institutions whose discursive formations, rules of intelligibility, worldviews, and meaning-making laws limit the sense we can make of any object — a poem, a gesture, a fish. Because we are overdetermined in a sense by our interpretive communities, "the 'you' who does the interpretive work," Fish explains, "is a communal 'you' and not an isolated individual." Because "the mental operations we can perform are limited by the institutions in which we are *already* embedded" (1980, 331), it stands to reason that an encounter with difference — and here I am thinking of cultural difference in particular — would be an exercise in either unintelligibility, a search for common "universals," value judgments, or — Fish's main point — the construction of something intelligible to one's own interpretive community. Thus, using Fish's text to read the fish as a text, we see clear binary oppositions at work: the girl, her parents, and her presumed community (i.e., "Indians") read — construct — the eelpout as a brother — a sentient, spiritual being deserving of respect. By contrast, most of the teachers, students, and principal (i.e., "whites") construct the fish differently — as a joke, a trophy, an ironic totem. Both groups comprise two different interpretive communities, constructing different meanings, different fish, out of the same "text." Problems emerge, however, when we start thinking of the "two" groups as discrete, sovereign entities. What are we to make of a young schoolgirl very capable of what Fish calls "doing studenting" (1980, 334) in the "white" school, who nonetheless breaks down across apparently cultural-epistemic lines? What about the other Indian kids who stayed in the audience, who may have done a little cheering themselves — are they now "white"? Assimilated? What about Bob? Or my father? In which communities are they embedded? Finally, as the young girl wants us to ask, what about what the fish thinks? While exhibiting tangible epistemological differences, the interpretive communities here are anything but discrete; to describe them as such seems to inevitably lead to a troubling and well-worn shift in discourse about Indian/white relations, particularly in the contexts of education: from talk about interpretive communities to the narratives of "assimilation."

Looking historically, we see that the assimilating drives of Indian education are undeniable. White policymakers suggested early on that the best path to assimilation was through school and the subsequent inculcation of Anglo American values and epistemologies. The infamous motto of the Indian boarding-school era, "Kill the Indian, save the person," was the rule of the day in the nineteenth and early twentieth centuries. The formative years of Indian education—from its genesis in Christian missions through the boarding-school years and beyond—show a remarkable awareness of the influence of culture and society on a human being. That is, the assimilationist pedagogies of early Indian educators operate from an understanding of what we might now recognize as a social-constructionist model of education or, to use Fish's terms, an *interpretive community model*. White people believed that schools should acculturate or socialize young Indian children into European social modes—Euro-interpretive communities—and assimilation, so crucial to the land grabs underway and the social construction of the new nation, would hurry along. (This, of course, was the humanist alternative to another option of the day: complete and utter genocide.) To assimilate the "person" while killing the "Indian" not only reifies the distinction between Indians and whites (or, worse, between Indians and "people"), but also suggests that the aims of education are to initiate students into preexisting, sovereign interpretive communities—white ones, no less— that is, to "civilize" Indians; that is, to kill them. How far have we really come from that?

While you would be hard-pressed to find a teacher who sees her or his role as "civilizer," much less murderer, the ways we distinguish between *traditional* and—what? *nontraditional? assimilated?—other* Indian students (in addition to Indians and non-Indians) reproduce the narratives of Indian/white relations and education: Indians and whites as discrete, different communities, school as civilizing instrument, learning as assimilative enterprise. It also leaves white people off the hook. Whether killing Indians to save people or multiculturally "celebrating difference" while abdicating responsibility for the material lives of others, common *laissez faire* reifications of difference belie white complicity and benefit in a culture supported by a history of Native American blood and land theft. They also ignore in uncritical fashion Indian complicity in the same. These narratives leave my own fish story woefully incomplete: a classically oblivious white school culture not knowing how to respond to what appears to be a traditional Indian culture—the solution being a physical removal of the Indian from "white" lands (only to see the Indian return for more indoctrination the following day), the whites going on as before, the fish dead and memorialized by formaldehyde. Captivities abound in this story, in part because thinking of difference this way—as the discrete differences of separate interpretive communities—is a bit imprisoning as well.

Pratt offers an interesting key to this dilemma in her seminal essay, "Arts of the Contact Zone" (1991), a critique of Western reading practices and theoretical refiguration of post-Colonial or multicultural spheres of intelligibility. Rather than thinking of cultures and human groups as "discrete, coherently structured, monolingual edifices," Pratt offers the model of the "contact zone"— "social spaces where cultures meet, clash, and grapple with each other, often in contexts of highly asymmetrical relations of power" (34)—to replace monolithic notions of both encounters with difference and ("imagined") constructions of what we frequently refer to as *community*. Critical of "utopian" language theories and pedagogies theorizing (interpretive) communities in this way, Pratt shifts critical attention away from a Fish-y notion of community meaning-making to more of a conflict-based idea of contested intelligibilities within the contact zone, an important move in an allegedly post-Colonial world. The conflict in the contact zone is dispersed not only *between* cultures— the white school and the Indian community, say—but *within* both white and Indian communities, which are themselves contact zones because they are formed not only together, but also in relation to each other and because that is how cultures work. There is no "assimilation" of the indigenous in the contact zone, but rather "transculturation," as Pratt points out, "processes whereby members of subordinated or marginal groups select and invent from materials transmitted by the dominant or metropolitan culture" (36). There is also the appropriation of the marginalized group's cultural forms, practices, and beliefs by the dominant—corn and wild rice, yes, but also the ironic retotemization of roughfish—in ways sometimes "acknowledging" of the debt (*à la* the corny Thanksgiving myth), in other ways that might be compared to theft or cultural genocide (e.g., those perplexing, ahistorical New Age movements), and in still other ways that have not yet been theorized enough (e.g., perplexing, ahistorical New Age movements). In other words, the "separate spheres," while certainly different and unequal in terms of access to power, are not as separate as they are usually made out to be, but rather mutually dialectical sites of both internal and external conflict: contact-zone heteroglots.

They are eminently mixedblood locales and so, in addition to the outburst of the little girl, it is the outburst of a mixedblood—my father, that mysterious director of Indian education—that signals to me the crucial need for rethinking race, reciprocity, and education. My father's recent outburst took the form of a surprising resignation from his job. After nearly a decade of serving students (a long career in Indian education), after ten years of mediation—between students and teachers, the school and Indian communities, the reservation and school administration, students and parents—my father, the quintessential mixedblood translator, "burned out" and walked away. "I'm tired and it's getting to the point where I don't think it's worth it," he says, "I used to get all fired up because I thought the kids were benefiting, but now I don't know." Today, his frustration is directed at a wide array of targets: stingy budgets (there were only three Indian education professionals for a Native American student population of more than two hundred), insensitive teachers, disengaged parents, distracted tribal leaders, and what he sees as a commodity culture few seem willing or able to deal with in thinking about our children's education. "I'm constantly getting it from all sides," he says. "I'm told by these folks to improve their test scores, by those people to integrate more Indian culture into the curriculum, and by them over there to explain why their kids are disinterested in school. Plus, television ads are telling the kids that what they really need are Starter jackets. Then everyone wants me to solve their problems, but they're not just *my* problems."

He takes with him some well-wrought wisdom, some of it meticulously made into oral aphorisms—"To understand Indian kids, you need to know Nike first, tribal culture second"; "Multiculturalism should go both ways"— and much of it conceived in complex tension with what he sees as the compromised positions of Indians and non-Indians alike. His and his students' local tribal council promised funds for his program, only to rescind them later. Most school officials and teachers he worked with tended to represent Indian students as "his area," rather than a collective responsibility, and thus treated him to such "favors" as assigning him alone to work closely with individual students and their particular situations. The community parent committees he met with frequently treated him as a sounding board for bellyaching, rather than as a resource for new thinking. Ultimately, it was his own particular feeling of captivity—that he and his students stood alone in a space viewed as distinct from and by both tribal affairs and mainstream education—that wore him out and prompted his leave. Caught in a dismal status quo between impossible options— assimilation versus separatism, whites versus Indians—my half-breed father, like his television western forebears, wearing the vestments of white culture with unmistakable Indian accents, quietly dropped out of the scene. The school will attempt to replace him with another Indian; the kids will sort out the mixed messages as best they can; the little Awasasiindoodem girl will enter the seventh grade and start noticing those really cool Nikes she does not have; and, in the principal's office, hanging on a wall amid diplomas and bookshelves, a large stuffed fish with glass eyes and a lacquer finish will continue to quietly gather dust.

Red, White, and Blue in North Dakota

The exclusive "Native American section" of composition that I taught for two years at the University of North Dakota (UND) was (and is) a mixedblood section, and it was there that I first started theorizing mixedbloodedness as a model for critical education and multiculturalism. In an effort to forge a theory of literacy instruction from what I saw as interstices between Anzaldúa and Pratt on the one hand, and Freirean discourses of liberatory pedagogy on the other, it was ultimately the contradictions of the Indian classroom itself—and the mixedblood strategies we all used to negotiate them—that taught me about both the pitfalls and promises of what Anzaldúa calls "straddling cultures" (1987, 80). Yet, as Rowlandson (1985) herself might say, Gentle Reader, be warned: The mixedblood classroom was no utopia (lest Ye suspect a Hero Narrative to emerge).

UND has one of the largest per-capita Native American populations in the country: Anishinabe, Metis, Lakota/Dakota/Nakota, Mandan, Hidatsa, Arikara, Crow, and other tribal backgrounds. Most of my students were from the Dakotas—from Turtle Mountain, Fort Berthold, Pine Ridge, Cheyenne River, Rosebud—but were also from Minnesota, Montana, Canada, and other places. Most of our students grew up on reservations, but many hailed from urban areas. In short, the Native American student body is anything but singular; Indian diversity is marked by a variety of lifeways—tribal, geographical, cultural, historical, religious, aesthetic, linguistic, and so on—creating complex social conditions in what announces itself as a unitary classroom (the "Native American" section). Some of our students come from the poorest regions in the country; some from backgrounds marked by alcoholism and extreme poverty, abuse, and violence; others from prominent and functional reservation families; and still others from predominantly white communities. It was, however, rare to meet students who strongly identified with white middle-class values and lifestyles or who were raised with a keen eye on the educational prize.

Indeed, these students might be viewed as what Ogbu calls "involuntary minorities," people marginalized by the acts and policies of "slavery, conquest, or colonization" (1991, 9). Compared to "voluntary" or "immigrant minorities"—people who migrated to America often to escape oppressive homeland conditions, and thus view some American myths and values as ideal goals ("assimilation," say, or mastering "standard English")—involuntary minorities have a tougher time operating within institutions like school because they were incorporated against their will and had no such expectation of educational success. Positive attitudes and "folk theories" of "getting ahead" get into the collective cultural narratives of voluntary minorities; stories of betrayal, resentment, and loss are characteristic of involuntary minority lore, as Ogbu observes (1991, 10–14). In the case of American Indians—people with recently suppressed oral traditions and forced literacies, with the cultural narratives of broken treaties and boarding schools in their epistemological pockets—concepts like higher education and literacy are frequently distrusted. Reading and writing are not valued among many of the people on the reservations of the Upper Plains, and sometimes even the very act of acquiring an education is represented as "turning white," as many of my students depicted in autobiographical writing.

But, as those autobiographies themselves attest, none of this suggests that education and literacy are not values held by our students. Indeed, they are here, coming to the university for a variety of complex reasons. Most of my students intended to return home to their reservation upon completion of their degree, frequently out of an activist desire to help their communities:

> After I finish with college and medical school, I plan to probably go back to the reservation and help with the shortage of competent medical professionals they have there. The Turtle Mountain reservation needs more doctors, and I plan to put my medical degree to good use for my people.

This response is typical. Health-care majors in particular are especially concerned with "giving something back," as are education and social-work majors. Other students, however, express their desire to leave the reservation entirely or, as one eighteen-year-old male put it, "to get the hell out." Still others try to

have it both ways, as is the case with this young eighteen-year-old male major-
ing in social work and music:

> [I want] to get an education to help better myself and my people, then start my
> music career and make an album and hopefully become famous!

This student's response is noteworthy because it typifies the tension many Indian students operate within at the university—that which is between community and individual impulses. While the medical student's response is clearly
and typically community-oriented, the musician's reply exhibits an overt mixedblood oscillation—a contradiction—between viewing education as a means to
community survival and flourishment and viewing it as a means to individual
success: a division representative of "two" sets of values. Dare we call the communitarian side the "Indian," and the individualist the "white"? Indeed, we do,
and what is more, we can see them as neither distinct nor coherent, but rather
fluctuating, dialectical, and different. That is to say, there are narratives of individualism in Indian communities and narratives of community in non-Indian
individuals, but they are spoken and thought of in different ways in different locales. On reservations, for instance, discourses of bourgeois individualism
(readily available on television or through other channels to "white society")
are tempered, even corrected, by frequent proclamations of communitarianism
(evidenced in both of my examples' typical use of the term "my people"). But
what are the dominant discourses of the university, of the writing classroom?

At our multicultural university, the Protestant epistemology still reigns
supreme: Individual success is the desired outcome of individual competition
and hard work, an ideology reflected in pedagogy—from the go-get-'em ethos
of the business school to the historically expressivist pedagogy of the Native
American composition section—that many Indian students find alienating, although a little alluring as well. Several of my students described this alienation
in our discussions and in their writing. Afraid to speak up in other classes,
worried about being singled out and called upon to represent all Indians, and—
above all—uncomfortable with the notion of competing (verbally and argumen-
tatively) for ideas, grades, and teachers' affections, Indian students frequently
remain silent (and sometimes drop out altogether), acts that have resulted in
them being inscribed by many teachers as somehow "culturally quiet." While
there is some truth to the generalization that some Indian students are raised to
listen to and not challenge their elders (including professors), what is usually
left out of those discussions are the facts that Indian students frequently feel
caught in a hostile environment when in predominantly non-Indian classrooms
and that the competitive, individualistic ethos of those classrooms is at odds
with the communitarian impulses of many students.

Take, for example, this class evaluation written by a young Rosebud woman
who compared the Native American section with a "regular" composition section she took (and dropped) the previous semester:

I think this composition class is the best class I am currently enrolled in. One of my fellow students said he wouldn't think of missing this class, that it made his whole day just to be in this class. In my white composition class, it was a chore everyday just to force myself to go to class. With the Native American class, I always knew there would be friendly smiles and faces to greet me every time I showed up for class, so I tried not to miss a single class unless I absolutely had to.

The community-centeredness of this commentary, from her dialogical reference to another student to the actual pressure she feels from her co-students to show up each day, is a telling reminder of the discursive discrepancies between reservations and universities, between communitarianism and individualism, and, I would say, between Indian and non-Indian students. For her, our section was a site of community and belongingness she could not find in other classrooms. That kind of community reinforcement was exciting to me in large part because of its political potential: a chance to work against the individuating discourses of the university at large and the many expressivist composition courses being taught at the time, an opportunity to promote some sort of collectivization that might be empowering to Indian students as a group. Consider the fair-skinned, reservation-bred student who wrote:

When I first enrolled in the Native American composition course, I thought that all it would be were all these Indian legends and things of that sort. I was surprised when we started to explore a lot more about ourselves as Native Americans. . . . I started to realize how much defense that I put up when people labeled me as different. The odd thing about it was that now I had started to accept the differences that made me special.

The transformation of her individual defensiveness to a group-identified "special" identity is a result of her feeling connected, not individuated, as "we started to explore a lot more about ourselves as Native Americans." At the time, this seemed well with me, akin to Freire's work (1990) with Brazilian peasants who collectivized in "culture circles" that critically interrogated their mass oppression by a dominant group.

But just as I came close to putting my faith in the collectivist utopian ideals girding the construction of my class, there happened an event that not only interrupted my cozy notions of pan-tribal community (a small-scale American Indian Movement group? a new tribe?), but also brought to the fore the all-too-tangible material politics of race, culture, and discourse at the "white" university. It was the fall semester of 1992 (a few months before the Eelpout festival), my second year of teaching the section, and a time when I really started to work hard on problems of liberatory pedagogy. I had significantly changed both the pedagogy and materials of the course from previous years: "Indianizing" the course further by reading more Native-American–centered and authored texts; constructing dialogical, student-centered writing assignments that required students to engage not only each other, but also the historical, social, political, and material milieus in which we operate; and overall, following Freire, promoting a critical literacy in which students might collectively empower and "name the world" for themselves. Equipped with both an Indianized curriculum and a faith in the possibilities of pan-tribal community I previously had come to know, I wanted to promote a literacy that, in contradiction to expressivist or current/traditional approaches, would privilege existing student capabilities and what Geertz (1983) calls "local knowledge," while at the same time remaining inextricably linked to the social or, as Robinson and Stock put it:

> A literacy that develops learners' consciousness of personal rights, literacy enacted as a process of search and creation, literacy that results in learners' critical presence in the world, offers promise of changing the world even as it changes learners' ways of being in that world. (1990, 272)

To me and my students, this resulted in a course that investigated (and valorized) *being Indian:* Indian knowledge, Indian practices, Indian identity. By writing and reading each other's narratives, we brought out our "differences" as we experienced them at the "white" university—problems, strengths, revisions— and examined these Freirean "generative themes" as a group ethnically (and, my hope, ethically) connected. Rewriting our captivity narratives as literacy narratives, engaging each other in what Pratt calls a "safe house"—"social and intellectual space where groups can constitute themselves as horizontal, homogeneous, sovereign communities with high degrees of trust [and] shared understandings" (1991, 40)—we forged a sense of community resulting in close feelings, group solidarity, and mutual interest: what in retrospect must have been a pretty naive sense of Indian identity.

That is not to say we erased our own differences from each other; on the contrary, in a unit on "Indianness," we eagerly wrote and read narratives of Indian difference: tribal differences, the politics of skin color, links between Indianness and cultural/religious practices, even mixedbloodedness. Jerilyn wrote a compelling piece about the pain of being light-skinned and having to "prove" her identity to Indians, while feeling "in the closet" around whites (who sometimes disparaged Indians in front of her). Larry, a self-described medicine man—older, darker, and longer-braided than the rest of us—assumed the position of Wise Elder early on and frequently offered proclamations resonating with the rhetoric of AIM-style pan-tribal nationalism, a stance he wanted others to assume. Several students were interested in exploring the meanings and metaphors of Indian medicine, and we enjoyed interesting discussions about the connections and divergences of Indian "traditional" religion and Christianity. It was exciting, stimulating, critical, usually comfortable, and—I thought— a strong, communal space, a safe house. So when a fight nearly broke out at the homecoming parade, I assumed we were ready to take a public stand.

The Indian Association float in the parade featured a group of women students and children dancing in powwow regalia to the always-stirring rhythms of a drum group, male sign and staff bearers following along. When the float passed by "fraternity row," a number of intoxicated young white men yelled racist epithets at the dancers, resulting in crying children and what might have been a riotous outbreak had it not been for the actions of some of the women that prevented clearly enraged men from approaching the offenders with fists and fury. A very close call, the event brought to the surface latent animosities between white and Indian students at the university, the usually submerged, historical divisions—even hatreds—between different groups occupying the same, historical, largely rural land. Within days, students and the administration demanded apologies from the fraternities whose members were involved (which were reluctantly given), an angry and activist Native-American–dominated student group formed (Students Organized Against Racism, or SOAR), and the strictly patrolled physical borders between Indians and whites became suddenly and frighteningly tangible. SOAR took as its first issue of change UND's sports nickname and mascot ("The Fighting Sioux"), made official statements about the university's historical complicity in racism and Indian disenfranchisement, demanded a name change as a token of sincerity and goodwill, and sparked a lively debate on campus and in the community as a whole.

Eagerly, I took up the events and debates as a class project. We read the editorials, essays, and letters that flooded the local media, investigated the issue as a nationwide movement (which, at the time, it was) and a historical discourse (which, clearly, it is), explored the arguments produced by people taking various positions on the issues and interrogated their investments in those positions, attended public lectures and debates on the name-change controversy, and listened to guest speakers from SOAR who visited our class. We also wrote arguments of our own. Representing the issues and unfurling events as a "cultural text" that can be read, written, and revised by us—critically literate Indians, a culture circle, academic activists, democratic citizens, a political group—I took a deep breath of brisk North Dakota air and waited for the community I worked so hard to forge and empower to raise their collective fist into the air and attack the fort (or, since we were—in a manner of speaking—*in* the fort, to at least hold it down; these fort metaphors understandably get a little tricky).

At first, my class seemed united in its outrage over the homecoming incident; students were quick to register their anger and frequently contributed similar stories of humiliation and harassment of their own. While they did not agree on the name-change controversy—arguments against the change usually focusing on its "meaninglessness" as a weapon against other forms of campus racism—they did seem interested in confronting many of the issues raised by SOAR. At the time, I thought that early work was still good: dissenting, but dialogical and political—some possibly productive seeds of a pan-tribal solidarity. However, as time went by and white anti-Indian sentiment grew on campus, students related personal accounts of harassment leading to greater levels of fear and tension. Dan, a single father of two small children, told the class how he sat down in his usual seat in another class only to find "Fuck prairie niggers" freshly written on his desk, and then another story about being threatened by two intoxicated young white students outside his student apartment complex. Rebecca told how uncomfortable she, the lone Indian student in her history class, felt when the professor brought up the issue for debate. "Some people were really mad," she said. "I could feel all eyes on me." It was not long before these captivity narratives started to dominate our discussions, and I soon realized I had trouble keeping the issues of representation and racial politics under review, much less notions of political solidarity. Instead, our space became a place to exchange tension.

Imagine my relief when Larry Wise Elder took on a leadership role in SOAR and tried to enlist the participation of other students. "The racism on this campus is worse than at other places," he announced one day, "because racism here is institutionally fostered. Fighting Sioux? We're mascots in the eyes of these people, we're not even real people!" As resident fullblood, Larry's booming, braided presence had until now been a source of strength and leadership in the class. With his sharp wit and traditionalist rhetoric, I fancied him a sort of Indian "organic intellectual": Antonio Gramsci meets Russell Means. But even he was not immune to the growing anger, frustration, and fear in the class that steadily increased throughout the semester. Students started arguing with him at best, tuning him out at worst, and one group of young Michifs even started rolling their eyes whenever he spoke. His particular appeals to "tradition" and post-AIM pan-tribalism—while appealing to me—did not sit well with his mostly age-twenty-and-under counterparts.

The class entered a period of decline. Students started complaining about our work: "We're sick of the issue." "It's boring." Some started skipping; those who stayed engaged in heated, sometimes downright mean, conversations (which contributed even more to the increasingly dismal attendance rate). Then, in an irony even the Trickster would admire, my pan-tribal culture circle started disintegrating along tribal lines. In a discussion about campus tribal politics, I told my students how a Lakota friend of mine told me she would not sign the name-change petition that was circling because "the only names on that thing were Chippewa." Bad move. "What's her problem?" a Chippewa student asked. "She's as racist as anyone else!" Others approvingly chimed in, as before my horrified eyes looks of outrage quickly appeared on the faces of my Lakota students. Finally, a Pine Ridge Lakota student turned around quickly, eyes snapping, and curtly said: "Well, what do *you* want to change the name to? The Fighting Chippewa?!"

This confrontation was nothing less than the reproduction of a centuries-old rivalry between Chippewa and Lakota/Dakota people, one usually invoked as pure humor these days, but which lost its punchline in the confines of my class. We survived the moment, but barely survived the semester. The vibrant, attentive group of the first part of the semester deteriorated into an unpredictable smattering of sometimes half-hearted, other times heated students who acted like classroom chain-gang workers. Their final portfolios typically consisted of early sweat-stained, lively essays on their literacy experiences and "Indianness," followed by later standard, often careless writings on the campus events. Evaluations were largely critical of the course, the majority pointing to our work with the ongoing campus events as "dumb," "too much out of nothing," and "a waste of time." I was personally targeted for a range of accusations: "siding with" both Chippewas and non-Chippewas, with pro-namechangers and anti-namechangers. Even SOAR took a few hits and I was accused of "propagandizing" for them (the evidence being my cousin—one of the parade dancers and a founder of the group—who came to speak to the class). Finally, Larry himself took written abuse from a number of students who objected to his assumed leadership as elder, medicine man, and traditional "fullblood" activist. "Is Larry a teacher or a student?" one student wrote. "I feel like when you talk to the class you always look to him for approval."

Which, in retrospect, I am sure I did. Throughout the semester, as I felt the tension thicken like *wojapi* and watched students cringe in ever-increasing numbers, I really started to doubt both my project and the way I was trying to pursue it. I also started to doubt my own connection to my Indian students. Trying to maintain both my political vision and pursuits of community solidarity (and feeling increasingly shaky about both), I found myself fading into an obscurity of sorts: irrelevant teacher, ineffectual politico, quite possibly the oppressive pedagogical bully some of my students made me out to be in their evaluations. As a light-skinned academic who left the reservation at an early age, I started feeling quite white: Considering the backlash on campus, and the fact that playing politics in Indian country can get one killed,[3] who would not want to if they could? Perhaps my students sensed that doubt in ways that eluded me; perhaps I was experiencing an identity crisis of sorts that, far from claiming a powerful "mixedblood" stance, instead suggested a momentary retreat into the more comfortable (or at least familiar) domains of race, identity, and power: When the going gets tough, hand it over to the "fullblood."

Mixedblood Literacies / Literate Mixedbloods

Looking back, I see the class as a whole—and the outbursts we performed— as perhaps caught in an identity crisis similar to my own. Our location in academe, the Native American section of composition, announces itself as a place to inscribe an ethnic identity, a condition I exploited in the name of fostering a pan-tribal community and politics. At first, my students appreciated the safe house, to which our successful (i.e., enjoyable) early days and compositions attest, but after homecoming and the name-change controversy, the crisis became a material threat, a tangible discourse on race and identity with bodily and narrative consequences. For most of my students, our course was the first chance they ever had in a school setting—and certainly at the university—to speak and write *as Indians* in the contact zone, to literally inscribe themselves not as disembodied subjects, romantic bourgeois individuals, or even noble savages, but as material producers of discourse in all their complexity, located along shifting and multiple axes in a larger sociocultural mileau: Indian, white, mixed-blood, student, elder, academic, subaltern subject, inheritors of oral traditions, students of literacy. This was new and exciting work. But the pleasures and promises of those initial efforts were challenged by what we must contend with as the material effects—and reinforcers—of discourse: racism, violence, exclusion, and conflict.

These challenges, born out of history and inscribed upon our day-to-day work, created the conditions out of which outbursts are made; however, the conflicts that emerged in our classroom should not be seen as purely contingent upon cultural and political conditions at the "white" university. Nor should they be condemned or avoided; rather, I think the conflicts of that semester also need to be seen as representative of the ongoing, conflictual construction of Indian identities on reservations and within Indians at large. Indian identities and cultures are being contested, reinvented, and (of course) threatened all across Indian country. What happened in my classroom is in one sense a reproduction of that creative, conflicted, rhetorical struggle: Our "internal" arguments, from reproducing Chippewa-Sioux rivalries to rolling our eyes at Larry, were in a very real sense a contentious struggle over the meanings of *Indianness*—a continuation of our earlier (and more naive) work—the formation of identity in a captivating site. But that is not to downplay for even a moment the frightening and painful conditions for Native American students at the university. They exist, and to address them discursively is to examine the complex nuances of our multiple forms of captivity. Clearly, the reinvention of Indian identity, culture, and community in my classroom was a multiplicitous, contradictory affair engaging the narratives of both reservation and university, history and the present, Indian and white—painful work in a post-Colonial world.

Sarris tells a similar captivity narrative in his essay on the reading practices of Kashaya Pomo schoolchildren, "Keeping Slug Woman Alive" (1993), which details the failed attempts of non-Indian schoolteachers to introduce "traditional" culture (i.e., Kashaya Pomo stories and myths) into the elementary-school curriculum. The young students on Sarris' California reservation reacted harshly to their teacher's (and Indian school board's) imposition of "Indian values" by hating the Slug Woman story required for class, calling it "devil worship," "not real," "a cartoon," and the work of "savages," while for Sarris and his elders, "Slug Woman is alive" (242). The distinction is jarring, and Sarris' point is not that his generation is "traditional" while the younger is "assimilated," but rather that the contexts differ: The story he relates is oral and contextualized by "life," while the kids read their story out of a decontextualized, ahistorical book in a tribal school. Tracing the diverse, heterogeneous history of both the Kashaya Pomo people (a mixedblood story about colonization, resistance, appropriation, and Mormonism) and diverse reading practices, Sarris argues for pedagogies of reading that do not decontextualize stories, but instead encourage students to "talk back, reinvent, and exchange with others" via texts (263), a process that recontextualizes not only stories, but also Kashaya Pomo ethnicity and individual identities. (One alternative example he likes is a coloring book in which students can illustrate tribal stories for themselves; for example, by drawing Coyote as a low-rider or hoodlum.) In this way, literacy moves from being an "effective colonizing device" (257) to "something that continues and re-creates culture" (264).

If the reading and writing subjects in Sarris' narrative performed outbursts against decontextualized literacies, my students and I were in an apparently opposite situation: We were so contextualized we did not know what to do. Our re-creation of culture and ethnicity was a political upheaval in the contact zone, and that meant engaging the "white" university in uneasy ways. Reading and writing were not merely on a page; they were in the room, alive, watching, waiting. Our lives, the campus, and the events we examined did not feel like something to which we could "talk back"; and for a time, we did not. Instead, there was our "boring," "savage," "devil-worshipping" work. We looked to the "Indian" (each other? the reservation? the section?) and the "white" (the university? literacy?) and felt compelled to make an impossible choice. For a while, like the little girl at my father's school, there seemed little else to do but kick and scream. We generated questions without clear answers. Was there a space for Indians at the university? What would that mean? What would be lost in the pursuit of education, of literacy? What would be gained? *Who are we, and what are we supposed to do now?* Our multiple contextualizations—the contentious formation of "Indian" identity in a contact-zone struggle, the impetus to act (or retreat), the various forms of assault directed toward students, a literal struggle to survive—bore down in heavy ways and forced us to consider our multiple captivities.

But unlike the little *ikwe*, we at least had a small place to speak, and somehow, through our mixedblood strategies—replete with pain and promise, learning and loss—we tried to negotiate the contexts. Most of us survived and all of us learned as we spoke. That is not to suggest that we were effectively heard; overall, we were not. Harassment did not die down until the issue did. (Incidentally, UND still uses "The Fighting Sioux" nickname.) And while most of my students left the course saying a lot of words, *empowered* was not among them. The Chippewa/Sioux conflict ended with no happy handshakes and jointly thrusted fists in the air. In my most annoying teacher evaluation, a light-skinned "quarterblood" Michif wrote: "Scott was an okay teacher for a white guy." But speak we did: we yelled, cajoled, accused, and name-called. We rolled, snapped, closed, and opened our eyes. We looked, looked back, looked at each other, and looked again. We also keenly felt ourselves being looked at. Looking was important: Because one type of work we did was the construction of our identities, the reinvention of ethnicity, we engaged in what Fischer calls "bifocality," a form of "ethnic search" in which we look and see "others against a background of ourselves, and ourselves against a background of others"

(1987, 8). As Pratt would point out, those backgrounds are contested and dangerous—at times threatening, at others alluring. So, as Anzaldúa might suggest, the bifocal gaze is a mixedblood stare: seeing others not only against a
background of ourselves, but *in ourselves*. Both our looking and speaking were
policed from inside and out—a contradictory captivity—but the fact that we
survived, even if painfully and agonistically, is a testament to the profound
mixedblood literacies Native Americans already possess and bring with them
to the classroom. I did not see them at first, my own vision blocked by a dream
of communal captivity; but, on second glance, I do.

The many contradictions of Indian students in the writing classroom were
underscored by the fact that the institution of the university, which in the eyes
of many was oppressing students with a culture of racism and exclusion, also
was trying to liberate them with a critical pedagogy and literacy. Lorde (1983,
1984) and Althusser (1971) come to mind, but is it not possible to recast these
contradictions as mixedblood ironies? A mixedblood theory of liberatory pedagogy and critical literacy might highlight the conflict and resistance in my
story as sites of not only captivity, but also possibility. In "The Politics of Literacy," Robinson and Stock argue for "a politics of education that makes for
openings, nourishes beginnings, no matter when they happen, and honors difference—even resistance—when it is uttered or inscribed or expressed in
meaningful silences" (1990, 313). To recast resistance (and even silence) as an
"opening" is to privilege outbursts, to acknowledge the realities of Indian and
white discourses and their material consequences. It also makes room for contradiction, tolerates ambiguities. Pratt's pedagogy of the contact zone, dismiss-
ing "community values and the hope of synthesis" for a student's "experience
of seeing the world described with him or her in it" (1991, 39) also "nourishes
beginnings" by constructing a world not as seamless or communal, but as sites
of domination, contest, and conflict—as a series of captivities—and owning
up to those histories while reinvigorating public discourse about them. By developing pedagogies of contact that interrogate the interstices between worlds,
groups, and conflicts, the institution of the "white" university can make a place
for Indian students while offering up itself for critique and acknowledging its
own mixedblood ethos.[4]

Clearly, my classroom was a mixedblood locale—not "Indian" or "universal," and certainly not "white"—and yet, its definition as a "racial" section
gave my students the strength to perform their outbursts. For that reason, I see
the section as important and necessary to maintain (although in need of rethinking). But while Pratt also argues for the maintenance of "safe houses" like
these for subaltern groups, Jarratt rightly questions the political efficacy of
what we might call "safe-house instruction" that posits community and privileges consensus as a means toward knowledge-making. Usually, when we think
a group is working well, someone—or some group—is being silenced: "Even
when teachers announce the desire to create a particular climate, they can't neu-
tralize by fiat the social positions already occupied by their students" (1991,

113). She is thinking of the "multicultural" classroom, but as I have argued, the social positions of supposedly "horizontal" Indian students are themselves heterogeneous and contradictory. Mixedbloods all, linked as "Indians" by historical, discursive, and institutional signifiers of neither their making nor choosing, my students acted in ways ironically appropriate to their otherwise terrifying circumstances. So while the class functioned as a safe house for many students, and perhaps during a critical time, it was not exactly what Pratt refers to as a "temporary protection from legacies of oppression" (1991, 40). It was, however, a captivating site where a mixedblood could speak. The course, like reservations and democracy itself, was a mixedblood contradiction: a failure, a success, a site of both regret and hope. And we still believe in Indians.

The vision I seek now is of post-community forged out of conflict. We need to understand in better ways the mixedblood literacies Native American students bring with them to academe, and respond in kind with pedagogies of conflict and contact that privilege student desire for community, while creating space for dissent toward discourses both internal ("Indian") and external ("white"). We should encourage students not to "compose identities"—they do that on their own—but rather to create space where they can examine the histories, power relations, and rhetorical play of Indian and non-Indian discourses, relationships, comminglings, and conflicts in what is already a mixedblood world (albeit one that thinks itself a "fullblood"). Indian students already possess the mixedblood literacies of negotiation we need—and need to know— and they need spaces to practice them. We need to bring the reservation into the classroom and historicize Indianness, while at the same time examining the nuances of mixedblood captivities. We must develop and promote a language of mixedbloodedness. This language—a "new mythos"—built and disseminated in coalition with students and communities of all backgrounds, might prove to dissolve notions of reified difference that block out so much and exclude so many, and replace them with a more complex, web-like network of histories, cultures, and power relations—torn here, taut there, but still connecting us all.

Endnotes

1. Non-Indian attacks on difference—from Hirsch and Bloom to the conventional wisdom of many of my colleagues—have undergone a good deal of crucial critique. Less known and understood (for obvious reasons) are separatist or nationalist sentiments expressed by some Native American thinkers and educators; for example, the interesting and troubling report by the Indian Nations At Risk (INAR) Task Force (which, among other things, describes a "secret war" perpetrated by the U.S. federal government against tribes, and calls for the implementation of what it calls "true" Indian education in opposition to the "pseudo" and "quasi" models it currently finds in existence). Still, the INAR report is eminently thoughtful in complex ways and certainly worthy of study. Less useful are the polemics issued by Means, whose frequent essentialist calls for a "return" to Indian Luddism and resistance to a monolithic notion of "Europe" (1995, 545–554) still find themselves rhetorically reproduced by some Indian educators.

2. "Chippewa" and "Ojibway" are both colonially imposed signifiers for the people who have historically referred to themselves as "Anishinabe." Today, all three are in common usage, as they are in this essay.

3. While I make this claim with some hesitation, a perusal of Indian political history and even a glance at today's tribal newspapers show how tribal politics on reservations can be nothing short of dangerous. That is not to suggest political activism in Indian country is always that way—far from it. It is merely to point out how reservation politics are governed by bloodier narratives.

4. Bizzell's recent work on contact-zone pedagogy is an excellent start (see "'Contact Zones' and English Studies" [1994], as well as her recent anthology edited with Herzberg, *Negotiating Difference* [1996]). Her emphasis on rhetorically reading historical contact is crucial, but if we are to retain Native American students, we also need to work with more immediate specificities of Indian student culture, literacies, and power in ways that promote mixedblood movement both ways. Likewise, Schriner's course at Northern Arizona University based on Bartholomae and Petrosky's work (1986), while "immediately" attempting to initiate Indian students into the university as "one person [in] many worlds," ultimately operates from a Fish-like interpretive community model of "worlds" that leaves the "white" university untouched (1992). Both (academic discourse) approaches have much to offer, but reproduce a "top-down" movement that promotes a form of captivity that still leaves Indian students and "white" institutions in unsettling opposition.

Response
"Mixedblood" Rhetorics and the Concept of "Outburst"

Patricia Bizzell

The concept of "outburst" is based in an assumption that there is a sort of normal classroom routine, which the outburst violates. The normal routine, I take it, is that the teacher directs classroom activity, which may sometimes entail making space for student initiatives and areas of control, and the students comply with the teacher's plans, following directions when asked to do so and taking initiative when invited. Of course, as every teacher knows, there can be surprises, both pleasant and unpleasant, in the "normal" classroom: unexpected responses, new discoveries, disruptions of routine by outside events, and so on. But the normal routine is still basically being followed when all present, teacher and students, feel that they are engaged in a common project of investigation, creation, and assimilation of knowledge, and that the project is proceeding productively for all concerned. It is precisely the accomplishment of this common project that the "outburst," as I understand it, is seen to interrupt or even to destroy.

We educators have become highly critical of the normal classroom routine. We have attacked it as oppressive—stifling cultural difference, serving social exclusion, and brainwashing students for restrictive roles in an exploitive politico-economic order. To the extent that one agrees with this critique, one might be inclined to see all classroom outbursts as understandable responses to an inequitable situation. All outbursts may not be progressive, in this view—because all may not function effectively as resistance to the inequities—but, at the very least, all ought to be recognized as legitimate responses to a repressive situation rather than as "discipline problems" subject to sanction.

I share this critical perspective to some extent. Yes, the social order is grossly unjust. Yes, schooling perpetuates that unjust social order. But no, I am not yet ready to say that this is all schooling does. I am not yet ready to give up on the normal project of the classroom. Wouldn't it be wonderful if teachers and students *could* investigate, create, and assimilate knowledge together? Are we sure that this project is now impossible? I am not. Therefore, I am not willing to acquiesce in all outbursts. Although I may see them all as understandable responses to inequity, I still may feel that it is legitimate for the teacher to exercise authority to redirect or suppress some of them.

109

To illustrate this analysis, I am aided by the descriptive clarity and admirable frankness of the three teachers to whose essays I am responding. It is extremely difficult to admit someone else to your classroom, not to mention a large reading audience, especially when the story you have to tell does not have a happy ending (as so many of our published accounts of pedagogy do). The kinds of outbursts chronicled by Dixon, Anderson, and Lyons illustrate a range of student responses to injustice and alienation that, I believe, require a range of teacher responses.

Dixon gives us a thoughtful meditation on challenges to her own "white feminist authority" in the classroom. Of the last of her three examples, she says:

> I now know that I have to use my authority even more prominently in this class, which already has been designed to ferret out people's prejudices. I have got to theorize groups better and I need to lay out more ground rules for the whole class, particularly with regard to racial difference.

Dixon's decision to exercise her authority more forcefully in this situation seems to be motivated primarily by the fact that the person who suffered the most from her failure to be more decisive was Native American. I would argue that this comment should apply to her other two examples as well, and I suspect that she did not see them that way because the principal "victims" in the other two cases were people more like herself; that is, white women feminists (in the second case, she herself could be said to be one of the "victims"). All of her classes, as she describes them, work to "ferret out people's prejudices"—given current cultural conditions, many classes in English studies function this way whether they were designed to do so or not—and so a firmer hand is needed from the teacher to keep the critical project going forward productively for the students.

I think it would be legitimate to say that the "gangs" in Dixon's three examples all comprise people behaving badly, as bullies or bitches. While one could argue that this bad behavior springs ultimately from alienating cultural conditions, it seems to me that what Dixon's classes were trying to accomplish, before disrupted by the bad behavior, was well worth doing, too valuable to be wasted. I would argue that in these cases, the "outbursts" should have been suppressed—by more explicit direction from the teacher in the undergraduate cases and by academic sanctions in the graduate case. In spite of the prevailing critique of schooling as oppressive, teachers still should not be afraid to use their authority in certain situations to save the class for the other students by exercising some control over the disrupters. It should not require a situation of obvious racial injustice before a teacher feels empowered to act.

Of course, once such a principle is articulated, the crucial question becomes how to decide—or who gets to decide—when the exercise of authority is called for. I do not think that question can be answered easily. In fact, I think it can be answered only locally, by individual teachers' judgments, over and over again, getting it right sometimes and sometimes getting it wrong. But I want to emphasize that I do not believe that the absence of a universally reliable rule for adjudicating such situations should make us afraid to exercise our authority at all.

Anderson shows us one teacher attempting to grapple sensitively with a subtle form of outburst situation. Her Deaf students fail, in varying degrees, to comply with her directions for writing. Should these failures be regarded simply as evidence of their limited skill with written English or as covert strategies of resistance? It seems to me that this is an important question, and Anderson approaches it carefully. I am not fully persuaded by her analysis of the first group of student papers. I am not convinced that these students are deliberately choosing to "front their identity in the *introductory* syntagmeme of the text" so as to "affirm that, from their perspective, self-identity is more salient than the topic provided by the essay prompt." Just as in my discussion of Dixon, I insisted that we have to allow for the possibility of bad behavior, here, too, I insist that we have to allow for the possibility of lack of skill.

Anderson's second group of examples, however, is more persuasive. It is easy to see the outburst aspect of student papers in which an attempt to meet the expectations of the assignment is abruptly broken off with the declaration that "this book is too hard for me" or "I don't like this book." Therefore, I think we would do well to keep in mind Anderson's concluding generalization:

> Deaf students—indeed, all minority students—regularly select to thematize viewpoints that differ from those who represent the mainstream. When they select an approach that is not familiar—particularly when they have just been told *how* they are *expected* to write an essay so that it conforms to majority patterns—then their texts, I would suggest, can be read as outbursts, as acts contesting existing social relations in the classroom.

At the same time, we must remember that not all such choices are deliberate strategies—"regularly," perhaps, but not always. This is particularly important if we wish to support Anderson's apparent intent to facilitate minority students' mastery of the mainstream, more academically successful discourse. And it is important if we wish to go farther, as Lyons' analysis suggests.

Lyons suggests that developing "mixedblood" rhetorics would be a better response to current cultural conditions than outbursts, a better use of the resistant energy that emerges in outbursts. Lyons begins to explain the concept of "mixedblood" with the illustration of himself and many other people of color in America today. "Mixedblood" people, first, are literally biologically mixed, combining in themselves several racial strands and, therefore, often in appearance are not easily assignable to any racial group (Lyons' example is his own nose, which may be a "Sioux" nose or a "Roman" nose, depending on who is doing the describing). In addition to being biologically mixed, "mixedblood" people are culturally mixed, conversant with more than one—and often highly divergent—cultural traditions, like the little girl in Lyons' "outburst" story who is receiving a mainstream American elementary-school education and, at the same time, has received enough instruction in Indian spiritual traditions to be deeply disturbed by the school's mockery and exploitation of the eelpout fish. Attendant upon these biological and cultural mixings is the generation of discourses that are themselves mixed, reflecting linguistic and rhetorical resources from many and varied cultural archives. As Lyons sums it up:

> In my story, *mixedblood* signifies both material bodies and discourse, *identity* and thinking, *race* and subjectivity: the moral of this story will be that these binaries do not hold.

Moreover, Lyons cites Anzaldúa as a mixedblood or *mestiza* whose thinking parallels his own, thus showing the potential for his analysis to cross (already blurred) ethnic boundaries.

Lyons recognizes that the condition of being mixedblood is culturally generalizable. He cites recent feminist theories that speak of female biological, cultural, and discursive identities as multiple in a similar sense. I think it is fair to say, as Lyons suggests later, that the mixedblood condition is becoming the paradigm case of American identity, as cultures churn in the Cuisinart of post-capitalist society. If so, then his diagnosis of the discursive consequence of mixedbloodedness is important not only for teachers of people of color, but also for teachers of all students.

It is crucially important that we understand Lyons' analysis of the discursive situation as profoundly mixed. We do not have a choir here, in which clearly distinctive cultural voices all sing their own part. Rather, there is a blurring of cultural boundaries. Lyons makes this point in showing how Fish's literary theory is inadequate to explain the situation of the Indian schoolgirl and the eelpout. He says that in Fish's model,

> Both groups ["Indians" and "whites"] comprise two different interpretive communities, constructing different meanings, different fish, out of the same "text." Problems emerge, however, when we start thinking of the "two" groups as discrete, sovereign entities. What are we to make of a young schoolgirl very capable of what Fish calls "doing studenting" (1980, 334) in the "white" school, who nonetheless breaks down across apparently cultural-epistemic lines? What about the other Indian kids who stayed in the audience, who may have done a little cheering themselves—are they now "white"? Assimilated?

And as Lyons shows in his account of his "Indian" section of composition at UND, such cultural blurring of boundaries gives rise to similarly mixed and multiple discursive strategies—what Lyons calls "mixedblood" rhetorics.

Hence, in Lyons' view, the thing to do with the outbursts he chronicles is to develop their potential for generating hybrid discourses. He states his pedagogical goals at the end of his essay:

We should encourage students not to "compose identities"—they do that on their own—but to create space where they can examine the histories, power relations, and rhetorical play of Indian and non-Indian discourses, relationships, comminglings, and conflicts in what is already a mixedblood world (albeit one that thinks itself a "fullblood"). . . . We must develop and promote a language of mixedbloodedness. This language—a "new mythos"—built and disseminated in coalition with students and communities of all backgrounds, might prove to dissolve notions of reified difference that block out so much and exclude so many, and replace them with a more complex, web-like network of histories, cultures, and power relations—torn here, taut there, but still connecting us all.

I want to call attention here to the move in Lyons' analysis from the situation of Indian mixedbloods to "a mixedblood world," in which the condition of cultural and discursive mixing has become normative.

Furthermore, I want to note the powerful optimism of his concluding call. He imagines—and I want to agree—that "mixedblood" rhetorics can be shared, that they can connect "us all," "all" being not only the many varieties of Indian mixedbloods, but also the many varieties of Americans. If we adopt Lyons' pedagogical agenda, we will not have abandoned the goal I noted previously implicit in Anderson's essay—that is, that everyone needs to master the mainstream discourse—but we will have gone beyond it in that we will have begun to imagine a cluster of discourses more culturally diverse than the current mainstream, yet still widely usable. If this is the direction in which we ultimately can channel the revolutionary energy of outbursts, we will be doing well.

Response
Beyond Liberal and Cultural Approaches to Social Justice

Elizabeth Flynn

These three narratives are wonderfully written and insightful, but also disturbing because they illustrate the enormous difficulties teachers face when teaching in multicultural classrooms. Dixon speaks of the gendered conflicts in her classroom in terms of gang life. She tells us that the use of the metaphor is tongue-in-cheek, but it is nevertheless the case that her stories are ones of unresolved hostility that do not seem to result in transformation or learning, except perhaps in the sense that they motivated Dixon herself to write and edit a book as a way of attempting to understand what she experienced. Anderson tells us of learning problems of Deaf students that are so deeply entrenched and so difficult to rectify that students and teachers alike become enormously frustrated. The outbursts Anderson describes, what she calls "textual anger," are deviations from "normal" essays, that make evident the helplessness and resentment of the Deaf students. Lyons describes a composition course for Native American students that starts off well but soon becomes a disaster. Students fight among themselves and with the teacher and seem to have learned very little by the end of the term. Lyons himself is able to write about the experience and to reflect on it, but at the time, the experience must have been extremely painful. Teaching in the situations described herein are clearly dangerous for faculty members, especially if they are untenured or minorities themselves.

The stories point to some limitations of the hybrid approach frequently used by universities to rectify social injustice, a combination of what I will call liberal and cultural approaches. The liberal approach emphasizes equity and inclusion, and is associated with initiatives such as affirmative action and the Americans with Disabilities Act. Structures are established to ensure that groups such as minorities, women, and the handicapped are included in institutions from which they traditionally have been excluded, and that they are given access to that which may help them succeed. The impulse here is assimilationist. The cultural approach (which is related to cultural feminism but unrelated to cultural studies as referred to by Dixon) emphasizes difference and is associated with initiatives such as women's-studies programs, black-studies programs, and special programs for the handicapped. The impulse here is separatist.

All three narratives illustrate both liberal and cultural approaches to social justice in that all three describe attempts to include groups that have been excluded from universities in the past—women, the handicapped, and Native Americans—and all three describe the establishment of special programs designed specifically for these groups. Dixon's classes are probably like most classes at universities these days, in that they include women as well as men, perhaps in roughly equal numbers. Dixon also speaks of teaching women's-studies courses, and the Modern Language Association Directory lists UND as having a women's-studies program. Anderson speaks of a sign language studies department and a culture that welcomed and supported Deaf students by providing them interpreters, preparing the faculty-at-large to teach Deaf students in workshops, having university administrators and faculty take an introductory ASL course. Anderson's university also provided remedial classes in English that were available to Deaf students and encouraged them to utilize the university's Center for Personalized Instruction, where they could receive tutoring. She also speaks of her institution making available competent interpreters and notetakers to assist Deaf students. Over time, however, training for faculty disappeared so that Anderson found herself teaching Deaf students in a composition class with virtually no special preparation for doing so. Lyons speaks of a special "Native American section" of composition at UND and of American Indian education programs in the school directed by his Indian father.

Clearly, though, these solutions are problematic and can be high risk for faculty. The difficulties that precipitate the problems described in the narratives are deep-rooted, and the solutions offered—inclusion and support—are not sufficient to reverse systemic sexism, racism, and ableism. Composition classes for Native Americans, for instance, are certainly a good idea, but they seem like little more than a gesture given the enormity of the problem—centuries of genocide and oppression. If Lyons or others in a comparable situation taught too many classes like the one he describes, which resulted in low student evaluations, the consequences could be devastating for untenured professors. Faculty might easily decide that, in the interests of their own survival in academe, they should teach such classes no more. Anderson and Dixon, too, might well eventually decide, as Lyons' father did, that the personal cost of attempting to rectify injustice is too high. Programs such as those described in the narratives clearly need increased support, and teachers involved in such programs need more training and a system of evaluation that makes allowances for the special challenges of their assignments.

However, the authors of these compelling narratives suggest a third approach to the achievement of social justice, one that needs to accompany liberal and cultural solutions. Dixon makes reference to post-structuralist theory, but Lyons spells out most clearly what a post-structuralist approach to social justice might look like. Lyons explains the limitations of an assimilationist approach. Assimilationist projects, he says, have resulted in socializing young Indian children into European modes; hence, eliminating their culture. Lyons sees that

Fish's conception of interpretive communities as discrete sovereign entities supports an assimilationist approach. I would argue, though, that Fish's work legitimates separatist programs and projects rather than assimilationist ones. It emphasizes the rigid boundaries that separate one group from another. The culturalist solution is preferable to the assimilationist one in that it does not aim to eliminate the culture of the minority, but recognizes its difference from the dominant culture and allows it to exist separately. A problem here, though, is that the minority culture may have little impact on the dominant culture, so the unequal power relationships remain intact. Also, the approach leads to essentialized conceptions of identity and can result in an isolationist and victim mentality.

The post-structuralist approach, though, is embodied in the image of the contact zone. Lyons summarizes Pratt's explanation of contact zones as "social spaces where cultures meet, clash, grapple, often in asymmetrical relations of power." Here the minority culture is neither eliminated nor separated, but rather allowed to engage the majority culture in struggle. The result is neither assimilation nor separatism, but rather *transculturation*. Minorities select and invent from the dominant culture, and the dominant culture, in turn, appropriates the marginalized group's cultural forms.

We need to find ways of institutionalizing contact zones toward the goal of eliminating social injustice. Dixon makes this point when she says that we need alternatives to victim narratives and suggests deconstructing the master narratives of race, gender, and class. Certainly, *Outbursts in Academe* is part of the solution. Writing the book clearly has been helpful to Dixon, Anderson, and Lyons, and will be helpful to teachers who read it as well. But we also need to create institutional and pedagogical structures that move beyond assimilationist and separatist tendencies.

I cannot resist concluding by offering a few outburst stories of my own. For a number of years, I have taught a 200-level course entitled "Literary Representations of Gender, Race, Class, and Ethnicity," the only course of its kind in the curriculum of our humanities department. Michigan Tech has no women's-studies program and few courses that focus on women's issues. This is no doubt, in part, a result of Michigan Tech's technological emphasis and relatively small number of women undergraduates—the ratio of undergraduate men to women is four to one.

The outbursts that I experience more often than not take the form of unpredictable enrollments. I have classes as large as thirty-five, the maximum allowable, and as few as eight. I also have had more dramatic outbursts, though. In one class, several black students complained in a presentation to the class that the stories we were reading included no representations of middle-class blacks. They were embarrassed, they said, by the repeated suggestion that all blacks are impoverished. In another class, a white woman burst into tears as she attempted to describe in a presentation to the class the struggles of her father to raise three daughters after their mother deserted the family.

I also frequently have to deal with the pervasive conservatism of many Michigan Tech students. A student this term, for instance, compared the class system in India with the class system in America, concluding that the two are totally different and that America does not have an underclass. When I asked about the homeless, he explained that he has read books that make clear that most homeless people have chosen and are satisfied with their situation.

Not all students take this line, though. I have had Asian students who were adopted and take the course because they want to better understand their special situation. I also have had biracial students attempting to understand why they cannot claim they are white if one of their parents is white. The strongest student in this term's class, a math major, is gay and has read widely in the areas of gay and minority literature. In a discussion of Willa Cather's "Paul's Case," he provided background on Cather's lesbianism and demonstrated that the story is a coded one that attempts to explore homosexuality without doing so overtly. Such a student is rare. This particular group, though, seems quite accepting of his perspective.

At this stage in our attempts to rectify social injustice, contact zones are frequently war zones. The injustices have been so extreme and so longstanding that contact among cultures often erupts into violence and destruction. The metaphor of an outburst, then, has a utopian aspect to it. An outburst, although an indication of inequality and frustration, is contained, momentary, something that can be dealt with. Perhaps these are stories of hope and promise after all.

Part III

Formations of "Multicultural" Selves and Institutions

Inter-view Two
Lost Outbursts
Kathleen Dixon

Following this inter-view will be the frankest outburst yet. Dierdre Glenn Paul's essay might itself be considered an outburst, even as it represents many anecdotes of outbursting from Paul's past. Dr. Paul is the only African American of three to have stayed with the *Outbursts in Academe* project to its publication. Clues as to why others may not have continued might be gleaned from her autobiographical narrative. From Paul's essay and from those of the lost outburst essays, and from some years of listening to and thinking about the subject, I have deduced that African American academics, maybe especially African American women, carry a heavy burden of responsibility for the history of discrimination against African Americans. Within academe, where African Americans are more likely to be junior faculty still needing to please tenure-granting colleagues; outside academe, where African American communities have placed high hopes in African American academics; in families, where African American women often bear the brunt of raising children who encounter racism daily — in all of these settings, the African American woman academic is expected to perform excellently and under conditions that are hardly auspicious. I am happy that one of three essays survived and sorry that two are lost to this volume; I hope they will be published elsewhere, as they looked to be most promising.

Probably as many outburst essays were "lost" as completed. Perhaps this is the usual process for edited collections. My guess, though, is that the same social and economic conditions that underlie the outbursts analyzed within these pages also underlie the revising and editing of the essays. The editing process was fraught; relationships were strained, some maybe beyond immediate repair. I say these things so those who celebrate post-structuralist "disruption" may be reminded that there are some forms of disruption that are not intellectually pleasurable. Nor is it always the "colonialist" who, as a result of disruption, considers the abandonment of a project.

It is with a certain relief that I turn to Doreen Stärke-Meyerring's essay, tonally the polar opposite of many in the collection: outbursts peek out now and again from within the scholarly Germanic prose. Because Stärke-Meyerring *is* German—East German, to be precise—her prose style comes as no surprise. Nonetheless, one is moved to rethink the notion of the outburst. Certainly, U.S. compositionists, at least, will need to look more closely than perhaps they would otherwise.

At the 1997 CCC Conference in Phoenix, Stärke-Meyerring spoke of the need to retheorize the notion of "writing" for the German context. Her paper was entitled, "German Writers and English Readers: Conscientization in an English Composition Class for German Students." In it, she argued that German students of the *Fachhochschule*, the new four-year technical college where Stärke-Meyerring taught, would need to reconceptualize the notion of *writer* if they were to make sense of U.S.-style composition pedagogy. There is no *writer* in German, only a *Schreiber* (copyist) or *Textproduzent* (text producer), on the one hand (most of Stärke-Meyerring's German students would probably think of themselves in these terms), and on the other, the elevated *Autor, Verfasser, Schriftsteller* (i.e., well-published author of literature, philosophy, criticism).

Outbursts in Academe might not even count as scholarship in Stärke-Meyerring's country, because it might appear to be in between one kind of "writing" and another. Some American readers might find it difficult to detect the intensity of Stärke-Meyerring's critique of American college composition texts that popularize notions of multiculturalism. She argues that such textbooks promulgate the notion of the "American" as a "salad bowl" or "vegetable soup"; many international programs on campuses invite students literally to ingest culture by eating ethnic foods during special "international" or "multicultural" celebrations. We can infer a little of Stärke-Meyerring's experiences as an international student at a Midwestern U.S. university; we might like her to retort, "It's *Gemüsesuppe* to you!"—but the circumspect Stärke-Meyerring would not be likely to satisfy our desires.

Instead, she turns her attention to pedagogical theory and to an empirical mode of understanding as she conducts an informal survey of 171 composition students from UND. She argues that the uniquely American notion of *multicultural education* probably unintentionally derogates the literacy potential of all students, and students can sense this. Stärke-Meyerring invites all of her U.S. students—including white students—to sound off on the topic of multicultural education. Answering the survey question, "Do you feel you have a culture? What is your culture?," one student writes boldly, "AMERICAN CULTURE! Enveloping and homogenizing all others." Stärke-Meyerring encourages us to read such outbursts as a sympathetic outsider might. Ultimately, the aggressive parody of this particular outburst gives way in the movement of Stärke-Meyerring's own thoughts to a poignant observation: The "white" Midwestern American, whose color is no color, experiences a culture that is oddly no culture—"all others" having been homogenized away. Because Stärke-Meyerring is poised to report and interpret outbursts from a position that is not aggrieved, her essay allows us to revisit other essays in the *Outbursts* volume.

6

Super-Mammy or Super-Sellout? Young, Black, and Female in Academe

Dierdre Glenn Paul

Some moments are indelible in memory. For me, such an occasion was my 1993 job interview at a state university located in a United States Eastern suburb. I was impressed with the campus' pastoral beauty, including the flowering blossoms and picturesque buildings I entered. I still recall the warm welcome of the interview team, including College of Education faculty and the Dean. After the interview, I felt confident, enthusiastic, and looked forward to the possibility that I would find, on that attractive campus and within the friendly department, my niche in academe.

I had just completed my doctoral work at Teachers College; only the writing and defense of the dissertation remained. My hopes were high of landing a job right out of school. When the official offer finally arrived, euphoria swept over me. My family, my then-fiancé (now husband), and I celebrated my entry into the "big time." As we say in the Bronx, "My shit was tight."

But the Bronx was a very different place. I had been a resident for twenty-two years and, after completing my undergraduate studies, I taught there as well.

Keepin' It Real: Classrooms in the Bronx

I had six years of experience in an intermediate school and a year-long stint as an elementary-school communication-arts teacher-trainer. My self-defined mission in those Bronx-based classrooms was to provide my Black[1] and Latino students with the means by which to demystify the rules of success (as defined by the dominant culture). I wished to enable them to use those rules for their

123

own benefit, as well as that of their communities. Determining an educational plan that would enhance their facility with language, providing them with greater access to society, and countering the social ills they regularly faced were of utmost importance to me (Paul 1997).

My concern was engendered as a result of growing up and attending school in the same community as my students, then receiving the opportunity to attend an exclusive boarding school in Massachusetts. The experience permitted me to see the disparity between education for the White elite compared with education for the working class and/or poor people of color. Differences could be seen in everything from the educational materials used to the instructional format (Paul 1997). As a teacher returning to the Bronx classrooms, I quickly realized that without the ability to read and understand the power inherent in the written word, a number of my students (as well as many of my public-school classmates) would be relegated to existences in which drugs, prison, dropping out, and poverty played inevitable roles (Paul 1997). In my estimation, there is a strong correlation between insufficient literacy development and dropping out. Wacquant and Wilson (1989) extend the connection by identifying ties between dropping out and poverty, asserting that "not finishing secondary education is synonymous with economic redundancy" (18).

Although my goals for my students were clearly defined, the strategies I used to teach them were not. In many instances, teaching was trial and error. I was unaware of the kind of theory that would support my beliefs or shape my pedagogical practice. Although the reader might find it odd, I had commenced teaching through an alternate certification route. There simply were not enough teachers to meet the demands of a growing New York City student population. Thus, at twenty-one years of age, with a degree in English/Journalism and without the benefit of an education degree—or even a literacy or children's and adolescent literature course—I was required to teach the students in my charge.

Although the task was daunting at first, it became easier. As time elapsed, teaching even became exciting and liberating. I grew to value the experiential, sending the message that reading and writing were fun and should result in social action. I desired that communication arts become relevant to students' lives and I attempted to ensure that class activities and projects reflected my values.

For example, my sixth- and seventh-grade students and I discussed social responsibility. The discussion emerged as a result of their interest in a book that I was reading. Subsequently, both groups determined (of their own volition) that they were not as socially responsible as they desired. As a result of our dialogue, the sixth-graders organized a school-wide canned-goods drive. They publicized the event, collected cans, and clearly defined their expectations of me. By all accounts, their project was a success. Most importantly, they left my classroom with the firm understanding that their actions had an impact on society.

My seventh-grade students were concerned about the environment. They decided to target McDonald's. A number of them decided to boycott until the chain stopped using Styrofoam cups and containers. Others decided that while they could not sacrifice McDonald's hamburgers, they could request that their Big Macs be placed in paper rather than Styrofoam. The seventh-graders also composed and circulated petitions and held a school-wide rally on the environment.

In another instance, students explored the question, "What is poetry?" In my experience, many students appeared to bring limited knowledge of the topic to discussions and understood only a narrow scope of the genre, such as a few traditional poets like Shakespeare and Edgar Allan Poe. Students seemed to associate poetry with boredom and antiquity. Through exposure to and discussion of nontraditional poets and definitions of poetry, I was able to assist them in establishing a broader conceptualization. They were encouraged to collaboratively define poetry in cooperative learning groups, as well as to define it through exploration of the "poetry" in various media forms, like art, song, rap, greeting cards, motion, dance, and nursery rhymes (Paul 1994). I was most excited by their enthusiasm over the discovery that rap music, an aspect of urban culture with which many of them were familiar, was a valid poetic form that included rhyme, meter, figurative language, and significant theme (Paul 1994; Purves 1993). Legitimately, rap could be classified as poetry because "regardless of a poet's culture, that poet uses rhythm, imagery, typography, grammar, and syntax as the medium of the poem" (Purves 1993, 358).

There were instances when I witnessed personal change of great consequence in individual students; for example, one of my students, who was most concerned with following the school rules and pleasing others, developed her own voice during one of our classes. After we had read a contemporary fiction book that featured a Latina heroine, this student courageously stated that she was tired of hearing everyone else's story, those of Blacks and Whites. She desired to hear more Latino/a stories. Soon after, she entered a piece in a writing contest on her experiences as a Latina, won, and was published in a local newspaper (Paul 1997).

As I became more proficient at teaching, children—even some of the most hardened—laughed and smiled in my classroom on a regular basis. I was often told by the children, their parents, and colleagues that the children loved both my class and me. Parents and colleagues were overwhelmingly supportive of my efforts. In many instances, we shared similar concerns and hopes.

I was passionate in my work, and I was confident about my burgeoning approach to education and literacy because it expressed my existing schema of the world. My experiences evoked the eros within. In this sense, *eros* is defined as "an assertion of the life-force . . . creative energy empowered" (Lorde 1978, 51). Simultaneously, I began taking education courses and, soon after, I commenced my doctoral studies in evening classes while continuing to teach during the day. In the process, I discovered theory focusing on multicultural education that strongly supported my practice.

Cross Questions and Crooked Answers: Students at the State University

I had been deeply affected by my classroom experiences, especially the context in which I taught, involving Black and Latino/a, working-class, and poor families. After my doctoral studies, I arrived on the university campus with a publicly acknowledged commitment to multicultural education.

But I found myself looking into the vast sea of primarily White female faces in my education courses and seeing (in a number of them) disdain for and a lack of comprehension of both the concepts I was addressing—and of me. In spite of the college's mission and commitment to innovative pedagogical practice, many of my students would place their notebooks neatly on the desk (at the start of each class) and wait for me to lecture. My questions were met with silence. Attempts to initiate dialogic exchange concerning the political and social dynamics of literacy instruction were often perceived as "a waste of time" or opportunities to attack liberal, progressive ideas.

Class assignments had to be reviewed (ad nauseum) until each minute detail was explained. This particular set of students, who were mostly early childhood majors, complained, "We won't be able to teach kids to read after this course." They seemed to disregard totally the fact that the course I taught was an introductory overview to the field of elementary/middle-school literacy.

Their scorn and/or lack of comprehension also was revealed in the student evaluations I received. For example, students wrote:

> . . . I strongly feel that most of her information is good but not appropriate for this class. Yes, multiculturalism can be tied into reading and literature, however, Mrs. Glenn has spent sooo much and too much time on this subject alone. . . . She comes across as very prejudice [sic] and is very offensive.

> The instructor was apparently a well-read person. . . . I felt her focus on African American content was distracting and quite offensive.

> Stop using racism as a drive for all lessons, readings, videos, and most class discussions.

> Often goes off on tangents.

I felt a similar contempt for them, many of whom, in my estimation, suffered from "Good White Girl Syndrome," as a White female colleague termed it. I quickly tired of what I perceived as their intellectual cowardice and grew exasperated by their attempts to make me the oppressor. I had come to appreciate the profession of teaching for its ability to transform and emancipate. Yet, it appeared as if a number of my students were prepared to enter teaching as a diversion . . . until "the right man" came along.

Surprisingly, complaints were not solely the province of my White students. It soon became evident that some of my students of color had labeled me a "sellout," to use the lingo of the city. In their eyes, I had forgotten where I came from and displayed little allegiance. To them, I was deemed unwilling to "keep it real." I recall most vividly the comment of an older Black female student (who had not completed assignments in a satisfactory manner, frequently arrived late to class, and slept through classes from time to time). She said, "I thought a Black professor would try a little harder to understand. I was wrong. When I teach, I will try to understand my Black students." With much chagrin, my response was something to the effect of, "Don't give me that. You won't be helping. Mediocrity is expected by the dominant culture. Black children should be made to understand *that* and, thus, understand the need for excellence in all of their endeavors."

A Latino male (who had a number of difficulties with spoken and written language) became so enraged after a discussion regarding the low grade he had received that he stormed out of my office saying, "It's no use talking to you." He previously had shared with me his negative educational experiences, resulting from his lack of facility with English and his previous teachers' lack of cultural understanding. As he left my office after that heated exchange, I was saddened. I knew that I would be added to his list of negative experiences. Yet, I also knew that I was obligated, as a teacher-educator, to the children that he would go on to teach.

There was a major difference, however, between my discontented students of color and those who were White. The White female students were much more apt to challenge my authority. Without hesitation, they went to more established, older, White professors to discuss secretly my "progressive, radical beliefs," my "racism," the "difficult assignments" I gave, and my "lofty" academic standards. A common student complaint was, "I just don't know what she wants. Why can't she just tell me what she wants and I'll give it to her!" While they claimed that they did not know what I wanted, I believed that I clearly knew what they wanted—boring, uninspired teaching.

My instructional decision-making was affected directly by the uncertainty and discomfort that I saw in their eyes. I had been told that many of them had never had a professor or teacher of color during their academic career. Once during class, a student freely shared, with a smile, her pleasure of having made my acquaintance. She said, possibly without realizing that the comment could be pejorative, "Usually when I look at the news, I say, 'Oh, the Black people are acting up again.' You've helped me to see that there is diversity, all Black people don't act that way."

There were other White students who chose to include me among the ranks of "honorary Whites," like Oprah Winfrey and Michael Jordan. Once again, I was told, in an apparently complimentary fashion, that I was different than other African Americans. As a result of my diligence and "brilliance," I had proven that one can pull him/herself up and become a productive member of society. Such comments were made without the benefit of much background information regarding my identity. I was always cognizant of students' attempts to place me into neat, stereotypical categories.

Unfortunately, similarly convoluted attempts were made by university colleagues, both White and Black.

Faculty and Me, A Woman Without a Country

On a regular basis, veteran colleagues would dismiss my concerns about students and assure me that student complaints were commonplace for new professors, regardless of race, creed, or color. Possibly such reassurances would have been more credible if these colleagues had shared similar experiences, recounting their own narratives of novitiate in academe. They did not. I cannot totally reject their premise and I realize that it does have some degree of validity. But I believe that their comments also reflected my White colleagues' desire to focus on similarity, universality, and racelessness as opposed to acknowledging that the interpretations, perspectives, and world views of people from traditionally marginalized cultures might be quite different from their own, and equally valid. Inherent in this discussion, as well, is the fact that my colleagues were often unable to acknowledge their White privilege and the undeniable advantage it provided them. Morrison eloquently explains this phenomenon by stating, "The habit of ignoring race *is* understood to be a graceful, even generous, liberal gesture. To notice is to recognize an already discredited difference" (1992, 9–10). She further states that "the world does not become unracialized by assertion. The act of enforcing racelessness . . . is itself a racial act" (46).

An unfortunate result of my perceptions regarding colleagues' lack of acknowledgment of and respect for my difference was self-imposed isolation. In an effort to preserve my independence and dignity, and to avoid failure, I stopped consulting with a number of colleagues. I began to reject offers to collaborate, as the very term seemed to contradict the essence of academe in spite of its claims. I frequently refrained from asking White colleagues for suggestions on teaching strategies or instructional materials because a schism had developed and solidified. Instead, I read a great deal and incorporated my new learnings into my pedagogical repertoire.

My feelings of isolation intensified as I noticed that even the discourse style employed by a number of colleagues, Black and White, was rife with "element(s) of one-upmanship" (Tannen 1990, 24). To me, this clearly established that I was in the subordinate position and others were in a "superordinate" one. I responded oftentimes with outbursts of hostility. For instance, during a semester-long faculty development program designed to assist in the retention of untenured professors, I noticed that our White male facilitator seemed to defer to a Black male colleague (who also happened to be a novice professor). It appeared as if my fellow novice were being touted as the authority on the position of untenured professors within this small group. I was especially sensitive to this distinction because my African American male colleague was the only other male present; the other participants were female.

During the course of the program, my awareness of this situation heightened, as well as my perception that this Black male colleague would interrupt as I spoke and attempt to solve problems I brought to the group, when I simply needed a listening ear. His behavior seemed sanctioned by the facilitator and the rest of the group. It is possible that I am merely hypersensitive, but it seemed to me that such behavior was repeated with frequency. So, as my female colleagues sat silently and/or appeared conciliatory, I spoke up. I told him that I resented his implication that his thoughts were more valuable than mine, and his patriarchal way of attempting to solve problems did not work for all participants. Furthermore, outside the program, there was another occasion when I addressed a Black male colleague's condescension and paternalism.

Needless to say, my behavior was not well received by some African American colleagues. An established Black female professor called me aside to caution against what she termed "my obsessive-compulsive tendencies" and the need to tone down my responses. While I found her choice of words objectionable, I felt there was little malice in her message. I believe she viewed me as young, confused, and needing direction. In her mind, my most significant concerns should have been to retain my position, gain political allies on campus, and ardently support other African American faculty. For me, however, the most significant concerns had been to retain my integrity and individuality at any cost.

Generally, I felt that faculty attempts to reinforce the power structure, in their exchanges with me, were based on my race and/or gender. I also believe, however, that the problematic nature of the situation was often exacerbated by my age, assertiveness, and desire to affect change after being on campus for a short while.

Problems arose when I suggested, after less than a month on campus, that my department explore the possibility of adding a course focusing on multicultural issues as they relate to pedagogy. My proposal was based largely on my campus-related experiences with students and my fear that they would do harm to underclass populations. While I freely admit that I did not understand the politics of adding courses to college programs or the ramifications of such a venture, I was motivated by a desire to help. From my perspective, the suggestion was not an attempt to criticize the existing program, which I considered meritorious, to a degree; it was an attempt to improve on it. A number of department members, however, viewed my suggestion as a bold affront. I expeditiously received the message that I had not yet "earned" the right to suggest changes. Granted, I understood their position that one should spend a certain amount of time within a structure before determining to change it.

Yet, when does one earn the right to suggest changes? Also, is not this sense of earned privilege another means by which to reinforce the hierarchical nature of academe that so many within express the desire to change? Do not such attempts to maintain power structures prohibit the development of community within academe and respective departments? I unabashedly expressed such sentiments with little concern for the effect of my words. With assaults coming from every direction and outbursts flying, I increasingly felt the need to insulate myself with an ever-thickening wall of hostility, an assertive and prepossessing style, and "shocking" comments.

I recognized that I was entering a battle . . . a battle to maintain my identity, define myself as a scholar on my own terms, and survive this experience emotionally intact in the face of adversity.

In retrospect, I am sure that faculty members were sometimes taken aback by my arrogance and desire to do things my way. I am also positive that a number of colleagues, Black and White, found working with me emotionally taxing. Yet, in my estimation and that of some others, I bring new energy to academe, a new perspective, an expanded definition of my field, and a new approach to scholarship, along with my arrogance. Such determinations are subject to interpretation.

Revelations . . . How I Got My Groove Back

Recently, I saw novelist Terry McMillan discuss her book, *How Stella Got Her Groove Back*. When asked to clarify the meaning of the title, she stated that, like the character, she had temporarily lost her way in life. The deaths of her mother and best friend precipitated her disconsolation and confusion. Then, like Stella, McMillan went to Jamaica and experienced a spiritual and emotional renewal. She had once again taken control of her life.

As I listened, I thought about the appropriateness of McMillan's title in relation to my own life. Although I had not traveled to Jamaica for emotional restoration, I had undergone a similar transformation.

In my Bronx classroom, I had developed a level of comfort with students and parents that made teaching an invigorating experience. I often left my classroom energized by the depth of my young students' responses. I also appreciated the support I received from colleagues of all races and ethnicities. The students, their parents, my colleagues, and I were in accord.

My positive experiences in the Bronx were predicated on my conscious desire to teach Black and Latino/a youngsters in an urban center. I felt and continue to feel a deep sense of commitment to and concern for the plight of oppressed people. Such commitment has been expressed similarly by Anna Julia Cooper, W. E. B. DuBois, Maria Stewart, Ida Wells-Barnett, and Carter G. Woodson, and continues to concern scholars of color internationally (Banks 1992). But it seems the expression of such concern and commitment within the confines of my new arena (i.e., academe) was considered "racist" by a number of White students and colleagues. Many of my students had been trained to believe that the act of teaching was apolitical and lacking eroticism. *Eroticism,* as defined in this context, focuses on the subjectivity and emotional interplay that occurs in the classroom between student and teacher (hooks 1994).

Specifically, they seemed to believe that education was treating all students "the same," as well as keeping one's personal feelings and politics out of the classroom. It might be more accurate to state that these were their expectations of me. Their feelings and politics were revealed frequently, as was their deference to other professors.

In my estimation, my students' expectations were retrograde. The term *apolitical teaching* seemed a contradiction of monumental proportion. The politics of education are inherent in decisions ranging from curriculum design to those that are pedagogical in nature, especially as they continually disadvantage people of color and women. The supposed need for objectivity seemed equally implausible because it subjugates the thought/intellect of women and people of color, since emotion is considered subordinate to intellect in this patriarchal society, which is dominated by "Western, metaphysical dualism" (hooks 1994, 113).

In spite of our ideological differences, I most resented this new set of students because of the power I felt they wielded, mainly in student evaluation forms, and the way in which that power affected my pedagogical decision-making. I lectured more frequently, increasingly focused on product as opposed to process, and spoon-fed them the information they were expected to learn. I also should state that some aspects of my decision-making, like the focus on lecture, were affected by my desire to clearly establish myself as the authority figure in this new classroom. My feelings were based on my status as an ABD (All But the Dissertation), as well as students' comments and actions. For instance, there were students who referred to me as "Mrs." or "that lady" despite the facts that I had introduced myself as "Professor" and the class syllabus clearly displayed the title. Other students refused to address me by any title. In contrast, these same students readily referred to White colleagues as "Dr." and/or "Professor."

I also felt students' proclivity toward deemphasizing and underestimating my intellect and their attempts to cast me in the position of "Super-Mammy," the nurturer. This nurturing role is one in which the dominant group is most comfortable placing Black females (Carroll 1982). For example, a few students would tell me what "a nice lady" I was or they first thought I would be, even though I knew such descriptions were inaccurate. They were inaccurate because I worked diligently to establish myself as distant, formal, and remote.

Some students of color and a few African American faculty/staff also misunderstood my views and politics, but it is important to add that I have received overwhelmingly positive responses from the majority of my students of color.

Although few in number, they have regularly expressed pleasure about my presence, the issues I address, and my lack of trepidation in regard to confronting White students' racism.

Yet, these few bright moments dim in the larger picture. While my purpose in the Bronx had been clear, I was less clear about my mission in this new setting. In fact, the mounting difficulties led me to question my reasons for even remaining on campus. I am positive, in fact, that I would not have remained if I had not made some significant self-discoveries in the process of thinking about leaving. The most influential dealt with taking responsibility for my own insecurity. I realized that, in a number of instances, I had attributed more power to White students and colleagues than they actually had possessed. I also realized that while I understood the relevance of a liberatory education (that is also multicultural) for me and the cultures to which I belonged or felt an affinity, I had not yet fully comprehended its significance or relevance for White people. During my early experiences with White students and faculty at the university level, I viewed both bodies monolithically. This view was established as a result of my perceptions of their lack of respect and empathy for me, as well as the antagonism those perceptions generated.

In the long run, students, colleagues, and my experience have helped me to confront assumptions of homogeneity and my tendency to overgeneralize. While I continue to believe the validity of my original claims concerning White students and colleagues' intolerance and/or overreliance on stereotypes, media images, and insincere flattery, I also accept responsibility for committing the same crime. Furthermore, I more fully appreciate the issue of diversity, especially as I become more involved in their stories. Once I began to truly listen to my students, I heard the stories of marginalization they shared. This "homogeneous" group became diversified as they spoke of oppression resulting from socioeconomic difference, language barriers, immigrant status, sexual orientation, interracial relationships, and transracial adoption. Some also talked about the distinct marginality associated with being female. Since experiencing this revelation, I have reconsidered my role in academe as it relates to both White students and students of color.

During my first couple of years at the university, I failed to acknowledge that, despite my self-description as a radical teacher, the methods I used silenced my students. Although well intentioned, I tended to talk *at* students. For example, I grew tired of their racist assumptions about their future students, so I spent time discussing the implications of such assumptions, as well as dealing with the issue through video presentations and readings. Yet, why weren't they getting the message? I currently believe that they failed to understand because I failed to engage them. While they are partially responsible for the learning environment created, I am also responsible for creating an atmosphere rife with apprehension and anxiety.

As time has progressed, I have matured and become more confident of my identities as pedagogue and person. Consequently, I have been better able to assist students, by encouraging dialogue and presenting diverse perspectives. I now realize that by encouraging the development of student voice and sharing my perspective in a less threatening manner, students are prompted to share in a similar fashion that will ultimately benefit their teaching. Additionally, they are encouraged to reexamine their thinking on certain issues. In fact, I encourage them to examine their identities as both citizens in an emerging democracy and teachers.

While I am no longer presumptuous enough to think that I will change student attitudes that have formed over a lifetime, I do think that I am capable of inspiring students to question their assumptions. By focusing more diligently on the development of student voice, I also am teaching them to agree to disagree. Furthermore, by encouraging dialogue and presenting my perspective on various issues, I believe I am helping academe as a whole. Academe should serve as an arena in which intellectual challenge and debate are fostered and the idiosyncrasy of thought is valued. The role of an intellectual is to encourage the growth of such an environment, with students and colleagues alike.

Some might consider this story to have a happy ending. While my discoveries have empowered me and enabled me to survive academe, to some degree, there have been consequential psychic costs. I have suffered a major health challenge that is stress-related, and I still trust very few and befriend even fewer. I continue to accept very few opportunities to collaborate professionally with colleagues within my department or on campus generally. In essence, I am still a woman without a country. Yet, to use a description of British Olympian Linford Christie, who refused to leave the track after being disqualified, I consider myself "perfectly balanced . . . [I] have a chip on both shoulders."

Despite my difficulties, I consider my work environment conducive to intellectual and personal growth. Such an environment is now reaffirming, whereas it was once hostile and unfriendly. But I do not delude myself. The double bind of racism and sexism, in addition to discrimination in all its forms, continues to affect me in the context of academe and will continue to do so. The way in which I cope with it, however, has changed forever.

Endnotes

1. The decision to use both the descriptors "Black" and "African American" is conscious and purposeful. In relation to the students to whom I sometimes refer, I use the term "Black" primarily because I am not solely referring to American students, but also to those whose families recently migrated from African and Caribbean locations as well. Also, while I clearly understand that a number of African Americans would like their African ancestry and connection to a specific geographic location emphasized, I personally do not find the term "Black" offensive or less appropriate than African American. As Madhubuti (1990) suggested before me, I view the term with the same reverence with which it was used in the late 1960s and early 1970s. In reference to use of the term at that time, Black theologian Howard Thurman asserts that:

"Black is Beautiful" became not merely a phrase—it was a stance, a total attitude, a metaphysics. In very positive and exciting terms, it began undermining the idea that had developed over so many years into a central aspect of White mythology: that Black is ugly, Black is evil, Black is demonic. (Thurman, as quoted in hooks 1989, 115)

Similarly, I descriptively use the term *Latino/a* to reflect the "deep connection among all . . . in the Americas who are descendants of native inhabitants, Spanish and other European colonizers, and enslaved Africans, or any combination of these groups" (Nieto 1992, 177). I do not use it to suggest that the group is monolithic.

7

"Lost and Melted in the Pot": Multicultural Literacy in Predominantly White Classrooms

Doreen Stärke-Meyerring

Multiculturalism is a term hard to define, especially if one seeks to define it by observing recent U.S. academic practices. Colleges and universities sponsor multicultural awareness weeks and invite students to eat "multicultural foods" with international students. Some campuses have instituted required courses in "multiculturalism." Although I am not aware of a multicultural requirement within composition programs, many composition teachers voluntarily adopt multicultural readers. "Multiculturalism" in this case seems to refer to a practice of informing students of the American mainstream about racial and ethnic differences, and requiring them to demonstrate their informedness in their writing.

Yet, with so much emphasis on "multiculturalism," why does there seem to be so little satisfaction in the results? In hallways, classrooms, and conferences, one frequently encounters complaints about students—especially white students—who perform outbursts in response to multiculturalism. Published cultural critics themselves have come close to outbursting in their commentary on the practices associated with multiculturalism, one making reference to multiculturalism as "a euphemism for the imperializing and now defunct melting pot," claiming that "dwelling on 'diversity' and multiculturalism . . . is a way of avoiding seriously dismantling Racism" (Anzaldúa 1990, xxii). Another refers to a "miserly tokenism" (Fusco 1988, 82). In this essay, I look further into such critique. As well, I consult composition research on the relationship between culture and literacy. And finally, through an informal survey, I consult 171 composition students, providing them with a forum for comment

135

and outburst. My goal has been to make initial inquiry into the nature of the problem that is "multiculturalism," especially as it appears in predominantly "white" composition classrooms. Although this essay does not provide a solution to a very complex problem, it is intended to provide teachers and researchers with some tools for analyzing "multicultural" education in "white" classrooms. Primarily, I argue for a change from content-oriented "informative" multicultural education—which ultimately cannot invite or explain outbursts—to a more process-oriented multicultural literacy, which might make constructive use of them.

A Perspective on Multicultural Literacy from the "The Rest of the World"

When I arrived in the United States, more exactly in the Upper Midwest, for the first time, one of my first impressions and one that has followed me ever since was that Midwesterners—most of whom I met were white—seemed to be very concerned about what they perceived as their ignorance of different cultures and countries. Already during the car ride from the airport, the director of the newly established Global Studies Institute, to which I was invited as a teaching assistant for German and Russian language and culture, mentioned this perceived ignorance of his students as he was introducing me to the organization and the rationale for the institute. As I found out during my work there, he was not the only educator concerned about this particular problem; many of his colleagues, as well as other educators I met later on, seemed to share his concern wholeheartedly. Not only professionals at educational conferences would be concerned about the so-called ignorance of white American students of other cultures and argue for new global-studies institutes or new multicultural curricula and textbooks, but also many of my colleagues would lament this problem in our daily conversations and tell me about their efforts to promote global thinking and multicultural literacy. This apparent self-criticism was quite surprising to me. Naturally, as an English major in the former German Democratic Republic with a specialization in American studies, I had been exposed to a considerable amount of criticism of the United States, but I had never heard of the problems about which my new colleagues seemed to be concerned. Having a somewhat multicultural major myself (i.e., a major in Russian and English language and culture; educated in Germany, Russia, and the United States), I was certainly fascinated by my new colleagues and their efforts to promote multicultural literacy among their students and to help their students understand people from different cultural backgrounds.

When I joined the English composition program at UND as a graduate teaching assistant, I was quite surprised and just as enthused to see that my new colleagues likewise were genuinely devoted to promoting multicultural literacy among their students. Not only was multicultural literacy an important part of our graduate courses on composition methodology, but also a number of teaching assistants as well as professors had identified multicultural literacy as the goal of their composition classes and had designed their syllabi accordingly. The difficulty, however, for anyone who has defined multicultural literacy as the class goal is to determine their approach to multicultural literacy in the specific cultural spaces in which they are working—in my case, in predominantly white classrooms. But I have found these spaces with their specific cultural dynamics to be particularly rare in composition scholarship on multicultural literacy.

By *cultural dynamics,* I mean the continuous process of movement and change in the relationships among individuals and groups (who might identify with different cultural categories such as gender, class, age, sexuality, race, and ethnicity) as they—in Brandt's terms—interact through literate means (1990). In the classroom, this refers to the relationships among individual students, groups of students, and teacher(s) and students. In any situation, the dynamics can range from the forming, breaking up, reforming, and changing of groups to the clashing, overlapping, and withdrawing from each other. They also include the negotiations of individuals and groups for power, as well as for public and private space, to pursue their interests or to secure acknowledgment, status, and support. These dynamics can be prompted by the instructor (e.g., for project work) or they can develop by themselves, without any prompts from an instructor (e.g., in class discussions). Essentially, these cultural dynamics are determined by a number of different factors, such as the concept of culture, the emotional and intellectual consciousness of cultural identity, the "self," and the "other," as well as the concept of and attitude toward multicultural literacy the students and the teacher bring into the class.

Naturally, cultural dynamics develop differently in every classroom and can never be predicted with any accuracy, but there are some tendencies that apply to most of the classrooms at UND. For example, because the student population on campus consists of more than ninety percent white students, who come mainly from the region of the Upper Midwest, most classrooms usually have a similar makeup. It is quite typical to have either only white students in a class or sometimes to have one or two students of color (e.g., Native Americans) in the class as well. Often, these predominantly white classrooms are described as *monocultural* or *culturally homogeneous*—terms frequently used to describe spaces that, for their lack of racial and ethnic diversity, are commonly not rendered multicultural. Yet, if the term *culture* is not understood as a strictly racial or ethnic concept, but as a "semiotic one . . . [as] webs of significance . . . man himself has spun" (Geertz 1973, 5), these classrooms hardly can be defined as "monocultural." For they are interlaced with multifarious "webs of significance"; they are spaces in which academic cultures and student cultures (e.g., Greeks and non-Greeks, urban and rural students) meet and interact, and, consequently, where different power relations between individuals and groups shape specific cultural dynamics in the classroom. With this understanding of culture as different semiotic webs people create and identify with, classrooms as well as students are inherently multicultural.

However, with multicultural literacy usually understood as a strictly racial or ethnic concept, I was asking myself questions, as many other instructors who teach in similar spaces might have been doing as well. If multicultural literacy means reading and writing about the world, race, and ethnicity, as some textbooks suggest, what kinds of groups and relationships along the lines of these concepts would form in the classroom? If there is only one student of color in the class—for instance, a Native American student—how would this student feel about discussing race and ethnicity, possibly their own (as suggested in some composition scholarship) alone in front of white students and a foreign white teacher, with whom he or she is not familiar? I also had heard about racial discrimination against Native Americans on campus in the discussions about changing the name of the UND athletic teams, "The Fighting Sioux," for its racist implications. With this context in mind, would the white majority of the classroom, or some of them, consciously or unconsciously make racist remarks toward the Native American student in the class as well? How would the Native American student respond to that? How would the white students, in turn, respond? How would all these potential variations and changes in the cultural dynamics affect the students and me and, consequently, our endeavor to further our development as multiculturally literate individuals?

Indeed, such questions are difficult to answer in any situation. Yet, whenever cultural dynamics, albeit limited to the racial and ethnic makeup of a classroom, are explored in composition readers and scholarship on multicultural literacy, most authors base their rationale for multicultural literacy on the assumption that the racial and ethnic diversity of the United States, and concomitantly the diversity in our classrooms, is increasing consistently. Gillespie and Singleton, for example, share the frequently quoted expectation that the proportion of immigrants to New York may exceed the historic 1910 high by the end of the millennium (1993, xvi). The authors point out that "these numbers and this diversity are reflected in our schools" (xvi). It is certainly true that the ethnic and racial makeup of the United States has changed over the course of its history and that racial and ethnic diversity in the United States is increasing today and will continue to increase. Undoubtedly, we need to adjust our teaching rationales, methods, and curricula to respond to and reflect these changes. Unfortunately, as much scholarship has rightly pointed out, "We have ample documentation of the failure of schools to honor the cultural identity of diverse learners" (Gomez and Grant 1990, 34).

Indeed, many educational programs, including many composition classrooms, have focused mostly on white middle-class, or so-called "mainstream," students and thereby have disadvantaged in particular students with different cultural and racial backgrounds. Thankfully, in the last few years, there have been a number of excellent studies (e.g., Heath's *Ways with Words* [1983] or Rose's *Lives on the Boundary* [1989]) that have started to analyze this situation and explore new ways and methods of responding in our teaching to the increasing ethnic and racial diversity in classrooms. Quite a bit of scholarship suggests, for example, providing instruction that "tap[s] into the experiences that students bring to their learning" (Cook and Lodge 1996, xii) or curricula that offer a " . . . focus on the lives of the students and their cultural and community contexts as sources of topics for writing" (Gomez and Grant 1990, 36).

There is no doubt that a multicultural literacy class can only benefit if the students draw from their own diverse backgrounds in their writing. However, I cannot quite agree with the authors (e.g., Gomez and Grant) when they then identify these "diverse learners" as students of color, including all kinds of colors, except white. If only students of color are considered to be "diverse learners," how would the students in my predominantly white classrooms fit in? How would the authors categorize these students? As "nondiverse"? And would this imply that the cultural identity of white students is always "honored"? Would the maxim of encouraging students to draw from their cultural and community contexts as sources of topics for their writing be applied only to "diverse learners" (i.e., students of color)?

Judging from the literature, in which most compositionists base their discussions of multicultural literacy on an "increasing cultural diversity in [their] classrooms" (Dean 1989, 23), I assumed that the predominantly white classrooms at UND must be an exception. However, when I read educational statistics, I was quite surprised to find that the student population in higher education of almost half the states of the United States consisted of only ten percent or less "minorities" (U.S. Department of Education 1991, 201)—i.e., those learners who had been identified as "diverse" and "students of color." While I welcome the focus in composition scholarship on creating a conducive learning environment for formerly and currently disadvantaged students, it seems to me that there is little discussion of cultural dynamics and multicultural literacy in predominantly white classrooms. In fact, the approach to students of color— that is, encouraging them to write about their own personal background, race, or ethnicity—seems to be merely transferred to classrooms with different dynamics (e.g., predominantly white classrooms). The only exception is that white students are not as much encouraged to write about their own personal background, race, or ethnicity, as about that of "other" cultures, usually meaning people of color or people in different countries. In essence, students of color are encouraged to write about themselves, while white students are encouraged to write about "other" racial and ethnic groups. Apparently, multicultural literacy and the concept of culture are limited to the categories of race and ethnicity with a clear-cut division between "self" and "other". In any classroom situation, however, the object of inquiry in student writing and reading seems to be the "other."

This strictly ethnic and racial concept of culture and of multicultural literacy as learning, reading, and writing about different races, ethnic groups, and countries, typically identified as the other, is also promoted in many composition textbooks that carry the label "multicultural reader." Consequently, most multicultural composition readers merely concentrate on writings by or about representatives of either various nations of the world or various racial and ethnic groups within the United States. They encourage students to inquire into the "other"; for example, to "write about important ideas associated with world cultures" to remedy their "lack of knowledge about the rest of the world" (*Writing About the World*, McLeod 1991), to "become better informed about our 'global village' . . . writing about the larger world" (*Ourselves Among Others,* Verburg 1991), or to "look beyond their own society and culture" (*Across Cultures*, Gillespie and Singleton 1993). Many of the books attempt "to challenge accepted beliefs by asking students to consider the lives, ideas, aspirations — and prejudices — of people who are very different from them" (*Crossing Cultures,* Knepler and Knepler 1991). Similarly, Gillespie and Singleton conceive of their reader with the "guiding image of a reaching out" (1993, xv). "Reaching out," then, mostly refers to "the other" or sometimes also to "the rest of the world." "The other" then is frequently defined as people of color and "the rest of the world" as cultures in countries other than the United States. That which is not "other" (i.e., white people) or which is not the "rest" (i.e., the United States) then is implied to be the center, from which people "reach out" to the "rest." In this notion of cultural identity, the "other" or the "rest" is strictly separated from the self in the center. In fact, the "other" seems to be viewed as the dualistic counterpart of the self. However, I am sure that just as I have not considered myself and my culture or country to constitute the "rest" compared to someone else, people of color might not necessarily have considered themselves someone else's "other." Not only people assigned to "the rest" or to the "other," but also white American students show difficulties grappling with the ethnically and racially constricted concept of multicultural literacy in which race and ethnicity are assigned to the "other." For example, Hoffman describes his classroom:

> As a white teacher in a roomful of white students, one of my biggest problems was making race *visible.* . . . Since we were a group of white people, many of my students were puzzled by my desire to think about the meaning of race: the question did not seem relevant or interesting or even askable in such an environment. (1991, 9)

As in the discourse around the multicultural in general, many textbooks and much composition scholarship on multicultural literacy essentially have excluded a discussion and questioning of this notion of identity, self, and other. Yet, as Trinh demonstrates, this notion is closely connected to "the self/other relationship in its enactment of power relations" (1990, 371). Trinh explains:

> Identity as understood in the context of a certain ideology of dominance has long been a notion that relies on the concept of an essential, authentic core that remains hidden to one's consciousness and that requires the elimination of all that is considered foreign or not true to the self, that is to say, not-I,

other. In such a concept, the other is almost unavoidably either opposed to the self or submitted to the self's dominance. (371)

This opposition of self and other is based on a binary and dualistic framework of thinking and consciousness and has thus lead to the objectification of people with devastating consequences. As Cliff explains, "through objectification—the process in which people are dehumanized . . . given the status of Other—an image created by the oppressor replaces the actual being. The actual being is then . . . denied selfhood—which is, after all, the point of objectification" (1990, 272). Thus, commonly centered on the "other," their "differences," and "diversity," multicultural discourse, in general as well as in composition textbooks, has perpetuated the objectification of people as "other." By equating "other" with people of color, much of multicultural discourse merely has reproduced the existing power structures with white culture being the central reference point, in the position to define the "other" and to set the standards according to which people belong to the "other" or the "rest." Not only has multicultural discourse reproduced the existing power structures, but according to several cultural critics, such as Anzaldúa (1987), hooks (1989, 1994), Trinh (1990), and Fusco (1988), it also has co-opted and exploited the discourse on race and culture to ensure the current power structures. Fusco, for example, maintains:

> . . . the "socially conscious" institutional engagement in "discovery" of the "other" is also . . . an engagement in collective amnesia of past entanglements and, in more recent memory, of dismissive rejection. Although the promotional mechanisms would have it otherwise, there is nothing new about the so-called "other" or its discovery. Western cultural institutions . . . have a history of rejuvenating themselves through the exploitation of disempowered peoples and cultures. (1988, 81)

Only very few composition textbooks explore such notions as "self," "other," "difference," and "identity," which are, however, crucial to the understanding of the dynamics between individuals and groups. Instead, with their focus on the "other" or the "rest of the world" as in a dualistic relation to the center, they might risk even perpetuating the existent preconceptions of relations between racial and ethnic groups, such as the dualistic opposition of self and other—and, consequently, the existing power structures—rather than promoting multicultural literacy, or—in their terms—a better understanding of and between cultures, which they originally had set out to promote.

There is no doubt that the proponents of multicultural literacy, including the authors of multicultural textbooks, are genuinely devoted to contributing to a better understanding among people of all cultural backgrounds. However, it might be this devotion that also tempts many proponents to look for a fast and idealistic means of achieving their goal without devoting any major attention to the contradictions, emotions, conflicts, and misunderstandings that occur when cultures interact in various forms. Gillespie and Singleton, for example, approach these conflicts only by recognizing that they cannot and do not attempt to "*hide* the difficulties and suffering sometimes caused by cultural diversity" (1993, xvii; emphasis added). This cultural diversity, then, seems to be the only "cause" Gillespie and Singleton identify to explain these "difficulties." Consequently, they believe that "these difficulties can be reduced when people know more about others and therefore are more accepting of them" (1993, xii). As in this example, many authors of multicultural readers do not include a discussion of cultural conflicts that overlap with social, economic, and political conflicts in their multicultural discourse, but rather resort to ethical perorations of being nice to the "other" or "accepting of them."

Such ethical perorations align these textbooks with a rather simplified and idealized concept of multicultural literacy, in which students are encouraged to view cultural dynamics in society through metaphors such as "salad bowl," "vegetable soup," or "mosaic." Most of the metaphors and concepts with which multicultural literacy has been approached seem to have the sweet and deceptive taste of food, art, or leisure activities, creating the impression that multicultural literacy is achieved by participating in an everlasting multicultural awareness festival "celebrating cultural diversity" or other "formal, fixed events or observable structures" (Schriner 1992, 100). Approaches based on such food- and folk-art–related metaphors present a painless and smooth path of simple and pure harmony to multicultural literacy, thereby leaving out the economic, social, and political interests, conflicts, and contradictions that permeate any cultural dynamics.

This concept of multicultural literacy as a content-focused model disseminating information about the so-called racial and ethnic other is based on a static understanding of literacy as a product. In this case, the product consists of knowledge about different races and ethnic groups—knowledge with which students can fill the perceived gaps in their information depository. However, as Brandt has shown in her study of literacy as social involvement, effective writers perceive literacy as a process, a process of using language to "sustain intersubjectivity, particularly the intersubjective work of reading and writing" (1990, 5). As such, the process has a highly social function and is very much dependent on how the individual understands human thought and communication processes and their determination by the social realities different cultures form. Regarding its function, Brandt shows that

> . . . literacy is the most social of all imaginable practices—hypersocial, actually, because it epitomizes the role of culture in human exchange and condenses into the channels of reading and writing some of the most crucial of our joint enterprises. To read or to write is to trade heartily—inescapably—on commonality and collectivity. (1990, 1)

Understanding the role of human culture means to understand how people learn to construct social reality, based on—in Geertz's terms—the "webs of significance" they grow up and live in, how they learn to deal with and transgress borders, how they learn to move in and out of different "webs of significance" (1973). It also means to understand how people in and between cultures use the way they construct meaning to pursue their interests, to negotiate for public and private space, or power—or, in Tannen's words—for being "one-up," "one-down," or level (1990). Essentially, understanding the role of human culture in human exchange means to understand how people and the cultures they are a part of interact with each other, how "they stick together through literate means" (Brandt 1990, 6); that is, it means to understand the cultural dynamics they shape in the exchange. In this sense, the term *multicultural literacy* is even tautological since literacy is by nature multicultural. After all, when we "trade on commonality," we move in and out of different cultures and their social realities by addressing and responding to readers and writers from different cultural backgrounds.

Therefore, multicultural literacy is more than "knowledge about others." Naturally, knowledge of different cultures and groups, their history, concerns, ideals, and values is a part of multicultural literacy, but it should not be the main goal. Rather than merely acquiring knowledge and information, a multiculturally literate person develops a new mental and emotional consciousness—in Freire's (1990) words, a consciousness of themselves as a "cultural and historical subject." According the concept of culture as Berlin and Vivion summarize it, the individual as a cultural and historical subject is conscious of "the ways social formations and practices are involved in the shaping of consciousness," and how this shaping is "mediated by language and situated in concrete historical conditions" (1992, ix).

As various cultural critics have observed, this new consciousness is already in the process of being formed. It is a new mental, emotional, and spiritual consciousness that enables people to juggle different cultures and to use contradictions and conflict for active and creative self-realization. Trinh, for example, defines her vision of this new consciousness as

> . . . a different terrain of consciousness [that] has been explored for some time now, a terrain in which clear-cut divisions and dualistic oppositions, such as science versus subjectivity, masculine versus feminine, may serve as departure points for analytical purposes but are no longer satisfactory if not entirely untenable to the critical mind. (1990, 372)

Similarly, Anzaldúa, another cultural critic, explores " . . . an 'alien' consciousness [that] is presently in the making—a new *mestiza* consciousness. . . . It is a consciousness of the Borderlands" (1987, 77). This new consciousness, Anzaldúa explains, is "a product of the transfer of the cultural and spiritual values of one group to another" (78). Like Trinh's concept of the new consciousness, Anzaldúa's notion focuses on the capability of mediating and "uniting" phenomena that "collide." Both of these concepts of the new consciousness are in many ways closely related to Freire's concept of "conscientization," a process that at the same time is the means and the goal of the struggle for literacy. Specifically, "conscientization," according to Freire, is the process of searching for the self as subject through critical thinking and thus dialogue so that the subject, conscious of her or his consciousness and its formation, can take an active part in the creation and re-creation of social reality.

Corresponding to these notions of a "new" or "critical" consciousness, anthropologists such as Geertz likewise have observed "the refiguration of social thought . . . [caused by a] culture shift" (1983, 19). Observing "an enormous amount of genre mixing in intellectual life in recent years," and a "blurring of kinds" (19), Geertz explains the significance of this refiguration:

> It is a phenomenon general enough and distinctive enough to suggest that what we are seeing is not just another redrawing of the cultural map—the moving of a few disputed borders . . . but an alteration of the principles of mapping. Something is happening to the way we think about the way we think. (1983, 20)

All these notions—Anzaldúa's *mestiza* "consciousness," Trinh's "critical consciousness," and Freire's process of "conscientization," as well as Geertz's observation of a change in the way we think about our thought processes—seem to be based on the assumption and vision of breaking down dualistic thinking; for example, between subject and object, between self and other. According to these cultural critics, anthropologists, and educators, dualistic thinking is in the process of turning into a thinking in continuums that allows people to move more freely among ideas, categories, and concepts without rigid boundaries.

It is in this context that multicultural literacy might be better understood as the development of such a new consciousness, or what Brandt (1990) calls "a new way of being in the world," that enables individuals to become conscious of themselves in the cultural dynamics they are entangled in through literate means. The individual not only develops a consciousness of cultural processes and their dynamics, but also a consciousness of how these dynamics shape the consciousness of the individual. Viewed in this way, multicultural literacy would be a dynamic concept, because it denotes a long, complicated, and nonlinear process—the process of developing a new consciousness through dialoguing and interacting in a world whose borders are becoming more and more blurred. It is this conscientization process of which a multicultural literacy class should be a part.

The first consequence of viewing the multicultural literacy class as part of this process would be to reconsider our approaches to teaching multicultural literacy. In much of composition scholarship—as well as in multicultural readers, in which the authors "challenge" or "invite" students (usually white) to explore the "other"—the students are more or less assumed to lack knowledge or to be ignorant of the "other." For example, Gillespie and Singleton, quoting Ronald Takaki, a Berkeley professor of ethnic studies, identify the "need to open the American mind to greater diversity" (1993, xvii), obviously assuming the students come with "closed" minds that instructors need to open.

Not only composition readers, but also classroom practices reflect this ignorance-based approach to students. For instance, in their project of "Internationalizing Freshman Composition I and II Through Literature and Film," Kehrer, Hunter, and McGlynn (1990) as instructors decided that citizens and thus their students "need greater understanding and acceptance of cultural practices" (360). Yet, the instructors did not consider it necessary to inform the students about their decision concerning the students' needs when the students registered for the classes: " . . . on registration print-outs, cross-cultural sections were listed with traditional approach sections, so students were not aware of having registered for 'special' courses until they arrived in the classrooms" (360). Students who were unable to use the class for their literacy development and, therefore, responded with evaluations like "I do not get a lot out of this class" or "[the class] went on about irrelevant things, nothing helpful" they merely categorized as "the ever-present loyal opposition" (370).

Similarly, Spear and her colleagues (1990), in their article about their Composition 101/World Civilizations course, base their rationale for their multicultural literacy class on Simonson and Walker's (1988) notion of American ignorance in view of increasing international interaction:

> As the world becomes more of a single economic [and social] entity, there is a corresponding need for all citizens to have not only a fundamental understanding of the cultures of their own culture (in part to conserve it), but also a knowledge of the rest of the world. However, citizens of the United States are profoundly ignorant of world literatures, histories, mythologies, and politics. (xii)

By approaching the students with this kind of medical vocabulary, suggesting that multicultural literacy is the "medicine" that will cure what the educator has identified as a deficiency of the students (i.e., their perceived ignorance), the instructors, as well as the textbook authors, categorize the students as unknowing and in need of being taught. In contrast, the textbook authors and the teachers are presented as knowing and offering the solution to the problem—providing the missing information that the students then only need to receive and file or—in Freire's words—to deposit in the "bank." Once they have this information about other cultures, they are considered literate and open-minded. However, being told that they deviate from the academic norm (with their unopened minds), the students are—in Freire's words—put in the position of spectators, not re-creators (1990). This approach fails to recognize students as cultural and historical beings, entangled in cultural dynamics—and, in fact, prevents them from becoming conscious of themselves as such.

Overcoming this remedial approach also means to inquire—in Pratt's terms—into the students' "pupiling" (i.e., "literate interaction" from the students' perspective), including their "submitting to [authority] or questioning it," as well as their "unsolicited oppositional discourse, parody, resistance, critique . . . " (1991, 38–39). As Pratt warns us,

> When linguistic (or literate) interaction is described . . . usually only legitimate
> moves are actually named as part of the system, where legitimacy is defined
> from the point of view of the party in authority. . . . If a classroom is analyzed
> as a social world unified and homogenized with respect to the teacher, what-
> ever students do other than what the teacher specifies is invisible or anom-
> alous to the analysis. (38)

Inquiring into students' "pupiling" and defining its place in our classrooms is essential in a multicultural literacy class if we conceive—as Brandt has shown—
of literacy as social involvement and of a literacy class as a space where students
are active and conscious creators and re-creators of the cultural dynamics—not
only as they exist outside the campus and the classroom, but also as they exist
in such a classroom itself. Because our approach to multicultural literacy needs
to be grounded in the cultural spaces and dynamics in which the students and
we are interacting, we need to understand how we—students and teachers together—shape these dynamics and what factors influence the dynamics in
what ways. However, we cannot understand the cultural dynamics by ourselves
without dialoguing with our students—without actively including their "pupiling"—and we cannot construct a multicultural literacy class if we do not understand the cultural dynamics. Therefore, we need to leave enough space for
the students to articulate their understanding and consciousness of the cultural
dynamics they experience and create in the classroom.

Finding scholarship on "pupiling" in multicultural literacy classrooms
to be scarce, particularly in predominantly white spaces, I decided to do an initial inquiry into some "pupiling" myself by means of an informal study. While
the student voices in this informal study certainly cannot yield any comprehensive insight into "pupiling" or cultural dynamics, and certainly cannot and
are not meant to be generalized, they can give us some inspiration for finding
new ways of redesigning our multicultural literacy classes through dialogue
with our students.

Student Voices on Multicultural Literacy

Considering the main purpose of my study to inquire into students on multicultural literacy, I chose the form of a survey to have a sizable number of
voices—not to claim that the study or the student voices are representative of
the whole UND student body or of white students in general, but to allow for
voices from many different perspectives and to get an impression where some
of these perspectives seem to diverge or converge. With this in mind, I personally distributed the survey in ten composition classes with 171 students altogether, administering it toward the end of the spring semester so the students
would have a fresh, at least one-semester-long experience of composition. All
ten classes were "regular" sections in the sense that they were not advertised as
sections offered specifically for Native Americans or speakers of English as a

Second Language. Two of the ten classes, however, had a "focus on multiculturalism." These classes used a "pluralistic reader" and, according to some of the students' responses to the question of whether they would like to write about multicultural issues, they already had written extensively in these classes. The focus on multiculturalism, however, had not been announced in the course schedule when the students registered for the classes.

Corresponding to both the "UND Student Profile" (University of North Dakota 1992) and my observations, the composition classes I surveyed consisted of more than ninety percent white students. Only four of the 171 students identified themselves as students of color (three Native and one Filipino American) and four identified themselves as Canadians when questioned about their culture. To avoid directing the students' answers to the concept of race or ethnicity in the question about their cultural identity, or to precondition them to a specific answer, they were not asked outright about their race or ethnicity.

The survey asked the students to answer some more general and some more specific questions regarding their concept of and experience with culture, multiculturalism, and multicultural literacy (see Appendix for all the questions in the survey). It consists of mostly rather open questions in order to avoid too many restrictions on the students' answers and to leave as much room as possible for their voices. Thus, I chose not to use multiple-choice–type questions because of their potential limitations for my purposes; the students might attempt to fit their answers into the more limited framework multiple-choice questions provide, rather than explore their own perspectives. Likewise, I chose not to specify possible responses in questions about their response to a concept or experience as "negative" or "positive," fearing the students either might not allow themselves more complexity or introspection in their answers or might resort to a rushed decision concerning the two categories. I realize that leaving questions more open increases the ambiguity of the responses and the difficulty of categorizing them clearly and definitively. However, having categorizable answers clearly was not my main goal. Rather, I wanted to have an initial impression of student voices on the issues as they perceived them and as they would offer them in a situation that was as "unthreatening" to them as possible (i.e., without any teacher that had the authority of assigning grades at the end of the semester). With this in mind, I also tried to meet the language of the students—to approach them as little as possible with my vocabulary or my concepts of the terms—by picking up on some of the phrases I had heard the students use in their in- and out-of-class discussions of cultural and multicultural issues among themselves and with me. For example, *multicultural literacy* was not a term they used, nor was it used much in multicultural discourse; therefore, I decided on the phrase *multiculturalism in composition* because it was used on campus as well.

For the purpose of this paper, I concentrate on three areas of inquiry. First, regardless of how we view multicultural literacy—whether we view it as a content-focused as well as ethnically and racially restricted model, or whether we view it in Brandt's and Freire's terms as a model based on social interaction and dialogue "epitomizing the role of culture in human exchange into the channels of reading and writing" (Brandt 1990), in which students develop as cultural and historical subjects—the students will need to think about their cultural identity and their experience with the term *culture*. Naturally, in the class they will proceed from their own experience with the concept and thus will shape the dynamics in the class. Therefore, it would be important to have an impression of how students might identify culture, including their own. Second, if the class is to focus on multicultural literacy and actually use the term *multicultural(ism)*, it also would be helpful to have some idea about the students' understanding of, their experience with, and their attitude toward multicultural literacy or the term *multiculturalism*, as it is often used in multicultural discourse. Third, it is important to see how the students would combine their perception of the term *multiculturalism* with their literacy development; for example, in a composition class with a so-called multicultural focus.

Students' Concept of Culture

With regard to the students' understanding of the concept of culture and of their own culture (i.e., Question Five in the survey), I found that many students in both types of classes had only vague ideas either of the concept of culture in general or of their own culture in particular. Almost seventeen percent of the questioned students claimed they had no culture and thirteen percent thought they had a culture, yet found it difficult to name or define it. One student pointed to the benefits of cross-cultural contact he lacked—to the possibility that others can show us our own culture in a way we are unable to see: "It's difficult to describe what your own culture is. This probably comes from being in that culture, being too close to it. . . . You would have a better answer asking someone not in my culture." Another student answered, "I do feel that I have a culture but I have a hard time defining it." In a previous question, the same student had claimed "since I was in grade school, I have learned of my own culture and race, but very rarely did I learn of cultures other than my own." It seems that she assumed she knew her culture very well; yet, when asked directly to identify her culture, she was not so sure anymore. Other students responded similarly: "I honestly would have to question what my culture is. I know I have a 'culture,' but I can't think of any aspects of my culture that are distinctively into its own"; or, "I'm not really sure what it [my culture] is though, but I know I belong to one."

Several students obviously were searching for cultural features such as culinary and folkloric diversity as they might have perceived them from consumer-oriented displays of the multicultural: "I don't really know if I have a culture or not. I know of different countries that eat particular things and do particular things around a certain time of the year. But I really don't feel that we are like that"; or, "My culture is not really anything noticeable. Most people in the

United States are the same. We dress alike, listen to almost the same music, and there is a lot of the same favorite foods across the country."

Another rather common theme in the student responses was the assumption that people lose their culture when their ancestors die or move away: "[I have] some [culture]—I feel we lost a great deal of this [culture] through the years by loss of grandparents and families moving away." The theme of culture as being determined by the ethnic background of one's ancestors and being "melted" recurred with about thirteen percent of the students. They recalled the various ethnic backgrounds of all their ancestors and found, for example, one-sixteenth Native American background, one-quarter of a different race or ethnic group. However, they often found that these fragments of ethnicity or race never had or had stopped having a major impact on their life. Some of the students pieced together all their ethnic background, while others could put only parts of their fragments together. Yet, none of the students who resorted to the ethnic and racial background of their ancestors made any attempt at defining aspects of the present that make up their culture. Considering the students who claimed not to have a culture or to be able to define it, along with those who tried to piece together their ancestral background, we look at a striking number of approximately forty percent of the students who did not identify anything in their current environment as belonging to their culture, let alone name their culture.

Only about a third of the questioned students defined their culture as American. These students often added that they perceived this culture to constitute the "majority" or norm. Typical answers were, "[My culture is] American—just as everyone who lives here should be looked upon as being" or "AMERICAN CULTURE! Enveloping and homogenizing all others." About twenty percent of the questioned students defined their cultural identity by referring to terms such as *Midwest small town* (about ten percent), *rural* (two percent), or *urban* (one percent). About five percent used the concept of race and defined their culture by the color of their skin—"average white"—and about two percent based their culture on religion.

The most significant result of the survey with regard to the question of the students' sense of their culture—the indication that more than a third of the questioned students seemed to have difficulties finding anything in their current environment that they would define as their culture—could have various explanations. First of all, achieving cultural literacy is a complex and challenging process because cultural meanings, or—in Geertz's words—"webs of significance" (Geertz 1973, 5) are not always easily visible. Thus, the students—although probably having some sense of their cultural identity—may not have thought about the meaning of the term *culture* yet. However, they also may have been influenced by the equation of culture with the concepts of race, ethnicity, or nationality common in multicultural discourse. As the discourse typically concentrates on ethnicity or race and assigns these concepts only to people of color, while leaving out white ethnicity, the students may have come to the conclusion that the absence of "whiteness" from the discourse and the focus on the colored "other" might mean that only the "other" "has race" and therefore "culture."

Students' Experience with Multiculturalism in General and in Their Education

Responding to the questions, "What is multiculturalism? What purpose does it serve?," almost all the students said they had some kind of understanding of the term *multiculturalism;* only five students responded that they did not know what the term meant. Apparently, the term is prominent enough for most students to bring varying preconceptions into the class. More than a third of the students, however, identified multiculturalism with the concept of the "melting pot." Also, most students identified it as inquiring into the "other," as something pertaining to "minorities" or people of color, and responded, "I think of mostly the African or Indian race"; "Other cultures trying to be heard around campus"; " . . . it's minorities trying to bring out and show their differences to the majority"; and "I think about people who are not white expressing their opinions and their beliefs to others."

Asked about their initial response to the terms *multiculturalism* and *celebrating cultural diversity,* almost forty percent of the students identified their response as positive, mostly hoping to gain more understanding of various cultures and thus to avoid misunderstandings; about the same number of students were not sure or neutral or simply repeated what they thought multiculturalism was; and a little more than twenty percent defined their response as negative. The negative responses occurred in classes both with and without a focus on multiculturalism. Some students exhibited plain resistance and dislike: "Boring!!"; "Another goof-ball high-budget low-turn-out production. . . . Might be interesting, but is it worth the time to find out?"; "It's a little overdone. I don't think we need to go through all of this rigmarole to make less than fifteen percent of the campus feel a little better." One student focused his negative response to multiculturalism more on the approach to the concept he had observed rather than on the concept itself:

> I'm a little disgusted with it [multiculturalism]. I do agree with what the phrases [multiculturalism and celebrating cultural diversity] are representing. . . .
> However, these phrases have become "buzzwords" for people trying to push different people together, often stressing the differences between different cultures, but if perhaps they took a different approach, they might have better results. After all, people really aren't that different when you get to actually know them.

Others felt threatened or disadvantaged by multiculturalism: "Oh, great, another way to do away with 'WASPS.' I feel that I'm becoming a minority in my own country"; "I think basically that it is irrelevant. I feel that minorities often use their differences for special treatment. . . . They want all of us to be aware of their differences, but I don't think that they take into account any of our beliefs and values."

Although only about forty percent of the students identified their responses to the terms *multiculturalism* and *celebrating cultural diversity* as positive, about two-thirds of the students found that multiculturalism has some kind of relevance to them personally when responding to that question. They identified as their main reason that the United States consists of many cultures and that "We all need to get along"; "I sometimes feel uncomfortable around people with a culture I don't understand. If I have the chance to understand their culture, I will no longer feel uncomfortable"; or, "We all have so much to learn from each other." Some found that the UND campus is "full of multiculturalism" (especially compared to the situation in their hometowns), referring in particular to multicultural awareness weeks or diversity forums on campus. A little more than a quarter of the questioned students, however, found no use for multiculturalism in their personal lives at all. Some students referred to their personal background; for example, "I don't think so because coming from this small city, I don't think there is much multiculturalism"; "I haven't really been in any multicultural situation"; "Not really, I don't feel I'm surrounded by multiculturalism"; "No, because everywhere I've lived has been one culture." Others minimized the meaning and consequences of culture and cultural differences: "No, not in the sense of what I've seen on campus. . . . I just accept my friends for who they are, not what they believe or where they come from"; "We are all the same"; and "No, because it really doesn't matter what culture a person is from."

Some students did not consider multiculturalism relevant for their personal lives because they perceived multicultural education as a remedy against racism, intolerance, and insensitivity. Because they felt they did not suffer any of these "diseases," they also had no need for this "medicine." They answered, for example, "No, because I respect other cultures"; and "Not really, I feel that I am a very open-minded person and that I'm not a target for multicultural help."

Other students considered multiculturalism and multicultural education as a way to "help" people of color and thus not relevant to themselves. Their responses were, for example, "No, I'm not a minority"; "No, not really, because when I think of multiculturalism, I think of others since I am white"; "No, I am an American, that is my culture. I practice my culture day in, day out"; "No, I'm perfectly content with how my own racial/ethnic situation treats me"; "No, because I don't care about other cultures"; "No, I really don't worry about other cultures"; and "No, because it doesn't bother me."

In their responses to the term *multiculturalism* and its relevance to their personal lives, the students seemed to echo much of the discourse around the multicultural: the limitation of culture to concepts of race and ethnicity; the absence of white ethnicity; the identification of people of color, or the "other," as object of inquiry; and the remedial approach of "helping" white people cure their racism. The student responses seemed to be astute—maybe unconsciously— in sensing the different power relations between white people and people of color, with white people as the "helpers" and therefore in power to "help" the powerless. What struck me most, though, was the fact that more than a third of the students had perceived multiculturalism exactly the way Anzaldúa (1987) had identified it: as being a different term, a *euphemism,* for the *melting pot.*

At the same time, reading the phrases "I don't worry," "I don't care," or "it doesn't bother me" in their voices, I was reminded of Mura's notion that the position of some cultures induces multicultural learning more than that of others. According to Mura, if a culture is in the position of power (thus suffering little or no racial or ethnic discrimination), its members are in the position to engage in multicultural learning at leisure; "for them, knowledge of a minority culture is a seeming . . . luxury; they can survive without it" (1988, 137). However, if a culture lives in an environment that is dominated by a different culture, multicultural learning becomes a necessity for survival. Obviously, some students perceive this situation either consciously or subconsciously—a perception that contributes to the shaping of the cultural dynamics in the classroom and thus needs to be addressed.

Most of the students must have formed their perception of the multicultural through their experience with it at the university and/or through information from the media. When asked if multiculturalism ever played a role in their education, about half responded positively, more often than not referring to their college experience. The remaining half found that multiculturalism had never played a role in their education. About seventy percent of those who never had any multicultural educational experience, however, would have liked it, though many added under the condition that it would not be "slammed down our throats." The other students either were not sure (fifteen percent) or would not have wanted any multicultural education (fifteen percent).

Asked about the advantages or disadvantages they perceived that multicultural education might have for them, almost eighty-five percent of the students identified advantages; about twenty percent identified disadvantages. Among the advantages, they listed learning to understand others, enrichment by learning from others, broadening horizons, learning "that your culture is special and not better than anyone else's," and "to answer more questions on *Jeopardy!*" While the latter student very well may have meant it jokingly, the answer also may reflect the focus in much multicultural discourse on disseminating "interesting information" about the "other." Regardless of her intention, her response also reflects the leisure/necessity motive of cross-cultural learning, as described by Mura (1988).

As for the disadvantages, the students identified the potential of their culture being judged and condemned for being the one in "super" power. Thus, students feared "constant criticism of my own culture," "liberal bias," or "biased teachers . . . [in] ignorant rural areas." Some students also feared losing affiliation with their own cultural values and their culture as a whole: they saw the potential danger of "losing sight of our own culture"; "we could be overexposed and lose our own culture"; "I wouldn't want ideas of other cultures to be forced on me"; or were afraid of forgetting "about basic history that's been taught for years." Furthermore, a number of students seemed to be concerned about "chances of hate emerging" and cautioned that "there is sometimes hostility and jealousy." Again, the answers did not seem to differ between the classes with and without the specified multicultural focus.

Students' Assumptions About Multiculturalism in Composition

The students' experience with multiculturalism on campus and in the media certainly has an impact on their expectations and attitudes toward a composition class with a multicultural focus, especially if the focus refers to reading and writing about racial and ethnic groups, as promoted in many multicultural readers. Asked if they would like to write about multicultural issues, a little more than forty percent of the questioned students said they would, about thirty-five percent might like to, and about twenty percent said they would not, fearing mostly not knowing enough about culture and multiculturalism. Their responses with regard to their perceived lack of personal experience with and knowledge of multicultural issues could be summarized quite well by this student's response: "I think that most composition students lack the breadth of experience to write cogently about multicultural issues. Spoon-feeding it to them will not create any understanding." A number of the students also thought that not knowing enough about the issue would put them at a disadvantage compared to students who have had more experience interacting with different cultures. As one student put it, " . . . having people write about the issue would put those who have not seen other cultures at a disadvantage." Again, the responses in classes with such a focus did not differ from those without such a focus.

While these were mostly the responses of white students, one would assume that students of color might like to write on multicultural issues in particular. After all, much composition scholarship encourages students of color to reflect on their specific ethnic and racial experience in their writing. While students of color might certainly benefit from such encouragement in racially and ethnically mixed classrooms, this might not necessarily be the case in predominantly white classrooms. Here, the cultural dynamics might differ in the sense that the power relations with regard to the intercultural interactions between the ninety or more percent of white students and the students of color may disadvantage the latter group. In their responses, for example, two of the students of color expressed fear of their culture being exposed to ridicule and misunderstanding. In short, they were concerned about cultural insensitivity on the part of other students—perhaps justified.

With these specific dynamics in mind, it seems only understandable when a Hidatsa woman claimed she would not have registered for the multicultural composition class she found herself in had she known of its focus. She explained, "I am very proud of who I am, but I have trouble doing justice in my writing to my heritage and then have trouble handing in papers regarding that subject." Especially in predominantly white classrooms, we must consider that in such spaces, students of color might sometimes undergo intense psychological stress when asked to write about their cultural and racial experiences, which—considering the phenomena of racism and discrimination—might have been traumatic for them in a way that members of the so-called "mainstream" may not fully comprehend—as Mura, Anzaldúa, and many other cultural critics frequently have pointed out. Some may argue that writing about traumatic or disturbing events can be healing, but as writing teachers and simply as human beings, we are not in the position to determine when a student might be ready for such an undertaking. Corresponding to this concern, almost ninety percent of the students answered "yes" to the question whether they would prefer to know before registering for the class if it is designed with a multicultural focus. Regardless of their attitude toward multiculturalism, most students considered it "only fair" or "their right."

When asked if they believed that their culture would be treated "fairly" in a composition class with a multicultural focus, barely half the students answered positively, and these often simply suggested that their culture *should* be treated fairly and equally rather than saying they believed it would. A little more than thirty percent believed that their culture would not be given fair treatment; the remaining students were not sure. However, the majority of students (sixty-three percent) considered it important. Those who thought their culture would be treated "equally" and "fairly" in a composition class with a multicultural focus, for the most part, either referred to the circumstance that their culture is "the majority" or "the norm around here," or relied on the students pushing for it: " . . . not many people would put up with a teacher that was unfair. . . ."

Those students who would not expect their culture to be treated fairly gave mostly the following reasons: "We ['WASPs'] are being pushed back—the melting pot is draining"; "Minorities seem to be the only group of people who get equal and fair time on this issue"; "I think people are allowed to slam WASPs more easily"; "In order to focus on different cultures, we would probably tend to 'assume' we know everything about ours (Midwest American)." One student even feared her culture would be condemned in such a class:

> . . . many minorities tend to include all whites in their discussion of racism and discrimination. While some of their anger is justified, most of it is not my

personal fault nor that of most whites today. We can't change the past, we can only learn from it. It would probably give me the opportunity to see what it's like to be condemned and discriminated against.

Other students expressed the same notion of an "attack" on their culture: "The current trend is to attack white dominant American culture"; "White people have done some terrible things and have treated people (cultures) terrible over the years. I would totally understand the different opinions"; "So many other cultures are so negative about my culture that people probably wouldn't be willing to fullheartedly accept this culture"; "The base root of multiculturalism is the downplaying and chastising of white culture because many cultures see white culture as the root of their problems"; "When people talk about cultures, usually only the minorities are talked about"; and "It would all be white American males' problem."

The students revealed a broad spectrum of complex and intense feelings, such as resentment, fear, insecurity, inferiority, hate, hostility, compassion, and pride. For example, while students of color in predominantly white classrooms seemed to express fear of racism, ridicule, or misunderstanding of their cultural background, a number of white students feared contempt, blame, or resentment for being part of the dominating culture. What the different student voices yielded for me more so than any composition scholarship I had read was the importance of the psychological and emotional dimension of multicultural literacy, whichever way literacy is understood. Whether it is understood as a model imparting information about different races and ethnic groups, or as a cultural and multicultural consciousness, these emotions do exist. In the same way as they are excited by the cultural dynamics, they also influence and shape the cultural classroom dynamics in different ways. For example, they might cause students to silence other students or to be silenced, or even to disappear from the class. Viewing multicultural literacy as a consciousness of cultural dynamics and, therefore, of the way these dynamics interact with the emotions of individuals and groups, will make these emotions as part of the student "pupiling" visible and, therefore, analyzable as part of our consciousness development. Yet, we too often limit literacy to its rational and intellectual dimension, while ignoring or reducing its emotional dimension. However, as Sosnoski (1991) argues,

> Students should learn to theorize their own pain and help others in similar situations to do so. As emergent intellectuals, they should be able to turn an inarticulate feeling into an articulate emotion, as well as to take an inchoate problem and articulate it as a theorem. Intellectuals deal with both emotions and ideas. (210)

In a multicultural literacy class, the students thus could articulate their emotions in the process of shaping the dynamics of which they are part and, consequently, become conscious of how their feelings and the cultural dynamics dialectically inform each other.

Altogether, the student voices on the cultural and multicultural most certainly can be interpreted in many different ways. Some might label them as lacking awareness or consciousness; others might label them as painful, racist, or culturally insensitive, and in need of being "set straight." Insensitive or not, they do shape the cultural dynamics of our classrooms directly or indirectly, visibly or invisibly. Therefore, considering the specific cultural dynamics in the spaces in which we work, as in my case in predominantly white classrooms, does not mean to "advocate" for any group of students. In just about any cultural space, including our classrooms, people—individuals as well as groups—will shape and be shaped by the different dynamics in which they negotiate for power, status, or space. It is exactly these dynamics that need to inform our approach to multicultural literacy, because learning how different people and groups "stick together through literate means" (Brandt 1990, 6) requires consciousness of what people do when they "stick together"; that is, how they shape the dynamics between each other. It also requires consciousness of how this "sticking together" influences the cultural consciousness of the student as an active participant, creator, and re-creator of the dynamics through which people "stick together." While the student voices might not necessarily yield a unified conclusion for ways to work with these cultural dynamics in our teaching of literacy (and were not meant to do so), they might indicate the emotional, psychological, social, and cultural complexity involved in the dialectic relationship between student "pupiling" and the shaping of these dynamics. This complexity also might show us in the voices—and the outbursts—of the students why multicultural literacy needs to be more than a content-focused model in which people supply and consume information about "the other" to be able to answer more questions on *Jeopardy!*

Appendix
Questions from the Survey

1. What is multiculturalism? What purpose does it serve?

2. What is your initial response when you hear the term *multiculturalism* or the phrase *celebrating cultural diversity?*

3. Do you feel multiculturalism has any relevance to you personally? Why or why not?

4. Have you had any personal multicultural experiences; for instance, with a friend, classmate, or family member from a different culture? How close are you to her/him? How often do you interact with her/him? Did you find anything different about interacting with that person as opposed to interacting with somebody from your own culture? What?

5. Do you feel you have a culture? What is your culture?

6. What aspects of your culture would you want to have taught to others?

7. Was multiculturalism ever part of your educational experience (high school or college)? If yes, what did you think about it? If not, would you have liked to have had it?

8. What advantages/disadvantages do you expect from being exposed to multiculturalism in your education?

9. Would you like to write about multicultural issues in a composition class? Why or why not?

10. If a comp class focused on multicultural issues, would you prefer to know about that focus before you register for that class? Why or why not?

11. In a class with a multicultural focus, do you think your culture would be given fair and equal treatment? Why or why not? Would it be important to you? Why or why not?

Response
Dangerous Critique: Academic Freedom and Institutional Constraint

Stephen Dilks

The point is not simply that, since our racial differences do not constitute all of us, we are always different, negotiating different kinds
of differences of gender, of sexuality, of class. It is also that these
antagonisms refuse to be neatly aligned; they are simply not reducible
to one another; they refuse to coalesce around a single axis of differ-
entiation. We are always in negotiation, not with a single set of oppositions that place us always in the same relation to others, but with
a series of different positionalities.

> Stuart Hall, "What Is This
> 'Black' in 'Black Popular
> Culture'?"

An té nach bhfuil láidir ní foláir dhó bheith glic.

> (*An Irish saying that means, "If
> you are not strong you had best
> be cunning."*)

Seventeen years' work in Western academe pursuing a B.A., an M.A., a Ph.D.,
and, since 1995, tenure has exposed me to numerous highly privileged "Marx-
ists," "Feminists," and "Liberatory Teachers" whose social behavior contradicts
their professed politics. How many academic defenders of "the oppressed" are
nonchalantly rude to librarians, students, and nonacademic university employ-
ees? How many are unapologetically elitist (often downright snotty!) in their
lifestyle and social manners? How much damage has been done to progressive
politics by those who talk and write about liberating the oppressed while living
according to notions of private luxury, personal advancement, and social pres-
tige advertised in *GQ, National Geographic, Playboy,* and *Vogue?*

Doreen Stärke-Meyerring and Dierdre Glenn Paul provoke a full-scale critique of academic progressivism by exposing its complicity with institutional and cultural practices that are fundamentally monogenic. Stärke-Meyerring demonstrates the damage done by dualistic, reductive definitions of "multiculturalism," asking us to attend to "the emotional, psychological, social, and cultural complexity involved in the dialectical relation and the shaping of [cultural] dynamics." Paul reveals what she learned from the clashing of different forms of essentialism, transforming a story about institutional hypocrisy, student hostility, and individual insecurity into a story about how resistance and disagreement can become central to the educational process. By attending more fully to the experiences of those who don't fit (culturally, politically, and otherwise), we can continue to make academic discourse increasingly inclusive: Stärke-Meyerring and Paul remind us that self-conscious attention to the relationships between our ideas and our practices is conducive to a process that might transform the elitist pretense of (merely academic) egalitarian politics into active, complex, liberatory praxis.

Paul is refreshingly honest in admitting her initial tendency to view "white students and faculty at the university level . . . monolithically." Who has not? And who has not been dangerously reductive in the pursuit of increased complexity? One lesson of Paul's essay is that liberatory intentions may have oppressive consequences. If we are to survive as progressive teachers without doing too much damage to our emotional, intellectual, and political health, we must attend, honestly and microscopically, to the contradictions, dissonances, awkwardnesses, and failings of our praxis. Paul does so.

Like any good teacher/scholar, Paul is interested in those moments when the realms of individual theory and institutional practice overlap, providing examples of Hegelian synthesis, of dialectical materiality, of engaged pedagogy. But her occasionally raw prose and her persistent discussion of personal alienation remind us that these blissful moments are rare. Describing herself as "a woman without a country," Paul's main experience has been conflictual. This is why, I think, her prose calls attention to itself. By reading Paul's essay, we experience firsthand the dissonance between what the individual says and what the institution does. Furthermore, Paul reminds us that academic practices, traditions, and expectations construct and constrain individuals by designating them as "teachers," "scholars," "students," "administrators," and "staff": those who do not "fit" comfortably into the assigned role become increasingly aware of their difference. Individual options for response are limited (particularly for untenured faculty): Paul retreated into a "self-imposed isolation," protecting her interests by reducing her participation; one alternative is to fight for everything you believe in, thus preserving one's integrity at the risk of souring one's prospects for tenure. My preference is to pick one's fights very carefully, focusing on specific achievable goals that have a gradual, cumulative effect on institutional practices.

If we remain in academe, we will continue to be produced (as "individual" academics whose freedom is bound by a network of conventions and decorums) in the perpetually negotiated complexity of relationships between our institutional positionings and positionings that are more obviously private, personal, nonacademic, noninstitutional. Institutions are built by, *not for,* individuals: Institutional conventions may assume individuality, but they do not prioritize the individual.

So, while universities and colleges frame their discourse in terms of "academic freedom," sanctioning numerous forums for personal expression, we are rarely free to say exactly what we think. Hired as a tenure-track assistant professor to direct the composition program at UND in 1995, I remain keenly aware that diplomacy and caution are my most trusted tools. Put another way, my daily practices develop out of the tense relationship between my punk-based Socialist Democratic politics and the politics of a conservative state institution that has deep-sixed its progressivist tradition in order to satisfy the proponents of educational functionalism. In a context where students are defined as "consumers" and where education is defined in terms of "credits," I necessarily spend much of my time and energy hiding my anticonsumerist politics. Like many teachers, I "grade" students even though I am fundamentally opposed to such a crude way of assessing educational success; like many directors of composition, I make daily decisions based on standardized testing, even though I firmly believe that tests only test one's ability to do a test.

My writing also is created out of a titration process that attempts to make new knowledge by bringing personal principles into active relationship with institutional conventions. As I test my personal passions against established ways of thinking, my raw, acidic prose is, somehow, alkalized, becoming less fiery, less personal, more balanced, more acceptable. Thus, I dilute the more risky, more emotional qualities (the "outbursts") that inspired me to write in the first place. Such is the method described by Wordsworth in the preface to the Lyrical Ballads: a poetic process in which a "spontaneous overflow of powerful feelings" is "recollected in tranquility," necessarily involving the attenuation of personal passions and commitments. Like poetic discourse, academic ways of working are created through personal negotiations with the spoken and unspoken rules that define professional behavior and speech: in other words, personal academic success *requires* us to sacrifice "integrity and individuality." Of course, while academic rules of behavior and speech dilute individual expression, they also provide opportunities for unified political action. By encouraging (Paul might say "forcing") us to come into accord with communal forms of expression, academic discourse has the potential to transform a messy array of idiosyncratic beliefs into a coherent political agenda that, ultimately, may change the "power structure."

So, just as we are well advised to begin our career as academic writers by positioning ourselves in relation to other academic writers, so we are well advised to consolidate our position in the academic milieu of our particular institution by cultivating "political allies." Very few of us can construct a successful academic career (which is a career that transforms academic discourse by making it both more inclusive *and* more complex) without such allies because so-called "academic freedom" actually involves a titration-like balance between "the tradition" and the individual talent. As Paul's essay demonstrates, this balancing act is most precarious, and most difficult, when we enter academe, becoming less and less so as we move up the academic hierarchy. Assistant professors must, then, "tone down" their responses, but they also must do as Paul did, figuring out ways to critique the institution even if it means being accused of "obsessive-compulsive behavior."

But this is not all. Not only is our academic freedom less and less constrained as we become more and more institutionalized, but—due to all kinds of historical and material asymmetries in institutional relationships of power (in which those with more power in any given situation determine which interpretations are acceptable and which are not)—some of us have to expend more energy than others if we are to fit in with academic standards and conventions. In other words: We all have to pay our dues, but the marginalized are charged at a higher rate; the less mainstream our political beliefs, the more cautious we have to be in expressing these beliefs.

Paul exposes the grim reality of a profession that works according to a complex system of economic, psychological, emotional, and other exchanges: grubby thumbs, hidden weights, biased measures, and uneven scales influence our work whether we like it or not. Paul gives a clear sense of this often-hidden system of exchanges as it manifests itself in the experience of a new tenure-track assistant professor whose position as a "novitiate" member of the intellectual elite is complicated by her position as a member of two groups that are sufficiently under-represented in this elite as to be favored by affirmative-action laws.

It is very tempting to dismiss Paul's response as her colleagues did, advising her to grow up and get some "direction," treating her proposals for reform as a "bold affront." The dissonance between teacherly success in one context and perceived failure in another might lead us to conclude that *she* is the problem. Indeed, institutional assumptions about what it means to be professional lead us to blame her: she is too idealistic, too reductive, too sophomoric, too angry. But, pandering to those who charge intellectuals with an absurd obsession with the politically correct, this evades the main lesson that might be learned from Paul's experience.

If academe is to continue its contributions to the development of a truly democratic social structure, it needs to figure out how to listen to those whose very presence reveals institutionally sanctioned behaviors and actions to be antiegalitarian, contradictory, hypocritical, deceitful, wrong. If education is to remain central to our institutional practices, we need to figure out how to read an essay like Paul's without resorting to clichés about diplomacy, maturity, and decorum.

While racism and sexism make Paul's story pertinent to academics identified in terms of two equally entrenched but differently experienced ways of categorizing the self, her essay is meaningful to *anyone* whose dreams of finding a "niche in academe" have been tested by the dissonance between personal desire and institutional reality. Her desire "to transform and emancipate" is perfectly consonant with the American academic claim to educational democracy and its carefully regulated process of affirmative action. Paul's critique reveals that the academic system, complex and sophisticated as it may be, needs to become even more complex and sophisticated if it is to accommodate the full spectrum of intellectual types that it produces. Paul develops a crucial critique of the academic apparatus—if we do not take it seriously, we truncate the very process of education that constitutes the central work of academe.

Applied to the academic apparatus, Stärke-Meyerring's call for a "more process-oriented multicultural literacy" might help us make progress in reconstructing academe as a place more adequate to the anger and frustration created by a culture that inclines too much in the direction of elitist monoculUralism. As a European, I was raised with the ambivalent understanding of America as a land of many cultures that insists on thinking in the monocultural terms of "the melting pot." Thus, I am familiar with and a little suspicious of Stärke-Meyerring's surprise at the apparent homogeneity of "white American" responses to "other cultures." Given the post-1945 McDonald's-ization of the world, such reductiveness is not exactly out of character. Still, Stärke-Meyerring's focus on "cultural dynamics" as a materialist concept is consonant with a European approach commonly associated with Adorno and Williams, with writers responding to the post-World War II Americanization of Europe; like Adorno and Williams, Stärke-Meyerring attends to the shifting historical experience of culture, pointing us back to the word's function as a "noun of process" (to quote Williams). Thus, she has a good go at complicating received understandings of "the other," recovering it for use as a triadic term that undermines the tendency of "multicultural discourse" to "reproduce[d] the existing power structures."

Fully aware that the road to hell may well be paved with good intentions, Stärke-Meyerring reminds us that political action is most effective when it engages in rigorous theoretical analysis of "the contradictions, emotions, conflicts, and misunderstandings that occur when cultures interact in various forms." She also reminds us that pedagogical and political rhetoric are most effective when we subject their metaphors and clichés to protracted critique.

Through such analysis and critique, "multicultural literacy" becomes a dynamic exploration of the relationship between a multiplicity of consciousnesses rather than a static description and "appreciation" of an elemental "other." Multiculturalism becomes a multilinguistic, inclusionary formation of the sort celebrated by James Joyce, Gloria Anzaldúa, and Jacques Derrida: Once we engage ourselves in a protracted process of self-review, outbursts, misunderstandings, and hostility become invaluable sites of learning. In this crucial sense, Stärke-Meyerring's essay is wonderfully complementary to Paul's.

Stärke-Meyerring argues for an empowering approach to multicultural literacy, replacing metaphors of remediation and cure with energy-based metaphors. Her survey engages students in the production of cultural knowledge, but it asks questions in a language that is so centered on "culture" and "multiculturalism" that it inevitably provokes reductive, even hostile, responses from students whose academic work has not been framed by a protracted analysis of the discourse of cultural studies. This reductiveness and hostility, of course, is produced by a media-dominated culture that is hugely invested in monoculturalism, monolingualism, monopolitics, and monoeconomics.

Progressive educational practices of the sort illustrated by this section of *Outbursts in Academe* set out to empower students by transforming their sense of personal agency. But the essays reveal that the discourse of progressivism has reached a dead end: the interconnected languages of multiculturalism and affirmative action have been shoved, exhausted, into an impasse built by those who perpetuate the debate over "political correctness." Distracted by discussions framed in terms defined by rightists and *laissez-faire* individualists (e.g., Rush Limbaugh, Margaret Thatcher, and Jesse Helms), social liberationists have put insufficient energy into praxis-based critique that attempts to unite our avocation with our vocation. Academe can only be improved if we work to bring personal principles into productive relationships with institutional practices. As we do this work, changing "our" language to make it less vulnerable to rightist ridicule and abuse, we should keep our eye on progressive democratic ends. This means learning to engage with "the system" (e.g., capitalist, academic, patriarchal) by drawing critical attention to the differences that make a difference. And it means learning how to accommodate those whose initial responses seem raw when viewed through the upper-middle-class lenses of academic discourse.

Works Cited

Addams Family Values. 1993. Film. Dir. Barry Sonnenfeld. With Raul Julia and Anjelica Huston. Hollywood: Paramount.

Althusser, L. 1971. "Ideology and the State Apparatuses." In *Lenin and Philosophy and Other Essays.* Trans. Ben Brewster. New York: Monthly Review.

Anderson, J. 1991. "Theme Management and Generic Formation in Deaf College Students' Texts." *Carleton Papers in Applied Language Studies 8:* 1–21.

———. 1993. *Deaf Student Mis-Writing, Teacher Mis-Reading: English Education and the Deaf College Student.* Burtonsville, MD: Linstok Press.

Anzaldúa, G. 1987. *Borderlands, La Frontera: The New Mestiza.* San Francisco: Aunt Lute.

———. 1990. "Haciendo Caras, Una Entrada." In *Making Face, Making Soul/Haciendo Caras: Creative and Critical Perspectives by Feminists of Color.* Ed. G. Anzaldúa. San Francisco: Aunt Lute. xv–xxviii.

Babbini, B., and S. Quigley. 1970. *A Study of the Growth Patterns in Language, Communication, & Educational Achievement in Six Residential Schools for Deaf Children.* Urbana, IL: Institute for Research on Exceptional Children.

Baca Zinn, M. 1994. "Chicano Men and Masculinity." In *Writing About Diversity.* Ed. I. I. Clark. Fort Worth: Harcourt. 527–539.

Bakhtin, M. M. 1981. *The Dialogic Imagination.* Ed. Michael Holquist. Trans. Caryl Emerson and Michael Holquist. Austin: University of Texas Press.

———. 1986. *Speech Genres and Other Late Essays.* Trans. Vern McGee. Eds. Caryl Emerson and Michael Holquist. Austin: Univ. of Texas Press.

Banks, J. A. 1992. "African American Scholarship and the Evolution of Multicultural Education." *Journal of Negro Education 61*(3): 273–86.

Bartholomae, D., and A. Petrosky. 1986. *Facts, Artifacts, and Counterfacts.* Portsmouth: Boynton/Cook Publishers, Inc.

Berlin, J. A., and M. J. Vivion. 1992. *Cultural Studies in the English Classroom.* Portsmouth: Boynton/Cook, Publishers, Inc.

Berthoff, A. E. 1981. *The Making of Meaning.* Portsmouth: Boynton/Cook Publishers, Inc.

Best, R. 1983. *We've All Got Scars: What Boys and Girls Learn in Elementary School.* Bloomington: Indiana University Press.

Bizzell, P. 1994. "'Contact Zones' and English Studies." *College English 56*(2): 163–69.

———, and B. Herzberg. 1996. *Negotiating Difference: Cultural Case Studies for Composition.* Boston: Bedford.

Blackwell, P., et al. 1978. *Sentences and Other Systems: A Language and Learning Curriculum for Hearing-impaired Children*. Washington, DC: A. G. Bell Association.

Bonvillian, J., et al. 1985. "Language, Cognitive, and Cherological Development: The First Steps in Sign Language Acquisition." In *SLR '83: Proceedings of the III International Symposium on Sign Language Research*. Eds. W. Stokoe and V. Volterra. Silver Spring, MD: Linstok Press. 10–12.

Brandt, D. 1990. *Literacy As Involvement*. Carbondale: Southern Illinois University Press.

Broyles, Y. J. 1986. "Women in Teatro Campesino: Apoco Estaba Molacha La Virgen de Guadalupe?" In *Chicana Voices: Intersections of Class, Race, and Gender*. Edited proceedings of the National Association for Chicano Studies, The Center for Mexican American Studies. Austin: University of Texas. 162–187.

Brummett, B. 1994. *Rhetoric in Popular Culture*. New York: St. Martin's Press.

Burke, K. 1969. *A Grammar of Motives*. Berkeley: University of California Press.

Butler, J. 1990. *Gender Trouble: Feminimism and the Subversion of Identity*. New York: Routledge.

Canaan, J. 1990. "Telling Jokes and Passing Notes: Gendered Strategies Among American Middle-school Teenagers." In *Uncertain Terms: Negotiating Gender in American Culture*. Eds. F. Ginsburg and A. L. Tsing. Boston: Beacon Press. 215–31.

Carroll, C. 1982. "Three's a Crowd: The Dilemma of the Black Woman in Higher Education." In *All the Women Are White, All the Blacks Are Men, But Some of Us Are Brave: Black Women Studies*. Eds. G. T. Hull, P. B. Scott, and B. Smith. New York: The Feminist Press. 115–28.

Charleston, G. M. 1994. "Toward True Native Education: A Treaty of 1992." *Journal of American Indian Education* 33(2): 7–57.

Christopher, W. 1994. Interview by R. MacNeil. *MacNeil/Lehrer News Hour*. Public Broadcasting System. June 16.

Clark, H., and S. Haviland. 1977. "Comprehension and the Given—New Contract." In *Discourse Production and Comprehension: Vol. 1 of Discourse Processes: Advances in Research and Theory*. Ed. R. O. Freedle. Norwood, NJ: Ablex. 1–40.

Cliff, M. 1990. "Object into Subject: Some Thoughts on the Work of Black Women Artists." In *Making Face, Making Soul/Haciendo Caras: Creative and Critical Perspectives by Feminists of Color*. Ed. G. Anzaldúa. San Francisco: Aunt Lute. 270–290.

Clifford, J. 1991. "The Subject in Discourse." In *Contending with Words: Composition and Rhetoric in a Postmodern Age*. Eds. P. Harkin and J. Schilb. New York: MLA. 38–51.

Clynes, M. E., and N. S. Kline. [1960] 1995. "Cyborgs and Space." *The Cyborg Handbook*. Ed. C. H. Gray. New York: Routledge. 29–33. (Reprinted from *Astronautics*.)

Cohen, L. H. 1994. *Train Go Sorry*. Boston: Houghton Mifflin Company.

Conrad, R. 1979. *The Deaf School Child: Language and Cognitive Function*. London: Harper.

Cook, L., and H. C. Lodge. 1996. *Voices in English Classrooms: Honoring Diversity and Change.* Urbana, IL: NCTE.

Covington, V. 1980. "Problems of Acculturation into the Deaf Community." *Sign Language Studies 28:* 267–85.

Crandall, K. 1982. "Reading and Writing Instruction for Deaf Young Adults." In *Deafness and Communication: Assessment and Training.* Eds. D. Sims, et al. Baltimore: Williams & Wilkins. 372–91.

Culley, M., and C. Portuges, eds. 1985. *Gendered Subjects: The Dynamics of Feminist Teaching.* Boston: Routledge and Kegan Paul.

Danes, F. 1974. "Functional Sentence Perspective and the Organizaton of Text." In *Papers on Functional Sentence Perspective.* Ed. F. Danes. The Hague: Mouton. 106–28.

Davis, B. Q. 1994. Videotape. *Machismo Versus Sexism.* With M. Alegria, C. Hernandez, J. Marquez, and M. T. Viramantes. For the Latina Leadershp Network Conference. Concord, CA.

Dean, T. 1989. "Multicultural Classrooms, Monocultural Teachers." *College Composition and Communication 40*(1): 23–37.

Dixon, K. 1995. "Gendering the 'Personal.'" *College Composition and Communication 46*(2): 255–275.

———. 1997. *Making Relationships: Gender in the Forming of Academic Community.* New York: Peter Lang Publishing.

Evans, L. 1982. *Total Communication: Structure and Strategy.* Washington, DC: Gallaudet College Press.

Firbas, J. 1966. "Non-thematic Subjects in English." *Travaux Linguistiques de Prague 2:* 239–56.

Fischer, M. J. 1987. "Ethnicity and the Postmodern Arts of Memory." In *Writing Culture: The Poetics and Politics of Ethnography.* Eds. J. Clifford and G. E. Marcus. Berkeley: California University Press. 194–233.

Fish, S. 1980. *Is There a Text in This Class? The Authority of Interpretive Communities.* Cambridge: Harvard University Press.

Fisher, S. D. 1982. "An Orientation to Language." In *Deafness and Communication: Assessment and Training.* Eds. D. Sims et al. Baltimore: Williams & Wilkins. 9–24.

Fitts, K., and A. France. 1995. *Left Margins: Composition and Cultural Studies.* Albany, NY: State University of New York Press.

Foucault, M. [1970] 1994. *The Order of Things: An Archaeology of the Human Sciences.* New York: Vintage.

Freire, P. [1968] 1990. *Pedagogy of the Oppressed.* Trans. Myra Bergman Ramos. New York: Continuum.

Fries, P. H. 1995. "Theme and New in Written English." Unpublished paper. Central Michigan University.

Fusco, C. 1988. "Fantasies of Oppositionality: Reflections on Recent Conferences in Boston and New York." *Screen 29*(4): 80–93.

Gaines, D. 1990. *Teenage Wasteland.* New York: HarperCollins.

Gallop, J. 1988. *Thinking Through the Body.* New York: Columbia University Press.

————. 1992. *Around 1981: Academic Feminist Theory.* New York: Routledge.

————. 1995. "The Teacher's Breasts." In *Pedagogy: The Question of Impersonation.* Bloomington: Indiana University Press.

Garcia, J., and S. L. Pugh. 1992. "Multicultural Education in Teacher Preparation Programs: A Political or an Educational Concept?" *Phi Delta Kappa 74:* 214–19.

Garth, T. R., and O. D. Smith. 1937. "Performances of Fullblood Indians on Language and Non-language Intelligence Tests." *Journal of Abnormal and Social Psychology 32:* 376–81.

Geertz, C. 1973. *The Interpretation of Culture: Selected Essays.* New York: Basic.

————. 1983. *Local Knowledge: Further Essays in Interpretive Anthropology.* New York: Basic.

Gillespie, S., and R. Singleton. 1993. *Across Cultures.* 2nd ed. Boston: Allyn and Bacon.

Gomez, M. L., and C. A. Grant. 1990. "A Case for Teaching Writing—In the Belly of the Story." *The Writing Instructor 10:* 29–41.

Gray, C. H., ed. 1995. *The Cyborg Handbook.* New York: Routledge.

Guilbault, R. 1989. "Series: Hispanic U.S.A.: 'Americanization Is Tough on *Macho.*'" *San Francisco Chronicle.* August 20: Sunday supplement. 6+.

Halliday, M. A. K. 1985. *An Introduction to Functional Grammar.* London: Edward Arnold.

————, and R. Hasan. 1976. *Cohesion in English.* London: Longman.

Haraway, D. J. 1991. "A Cyborg Manifesto: Science, Technology, and Socialist-Feminism in the Late Twentieth Century." In *Simians, Cyborgs, and Women: The Reinvention of Nature.* New York: Routledge.

————. 1992. "The Promise of Monsters: A Regenerative Politics for Inappropriate/d Others." *Cultural Studies.* Eds. L. Grossberg, C. Nelson, and P. A. Treichler. New York: Routledge. 295–337.

————. 1993. "Otherwordly Conversations; Terran Topics; Local Terms." In *Science As Culture 3.* London: Free Associated Press. 64–93.

Heath, S. B. 1983. *Ways with Words.* Cambridge: Cambridge University Press.

Hewitt, M. A. 1993. "Cyborgs, Drag Queens, and Goddesses: Emancipatory-Regressive Paths in Feminist Theory." *Method & Theory in the Study of Religion 5(2):* 135–154.

Hirschberg, S. 1992. *One World, Many Cultures.* New York: Macmillan.

Hoffman, A. 1991. "Multicultural Literacy in the Composition Classroom: Report on a Pilot Project." ERIC Document ED 337 778.

Holcomb, T. K. 1990. *Deaf Students in the Mainstream: A Study in Social Assimilation.* Rochester, MN: The University of Rochester Press.

hooks, b. 1989. *Talking Back: Thinking Feminist, Thinking Black.* Boston: South End Press.

———. 1994. "Eros, Eroticism, and the Pedagogical Process." In *Between Borders: Pedagogy and the Politics of Cultural Studies*. Eds. H. Giroux and P. McLaren. New York: Routledge. 113–18.

Hughes, R. 1993. *Culture of Complaint: The Fraying of America*. New York: Oxford University Press.

Irigaray, L. 1985a. "Plato's *Hystera*." In *Speculum of the Other Woman*. Trans. G. C. Gill. Ithaca, NY: Cornell University Press.

———. 1985b. *This Sex Which Is Not One*. New York: Cornell University Press.

Jameson, F. 1991. *Postmodernism or The Cultural Logic of Late Capitalism*. Durham: Duke University Press.

Jarratt, S. 1991. "Feminism and Composition: The Case for Conflict." In *Contending with Words: Composition and Rhetoric in a Postmodern Age*. Eds. P. Harkin and J. Schilb. New York: MLA. 105–23.

Johnson, E. A. 1992. *She Who Is: The Mystery of God in Feminist Theological Discourse*. New York: Crossroads.

Kanellos, N. 1989. "Two Centuries of Hispanic Theater in the Southwest." *Mexican American Theatre: Then and Now*. Ed. Nicolás Kanellos. Houston: Arte Público Press. 38.

Kehrer, G., J. Hunter, and H. McGlynn. 1990. "Internationalizing Freshman Composition I and II Through Literature and Film: A Cross-cultural Approach." *Community/Junior College 14:* 359–70.

Kelly, L. P. 1989. "Does Deaf Students' Concern with Applying the 'Rules' of Grammar Impede the Writing Process?" *Perspectives for Teachers of the Hearing-impaired 7:* 21–23.

Knepler, H., and M. Knepler. 1991. *Crossing Cultures*. 3rd ed. New York: Macmillan.

Kohn, M. L., et al. 1990. "Position in the Class Structure and Psychological Functioning in the United States, Japan, and Poland." *American Journal of Sociology 95*(4): 964–1008.

Lemke, J. L. 1995. *Textual Politics: Discourse and Social Dynamics*. London: Taylor & Francis.

Levine, E. S. 1981. *The Ecology of Early Deafness*. New York: Columbia University Press.

Liben, L. S. 1978. "Developmental Perspectives on the Experiential Deficiencies of Deaf Children." *Deaf Children: Developmental Perspectives*. Ed. L. S. Liben. New York: Academic. 195–216.

Liebow, E. 1993. *Tell Them Who I Am: The Lives of Homeless Women*. New York: Free Press.

Longacre, R. E. 1983. *The Grammar of Discourse*. New York: Plenum.

Lorde, A. 1978. "Uses of the Erotic: The Erotic As Power." In *Wild Women Don't Wear No Blues*. Ed. M. Golden. New York: Anchor Books. 45–55.

———. 1982. *Zami: A New Spelling of My Name*. Freedom, CA: Crossing Press.

————. 1983. "The Master's Tools Will Never Dismantle the Master's House." In *This Bridge Called My Back: Writings by Radical Women of Color.* Eds. C. Moraga and G. Anzaldúa. Brooklyn, NY: Kitchen Table Press.

————. 1984. *Sister Outsider: Essays and Speeches.* Freedom, CA: Crossing Press. 124–33.

Madhubuti, H. 1990. *Black Men: Obsolete, Dangerous? Afrikan American Families in Transition: Essays in Discovering Solutions and Hopes.* Chicago: Third World Press.

Makler, A. 1991. "Imagining History: A Good Story and a Well-formed Argument." In *Stories Lives Tell: Narrative and Dialogue in Education.* Eds. C. Witherell and N. Noddings. New York: Teachers College, Columbia University Press. 29–47.

Mann, W., and S. A. Thompson. 1987. "Rhetorical Structure Theory: Description and Construction of Text Structures." In *Natural Language Generation: New Results in Artificial Intelligence, Psychology, and Linguistics.* Ed. G. Kempen. Dordrecht, The Netherlands: Martin Nijhoff. 85–95.

McCarthy, C., and W. Crichlow. 1993. *Race, Identity, and Representation in Education.* New York: Routledge.

McIntire, M. 1977. "The Acquisition of American Sign Language Configurations." *Sign Language Studies 16:* 247–66.

McLeod, S., et al. 1991. *Writing About the World.* New York: Harcourt.

Means, R. (with M. J. Wolf). 1995. *Where White Men Fear to Tread: The Autobiography of Russell Means.* New York: St. Martin's Press.

Meisel, C. J. 1986. *Mainstreaming Handicapped Children: Outcomes, Controversies, and New Directions.* Hillsdale, NJ: Lawrence Erlbaum.

Modleski, T. 1997. "Doing Justice to the Subjects: Mimetic Art in a Multicultural Society: The Work of Anna Deavere Smith." In *Female Subjects in Black and White: Race, Psychoanalysis, Feminism.* Eds. Elizabeth Abel, et al. Berkeley: University of California Press.

Moi, T. 1985. *Sexual/Textual Politics: Feminist Literary Theory.* New York: Methuen.

Moraga, C., and G. Anzaldúa. 1983. *This Bridge Called My Back: Writings by Radical Women of Color.* Brooklyn, NY: Kitchen Table Press.

Morgan, J., and G. M. Green. 1980. "Pragmatics and Reading Comprehension." In *Theoretical Issues in Reading Comprehension: Perspectives from Cognitive Psychology, Linguistics, Artificial Intelligence, and Education.* Eds. R. Spiro, E. Bruce, and W. Brewer. Hillsdale, NJ: Lawrence Erlbaum. 113–40.

Morrison, T. 1992. *Playing in the Dark: Whiteness and the Literary Imagination.* New York: Vintage Books.

Mura, D. 1988. "Strangers in the Village." In *Multicultural Literacy: Changing the American Mind.* Eds. R. Simonson and S. Walker. St. Paul: Graywolf Press. 135–54.

National Center for Health Statistics (NCHS). 1994. Data from the National Health Interview Survey. Series 10, Number 188, Table 1.

Nieto, S. 1992. "We Have Stories to Tell: A Case Study of Puerto Ricans in Children's Books." In *Teaching Multicultural Literature in Grades K–8*. Ed. V. Harris. Norwood, MA: Christopher-Gordon Publishers, Inc. 171–201.

Ogbu, J. U. 1991. "Immigrant and Involuntary Minorities in Perspective." In *Minority Status and Schooling: A Comparative Study of Immigrant and Involuntary Minorities*. Eds. M. A. Gibson and J. U. Ogbu. New York: Garland. 3–33.

Ong, W. 1981. *Fighting for Life*. Ithaca, NY: Cornell University Press.

Ortiz Cofer, J. 1994. "The Myth of the Latin Woman: 'I Just Met a Girl Named Maria.'" In *Common Ground: Reading and Writing About America's Cultures*. Eds. L. G. Kirszner and S. R. Mandell. New York: St. Martin's Press. 220–27.

Padden, C., and T. Humphries. 1988. *Deaf in America: Voices from a Culture*. Cambridge: Harvard University Press.

Panunzio, C. 1991. "'In the American Storm' from *The Soul of An Immigrant*." In *American Mosaic: Multicultural Readings in Content*. Eds. B. Roche Rico and S. Mano. Boston: Houghton Mifflin Company. 16–23.

Paul, D. G. 1994. "Exceptionality and Poetry." *New Jersey English Journal 3:* 46–48.

———. 1997. "Toward a Multicultural Perspective." In *Multi-ethnic Literature for Children*. Ed. V. J. Harris. Norwood, MA: Christopher-Gordon Publishers, Inc.

Pinter, R., and D. Patterson. 1916. "A Measurement of the Language Ability of Deaf Children." *Psychological Review 23:* 413–36.

Pratt, M. L. 1991. "Arts of the Contact Zone." *Profession 91:* 33–39.

Prinz, P., and E. Prinz. 1979. "Simultaneous Acquisition of ASL and Spoken English." *Sign Language Studies 25:* 283–96.

Purves, A. C. 1993. "Toward a Reevaluation of Reader Response and School Literature." *Language Arts 70*(5): 348–61.

Pyles, T., 1969. "How Meaning Changes." In *Exposition and the English Language*. Eds. J. L. Sanderson and W. K. Gordon. New York: Appleton-Century Crofts. 250–52.

Quigley, S., et al. 1976. *Syntactic Structures in the Language of Deaf Children*. Urbana, IL: Institute for Child Behavior & Development.

Robinson, J. L., and P. L. Stock. 1990. "The Politics of Literacy." In *Conversations on the Written Word: Essays on Language and Literacy*. Ed. J. L. Robinson. Portsmouth: Boynton/Cook Publishers, Inc. 271–317.

Rose, J. 1991. "Peter Pan and the Commercialization of the Child." In *Popular Fiction: Technology, Ideology, Production, Reading*. Ed. T. Bennett. London: Routledge. 413–22.

Rose, M. 1989. *Lives on the Boundary*. New York: Penguin Books.

Rowlandson, M. 1985. "A Narrative of the Captivity and Restoration of Mrs. Mary Rowlandson." In *Concise Anthology of American Literature*. 2nd ed. Ed. G. McMichael. New York: Macmillan. 121–31.

Russell, S. 1986. "The Hidden Curriculum of Schools: Reproducing Gender and Class Hierarchies." In *The Politics of Diversity*. Eds. R. Hamilton and M. Barrett. London: Verso. 344–60.

Sarris, G. 1993. "Keeping Slug Woman Alive: The Challenge of Reading in a Reservation Classroom." In *The Ethnography of Reading*. Ed. J. Boyarin. Berkeley: California University Press. 238–69.

Scheler, M. 1961. *Ressentiment*. Glencoe: The Free Press.

Schilb, J. 1991. "Cultural Studies, Postmodernism, and Composition." In *Contending with Words*. Eds. P. Harkin and J. Schilb. New York: MLA. 173–88.

Schlesinger, H. S., and K. Meadow. 1972. *Sound and Sign: Childhood Deafness and Mental Health*. Berkeley: University of California Press.

Schriner, D. K. 1992. "One Person, Many Worlds: A Multicultural Composition Curriculum." In *Cultural Studies in the English Classroom*. Eds. J. A. Berlin and M. J. Vivion. Portsmouth: Boynton/Cook Publishers, Inc. 95–111.

Scouten, E. L. 1984. *Turning Points in the Education of Deaf People*. Danville, IL: Interstate.

Silko, L. 1986. "Language and Literature from a Pueblo Indian Perspective." In *English Literature: Opening Up the Canon*. Eds. Leslie Fiedler and Houston Baker, 54–72. Baltimore: The Johns Hopkins University Press.

Silverman, K. 1988. *The Acoustic Mirror: The Female Voice in Psychoanalysis and Cinema*. Bloomington: Indiana University Press.

Simonson, R., and S. Walker. 1988. Introduction. In *Multicultural Literacy: Changing the American Mind*. Eds. R. Simonson and S. Walker. St. Paul: Graywolf Press.

Sosnoski, J. J. 1991. "Postmodern Teachers in Their Postmodern Classrooms: Socrates Begone!" In *Contending with Words*. Eds. P. Harkin and J. Schilb. New York: MLA. 198–219.

Spear, S., et al. 1990. "Multicultural Literacy: A Context for Composition." *Teaching English in a Two-Year College 17:* 247–52.

Stanworth, M. 1987. "Girls on the Margins: A Study of Gender Divisions in the Classroom." In *Gender Under Scrutiny: New Inquiries Into Education*. Eds. G. Weiner and M. Arnot. London: Hutchinson. 198–212.

Sullivan, C. A. 1993. "*Macho* and *Machismo* as Loan Words to American English." In *Side by Side: A Multicultural Reader*. Eds. H. S. Wiener and C. Bazerman. Boston: Houghton Mifflin Company. 218–23.

Tannen, D. 1990. *You Just Don't Understand: Women and Men in Conversation*. New York: Ballantine Books.

Telford, C. W. 1932. "Test Performance of Full and Mixed Blood North Dakota Indians." *Journal of Comparative Psychology 14:* 123–145.

Tokarczyk, M., and E. Fay. 1993. *Working-class Women in the Academy: Laborers in the Knowledge Factory*. Amherst, MA: University of Massachusetts Press.

Trager, J. 1992. *The People's Chronology*. New York: Henry Holt.

Trinh, M. 1990. "Not You/Like You: Post-Colonial Women and the Interlocking Questions of Identity and Difference." In *Making Face, Making Soul/Haciendo Caras:*

Creative and Critical Perspectives by Feminists of Color. Ed. G. Anzaldúa. San Francisco: Aunt Lute. 371–75.

University of North Dakota. 1992. *University of North Dakota Student Profile, 1992–93.* Grand Forks: Office of University Placement.

U. S. Department of Education. 1991. Office of Educational Research and Improvement. *Digest of Education Statistics.* Washington, DC: Government Printing Office.

Verburg, C. J. 1991. *Ourselves Among Others.* 2nd. ed. Boston: Bedford Books.

Vizenor, G. 1984. *The People Named the Chippewa: Narrative Histories.* Minneapolis: Minnesota University Press.

Wacquant, L. J. D., and W. J. Wilson. 1989. "The Cost of Racial and Class Exclusion in the Inner City." In *The Annals of The American Academy of Political and Social Science.* Ed. W. J. Wilson. Newbury Park, CA: Sage Publications. 8–25.

Wells, Susan. 1996. "Rogue Cops and Health Care: What Do We Want from Public Writing?" *College Composition and Communication 47:* 325–341.

Whitford, M. 1986. "Luce Irigaray and the Female Imaginary: Speaking as a Woman." *Radical Philosophy 43:* 3–8.

Wilbur, R., et al. 1975. "Syntactic Structures in the Written Language of Deaf Children." *Volta Review 77:* 194–203.

———. 1976. "Pronominalization in the Language of Deaf Students." *Journal of Speech and Hearing Research 19:* 120–140.

Wilbur, R., and S. Quigley, et al. 1975. "Conjoined Structures in the Language of Deaf Students." *Journal of Speech and Hearing Research 18:* 319–35.

Williams, R. 1983. *Keywords.* New York: Oxford University Press.

Winkelmann, C. L. (In press). "Unsheltered Lives: Battered Women Talk About School." In *Literacy and Democracy: Essays on Critical Literacy and Educational Reform.* Festschrift in honor of J. L. Robinson. Eds. C. Fleischer and D. Schaafsma. Urbana, IL: NCTE.

Witte, S. P. 1983. "Topical Structure and Revision: An Exploratory Study." *College Composition and Communication 34:* 313–41.

Contributors

Jacqueline Anderson was Professor of English at Madonna University until her death in January 1997. Her teaching and research interests ranged widely, from composition/rhetoric to linguistics to feminist literary criticism. Her book, *Deaf Student Mis-Writing, Teacher Mis-Reading: English Education and the Deaf College Student,* was published in 1993 by Linstok Press.

William Archibald is a doctoral student at the University of North Dakota. He received his master's in composition and rhetoric from California State University, San Bernardino. In addition to composition/rhetoric, his interests include eighteenth-century British literature, cultural studies, and teaching pedagogy.

Patricia Bizzell is Professor of English and Director of the College Honors Program at the College of the Holy Cross. She directed the College writing programs for many years, and teaches first-year composition, American literature, and composition theory and pedagogy. Among her publications are *Academic Discourse and Critical Consciousness* (Pittsburgh, 1992), a collection of her essays; and, with Bruce Herzberg, *Negotiating Difference: Cultural Case Studies for Composition* (Bedford, 1996), a reader in American rhetoric.

Barbara Quevedo Davis is Assistant Professor of English at Contra Costa College in San Pablo, California.

James Degan has taught writing at UC San Diego and The Ohio State University. He has published articles and essays on Raymond Carver, Graham Greene, and the Nuclear Age. His book, *The Irony of Exile: Memory and the Experience of Exile,* is forthcoming from Peter Lang Publishing.

Steve Dilks is Assistant Professor at the University of Missouri, Kansas City, where he collaborates in directing several writing programs and teaches twentieth-century British and Irish literature, critical theory, and interdisciplinary studies. Defining himself as a critical mediator, Steve is working on a book called *Baring the Devices: Teaching Reading and Writing After Postmodernism.* From North Hykeham, Lincolnshire, he learned his trade at St. John's Comprehensive School of Cyprus, the Robert Pattinson Secondary Modern in England, the University of Stirling in Scotland, and, in the United States, at the University of Kansas and Rutgers, the State University of New Jersey.

Kathleen Dixon is Associate Professor of English at the University of North Dakota, where she teaches composition/rhetoric theory and practice, women's studies, and cultural studies. Her essays have appeared in Karen Fitts and Alan Frances' collection, *Left Margins: Composition and Cultural Studies* and in *College Composition and Commu-*

nication and the *Journal of Basic Writing.* Her book, *Making Relationships: Gender in the Forming of Academic Community,* was published in 1997 by Peter Lang Publishing.

Elizabeth Flynn is a Professor of Reading and Composition at Michigan Technological University. She is co-editor of *Constellations* (1992; 1995), *Gender and Reading* (1986), and the journal *Reader.* She has published essays in *College English, College Composition and Communication,* the *Journal of Advanced Composition,* the *Journal of Business and Technical Communication, The Writing Instructor,* and in numerous essay collections. She has served as president of the Women's Caucus for the Modern Languages and as chair of the CCCC Committee on the Status of Women in the Profession.

Scott Lyons (Ojibwe) has taught in settings as varied as Upward Bound and Concordia College, a four-year Lutheran college in Moorhead, Minnesota. He is now a doctoral student at Miami University in Oxford, Ohio, where he specializes in rhetoric and composition. He plans to return to the Leech Lake Chippewa Reservation in Minnesota to study Indian education.

Dierdre Glenn Paul is Assistant Professor of Reading at Montclair State University in Upper Montclair, New Jersey. She has written on teaching language arts in a multicultural classroom, multicultural children's literature, and the development of a multicultural perspective.

Annemarie Pérez is a Graduate Fellow in English at the University of Southern California, specializing in Chicana Feminist and Post-Colonial Literatures.

John Schilb is the Culbertson Chair of Writing at Indiana University. He is the author of *Between the Lines: Relating Composition Theory and Literary Theory,* also published by Boynton/Cook. In addition, he has co-edited *Writing Theory and Critical Theory, Contending with Words: Composition and Rhetoric in a Postmodern Age,* and *Constellations: A Contextual Reader for Writers.*

Doreen Stärke-Meyerring was born and raised in East Germany, where she received her undergraduate degree in English, Russian, and Education. She studied at the University of Rostov-on-Don in Southern Russia for a year; the following year, she was invited by the Institute of International Education/Fulbright Chicago to work as a teaching assistant in Russian language and culture at the Northwestern Minnesota Global Studies Institute. After completing a master's degree in rhetoric and composition (at the University of North Dakota), she returned to Germany. She taught technical writing at the University of Magdeburg (Fachhochschule Magdeburg). She is currently pursuing her doctorate at the University of Minnesota.

Jane Varley is an editor and writer. She has published poems and reviews in journals such as *Prairie Schooner, The Iowa Review,* and *North Dakota Quarterly.* She studies and teaches at the University of North Dakota, where she is earning a Ph.D. in creative writing.

Carol Winkelmann is Associate Professor of English at Xavier University in Cincinnati, Ohio. She teaches linguistics, sixteenth- and seventeenth-century women's literacy, and a women's/peace studies course on women and violence. She facilitates a literacy/storytelling circle at a shelter for battered women. Her essays have appeared in anthologies and in *Computers and the Humanities, English Education, Frontiers: A Journal of Women Studies,* and *Linguistics and Education: An International Research Journal.* Currently, Winkelmann is working on an ethnolinguistic study of the language practices of battered women.